WESTMAR COLLE

VIETNAM

A Diplomatic Tragedy

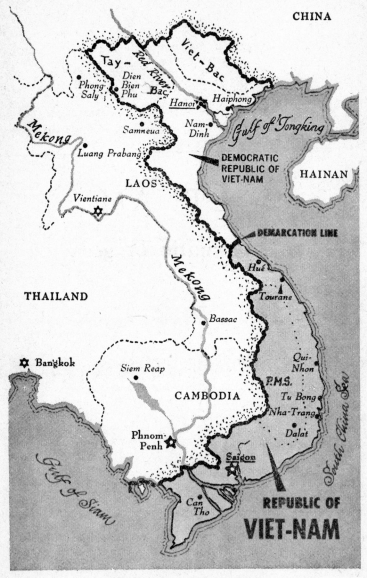

THE TWO VIET-NAMS

VIETNAM

A Diplomatic Tragedy

The Origins of The United States Involvement

By

Victor Bator

Oceana Publications, Inc.

Dobbs Ferry, New York

1965

Quotations from *The White House Years: Mandate For Change 1953-1956* in Chapters I through 5, 7 through 13 and 14 through 17 are reprinted by permission of Doubleday & Company, Inc. Copyright © 1963 by Dwight D. Eisenhower.

The map of Vietnam on page ii is by Professor Bernard B. Fall and is reproduced by permission of Frederick A. Praeger, Inc.

The cartoons by David Low on pages 4, 106 and 126 are reproduced by permission of the London Daily Express.

The cartoon on page 186 is reproduced by permission of the artist, Bill Canfield.

The Cartoon on page 188 reproduced by courtesy of the *Chicago Sun-Times*, © 1964 by Bill Mauldin.

Library of Congress Catalog Card Number 65-17939

Manufactured in the United States of America

To

three true friends, my sons

Francis, Peter and Paul

and

to the memory of Franci, an unforgettable woman.

Contents

1   Eisenhower and Dulles reverse United States policy
towards Britain and Western Europe — Equal alliance rank
considered for Asiatic countries.   1

2   The French war in Indochina acquires global importance for anti-Communist coalition — Effects on French
policy of fading colonial status and burden of war effort —
Dilemma of choice for United States between loss of Indochina to Communist powers and large scale intervention —
Four Power Conferences in Berlin—Agreement on a conference in Geneva on Korea and Indochina with Chinese
participation — Opposition in America — Prospect of concessions to Communists endangers military situation.   9

3   Military strategy for ending the war (Navarre plan)
— Recognition by France of independence of three states in
Indochina — Navarre's decision to engage Vietminh in major
battle at Dien Bien Phu — General Ely's mission to Washing-
ing — Ely and Admiral Radford agree on aerial intervention
by United States for relief of Dien Bien Phu. — Dulles' plan
for general intervention by European-Asiatic coalition — Resentment of allies towards Dulles' plan — Dulles and Con-
gress veto Radford-Ely plan.   23

4   Diplomatic manoeuver by Eisenhower and Dulles to organize militant coalition against Communist aggression in Indochina — Dulles' mission to Europe — British and French refusal misinterpreted as consent — Dulles convokes ambassadors for conference on Southeast Asia Defense pact — Veto by Eden. 51

5   General Navarre demands immediate American aerial support for Dien Bien Phu — Eden returns to London to obtain Cabinet decision — Cabinet refused intervention. 67

6   Eden agrees to military staff meetings as face-saving diplomatic substitute for conference on coalition — Eisenhower, in public statements, interprets staff meetings as conference for immediate alliance — Churchill denies. 75

7   Washington plans coalition without Britain — Australia, New Zealand refuse — American proposals for internationalization of Indochina war with United States joining France — French policy changes from conditional agreement to refusal after Dien Bien Phu defeat — American delegation sabotages settlement in Geneva. 81

8   Height of crisis within the alliance — Reciprocal reproaches and accusations of disloyalty — Conflict of policies — Eden's diplomacy turns the corner in Geneva — Personal antagonism between Dulles and Eden — British Locarno-type guaranty plan for Geneva settlement — Sharp condemnation by Washington. 97

9   Conciliatory journey of Churchill and Eden to Washington — Southeast Asia alliance conceded without Asiatic Commonwealth nations — Refusal of diplomatic action before end of Geneva Conference — Eden and Mendès-France return to Geneva — Success in sight — Limited United States support to achieve settlement. 113

10 Geneva Conference succeeds — American militancy claims success of Conference. 123

11 Four anomalies in Geneva Agreement — Absence of signed documents; pretext of non-political nature and temporary character; absence of mutual obligations. 133

12 Omens of internal debacle and external dangers to South Vietnam — United States refuses guaranty by Conference participants — United States becomes sole quasi-guarantor of Cambodia, Laos and South Vietnam. 149

13 Dulles' international guaranty scheme realized at Manila — House of Commons debate for ratification — Weakness of SEATO. 157

14 French policy in Vietnam after Geneva settlement — General Ely's mission — Conflict between Ely and Diem — United States supports Diem — France and Britain fail to maintain presence in Indochina. 171

15 Anti-colonialism and anti-imperialism in United States policy before and during Eisenhower-Dulles Administration — Analysis of both concepts. 191

16 Analysis of United States policy toward France in Indochina crisis — Background and determinants of policy — Decisive influence of domestic politics. 205

17 In 1954, United States policy for victory changes into policy of containment — North Vietnam's interest in independence as basis of political status quo. — Militancy versus diplomacy in United States policy. 223

Appendices

I. Letter of President Dwight D. Eisenhower to Sir Winston Churchill, dated April 4, 1954 231

II. Final Declaration of the Geneva Conference, July 21, 1954 233

III. Statement of President Dwight D. Eisenhower in regard to the results of the Geneva Conference 236

Notes 237

Bibliography 251

Index of Names 253

Index of Subjects 255

Introduction

This book is a study of the policy and diplomacy of the United States during the three-year period from the middle of 1953 to 1956 in the Indochina crisis and its temporary dénouement at the Geneva Conference. It is not the history of military and political events in Indochina itself. Insofar as these will be narrated they serve only the purpose of making possible the exposition and interpretation of American foreign policy dealing with the problems of the Indochina situation and give to the policy its full meaning. I shall attempt to lift the Indochina policy beyond its local and temporal significance to present some of the general features of the Eisenhower-Dulles era in United States history.

This chapter of American history might have become the theme of a book which is history for history's sake, a contribution to the annals of the United States but staying within the framework of the generally recognized foundations and traditions of American external relations, without attempt at a more general or exceptional enlightenment. As our national history must record all periods in uninterrupted continuity it would have been a worthy subject for a scholarly book in any event. But as any observer of daily events in the Nineteen Sixties may guess and the readers of this book soon will discover, this particular chapter of our foreign policy has a special image.

In 1953, General Eisenhower became President. The majority of the American people voted for the Republicans after twenty years of government by the Democratic Party. The new President interpreted the vote *not* as authority for the continuation of the external policy preceding his administration but as a clear mandate for change. Thus, he selected for his administration's highest cabinet post, for Secretary of State, John Foster Dulles, a man who had the self-confidence, talent, and intellectual courage to bring the change in operation. Dulles had the ambition to leave his personal mark on world affairs. The Republican Party platform drafted by him marked out the changed course. This distinguished the program written into the election platform of Eisenhower from the usual pattern of foreign policy statements in Western countries when a new head of State or the government of a party emerging from opposition takes office. In domestic policies very often, perhaps always, the newness, the differences are emphasized. But in regard to external relationships the new rulers usually give reassurance that the traditional policies will be continued. Instead of this, the Eisenhower platform promised the abandonment of what was referred to as the "Asia last" policy, it promised the end of neglect of the Far East and of its sacrifice to gain time for the West, and thereby, the strengthening of the morale of the peoples of the Far East. It promised the end of the defensive containment of communism and asserted firm will to defeat it and roll back Communist Russia into its pre-war orbit. It held out the promise of depriving International Communism of the political and military initiative.

Eisenhower was not the kind of politician who would take his election platform with a grain of salt. After all, his Secretary of State drafted it; he himself weighed its every word with attention. And as a man of strong moral fiber, he could be expected to abide by it. It is with this background in mind that we have to follow his and Dulles' footsteps in these new directions. This is all the more so because it was not in the Republican Party platform that these thoughts, plans, and principles had been first voiced by Dulles. In an article[1] written by him in 1952, a few months before he became Secretary of State, he set forth that "those who think only of Western Europe and of making it 'impregnable'— without regard to the Near, Middle and Far East and Africa —are just as blind as those who think only of the United States and of making it 'impregnable.' Policies that do not defend *freedom in Asia** † are fatally defective." The article gave special emphasis to the "20 odd *non-Western** nations which are next door to the Soviet world." Today, (that is, before the coming into office of the Eisenhower administration) "they live close to despair because the United States, the historic leader of the forces of freedom seems dedicated to the negative policy of 'containment' and stalemate." This promise of new policy was put in words which could not vouch firmer determination for change. "We must *move promptly* to get *out of the present morass*."* This was not meant to be one of the ideas in a statement that might permit flexible interpretation. On this point "I do venture to be *dogmatic*," he wrote. It would "commit our *offensive** military power to the deterring of aggression and the preservation of peace." The policy in the Indochina crisis was one of the major attempts for the application of the promised novel, aggressive program after the new President and his Secretary of State had taken the reins of command in their hands.

Chapters 1 to 10 of this study chronicle the diplomatic history of the first period of the Indochina crisis terminating with the Geneva Conference in July 1954. The conflict between the United States and Great Britain during this period

---

† The cross signifies explanatory text at the bottom of the page.

* The asterisk signifies *added italics* within verbatim quotations.

Numbers refer always to source of information appearing as notes at the end of the text, beginning on p. 229.

will be the chief concern of these chapters. Chapter 11 analyzes the agreements and documents produced at Geneva. Chapters 12-14 relate the political events during the following two years, from July 1954 to June 1956, events which ultimately landed the United States in the second Indochina war. Finally, chapters 15, 16 and 17 describe and analyze the political factors and motives which led the United States into the Vietnam morass which has now become one of our major political and military problems.

This study makes no claim to new independent research nor to use of materials which would not be available to any scholar, but it was greatly helped by another circumstance. All the principal actors of the drama—in alphabetical order: Anthony Eden, then Foreign Secretary of Britain; Dwight D. Eisenhower, then President of the United States; General Paul Ely, the special envoy of France who was Chief negotiator of French policy in Washington in March 1954 and later in 1954, the political and military Plenipotentiary of the French Government in Vietnam; Joseph Laniel, Premier of France in 1953-1954; General Henri Navarre, French Commander General in Indochina in 1953-54 before General Ely's appointment—published their memoirs in book form.† Countless contemporary speeches, statements from these statesmen and from others closely related to the events which gave shape to this chapter of history are available here and abroad. The official documents are published. The daily press and the periodical literature followed closely the events. Two major books have been published which present in masterly detail and summary different aspects of the political, diplomatic and military events of the Vietnam

---

† Anthony Eden, *Full Circle* (Houghton Mifflin Co., Boston, 1960). Dwight D. Eisenhower, *Mandate For Change* (Doubleday & Co. New York, 1963). Général Paul Ely, *l'Indochine dans la Tourmente* (Librairie Plon, Paris, 1964). Joseph Laniel, *Le Drame Indochinois* (Librairie Plon, Paris, 1957). Henri Navarre, *Agonie de l'Indochine* (1953-1954) (Librairie Plon, Paris, 1956).

crisis.†† These sources of information have made it possible to write a confident history.

In spite of the overwhelming attention that the diplomatic events of the British-American crisis had received contemporaneously, in the summer of 1954, its history, its critical chaos, its threat to allied unity are almost forgotten. A book of a noted author[2] written on British-American political relationships refers more than ten times to the Suez crisis of 1956 as an outstanding instance of Anglo-American disagreements, but mentions only once, casually, the just as deep and similarly ominous breakdown of the alliance in 1954 caused by the Indochina debacle. Hans J. Morgenthau considers the Anglo-American Alliance as all inclusive and world-embracing, based upon common culture, political institutions and ideals, transcending the limitations of material interests undisturbed until *the British invasion of Egypt in 1956.*[3] He does not seem to be aware of the previous breakdown of the spirit of alliance in 1954. This is all the more surprising as the effects of the Suez crisis are, fortunately, hardly noticeably any longer in the relationship of the two nations while in Vietnam the regrettable results of the disagreement are very much in appearance. Thus, it is surprising that the Indochina crisis of 1954 and its immediate aftereffects in 1955-56 have not yet reached that level of recognition that their importance would deserve.

†† Jean Lacouture and Philippe Devillers, *La Fin d'une Guerre— Indochine 1954* (Editions du Seuil, Paris, 1960). Bernard B. Fall, *The Two Vietnams* (F. Praeger, New York, 1963).

1

THE UNITED STATES IS NOW, IN 1965, ENGAGED IN VIETNAM in a serious guerilla war, not unlike that with which France was cursed from 1946 to 1954. It is the same conflict, by and large, with the difference that the United States stepped in and, instead of France, now holds the command position in that local battle of the global confrontation between the Free and the Communist worlds.

The transition of the command and local responsibility in Vietnam from France to the United States was achieved relatively smoothly with only minor frictions between them. Its history is narrated in Chapter 14 of this study. But this operation brought about a major political clash between the United States and Britain. The history of this conflict will be the main topic of Chapters 2 to 10 of this book.

Despite the identity of interests and ultimate purposes of the two countries in regard to the Vietnam situation they had strongly conflicting views about the means for their achievement. The disagreements were so deeply imbedded in their domestic politics and in their other international commitments that they brought their partnership danger-ously close to breakup. This debacle was averted at the last minute by the intervention of Sir Winston Churchill who not only used his prestige, his personal ties to the political leaders of the United States and his authority with President Eisenhower, but who, to achieve this, had to make substantial concessions to United States policy.

The proximate cause of the discord lay in the "new look" that the Eisenhower-Dulles administration gave to the alliance with Britain. During World War II the partnership had not been without disagreements either, but the personal attachment between President Roosevelt and Prime Minister Churchill would never permit bitter feelings, recriminations or any substantial parting of the ways. When, in 1945 this intimacy at the top disappeared, the alliance might have receded to secondary consideration in American foreign policy if Stalinist imperialism had not engendered the cold war. But, in 1946, the threat of Soviet conquest all around the periphery of Russia reestablished the alliance as a cold war instrument and, within the Atlantic Community, the partnership with Britain was considered by many to be the first peace-time alliance of America.

With the establishment of NATO and the creation of the working partnership in the nuclear deterrent there came into being again an informal Anglo-American alliance which, *mutatis mutandis,* incorporated most of the essential features of the wartime relationship.[1] Thus, between 1945 and 1952, the official alliance policy of the two governments reached that warmth that majority public sentiment in the two nations has invariably shown between the two nations.

Though during the Truman Administration the alliance was different in style from the Roosevelt-Churchill partnership, yet in many ways it was even more harmonious. On occasions, President Roosevelt had toyed with the idea that Russia was another kind of democracy closer in spirit to the international policy of America than was imperialist Britain, that Uncle Joe was, in a sense, a truer democrat than Seigneur Churchill, but Stalin promptly prevented this feeling becoming truly potent. His clumsy, overbearing attitude

2

soon delivered the cold douche to such dreams. On the other hand, Acheson "never forgot what was due to an ally and worked in the spirit of an equal partnership, even though the United States carried so much the heavier load."[2] Thus, on account of the intimacy on the highest diplomatic level the inadequacy did not harm the harmony of the partnership. An incident recounted by Eden sheds strong light on this aspect of the relationship.

> "On one occasion I [Eden] showed him a telegram from Selwyn Lloyd, the Minister of State, giving an account of [critical] feeling in the House of Commons with regard to Korea. After reading the telegram, Acheson said: 'In fact you would like us to make fewer mistakes, and keep you better informed when we make them!' He went on to welcome the visit of Lord Alexander, then Minister of Defense, and Lloyd to Korea. 'I understand' he said 'the anxieties which the British public must be feeling, and I hope that this will do something to dispel them.' "[3]

The crisis in 1954 was the result of the reappraisal by the Eisenhower-Dulles Administration of the relationship of the United States to Britain. "The agonizing reappraisal" of the relationship to France, threatened by Dulles in a speech at the meeting of the North Atlantic Council in Paris, on December 14, 1953[4] has received prime political and historical publicity ever since, though it remained one of those crash and shock utterances of Dulles such as "liberation," "rollback," and "instant retaliation," which never went beyond oratory. In contrast, very little prominence has been given so far to the much stronger, publicly *undeclared* but *de facto* change of American policy toward Great Britain. Although this change of policy did not receive all-embracing positive emphasis in a public pronouncement it was referred to publicly, and clearly expressed towards Churchill and Eden on a conference level several times. Secretary of State Dulles, in his first official broadcast did not except Britain from his threat that "if France, Germany, and

3

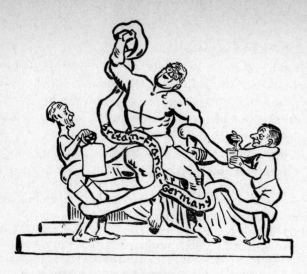

"LOOK OUT! HE'S MAKING AN AGONISED REAPPRAISAL"

England should go their separate ways, then certainly it would be necessary to give a little rethinking to America's own foreign policy in relation to Western Europe."[4a] Even though the ANZUS Treaty between the United States, Australia, and New Zealand was concluded prior to the take-over of administration by Eisenhower, it is generally believed that exclusion of Britain from it, strongly resented by Churchill and Eden, was Dulles' idea and that he played a major part in bringing it about.[5]

A generalized formulation of this new policy towards Britain was first done during the Bermuda Conference of Eisenhower, Churchill and Premier Laniel in December 1953. The topic that brought it out was the unsettled state of the European Defense Community (E.D.C.). The point to be made here is not the substance of the proximate cause, E.D.C., the Four Power Summit Conference or any other policy matter but the fact that the Eisenhower-Dulles team was willing to generalize the disassociation, to change the alliance structure to an occasional partnership, subject to changing conditions, limited to cases of convenience. Dulles "could not take the responsibility that Congress would con-

4

tinue its firm and loyal support of NATO"[6] if positive action toward European unity were not taken within two to three months. At that time, this in reality meant that is was President Eisenhower (firmly in the saddle during the honeymoon of his presidency) and Dulles who might not continue the firm and loyal support of NATO.

In fact, Eden reports that three days later, following the day (December 15) when the agonizing re-appraisal was threatened towards France, Dulles told him that

> "the United States and Britain were approaching a parting of the ways with regard to American policy. If things went wrong [with the European Defense Community] the United States might swing over to a policy of Western hemispheric defense, with emphasis on the Far East. . . . [that] the consequences of a swing of American policy towards hemispheric defense, were of obvious concern to Great Britain."[7]

This was not the first time that Dulles hinted at a possibility of rethinking of American foreign policy in relation to Western Europe, including Britain. Quite a few of Dulles' early diplomatic actions in 1953, especially in the Middle East were, in essence, such declarations of independence prompted, or at least, firmly approved, by President Eisenhower.

We have other reliable testimony confirming this approach of Dulles to the alliance relationship. At a conference with the leaders of the Senate held in early 1955 Dulles said emphatically that

> "we could not allow our policies in Asia to be dictated by our European allies . . . He was deeply annoyed by the hesitancy of the British and the French to join with the Americans in making a bold and unified stand against the Red Chinese. . . . He showed then some . . . willingness to pull away from the traditional partnership with the British and the French. . . ."[8]

Eisenhower himself also approached the alliance relationship with detachment and casualness. He used his first meeting with Churchill and Eden in Bermuda in 1953 to advise them of this policy. When Churchill in Bermuda

"had much to say about the need for Washington and London to coordinate and crystallize their views whenever they had mutual interests in any spot on the globe —for example, India, Egypt, Iran—and then to publicly present a solid front to the third party in the dispute. I gave my approval to part of his argument—to confer confidentially in searching for joint solutions *that would be approved by world opinion as just, equitable and considerate.** But I expressed the thought that if any other party in the dispute had the *slightest semblance** of justice on its side, it now could appeal to the United Nations. Unless we recognized the equality of member nations of that body, we could, in many cases, be made to look like arbitrary imperialists if we tried to 'gang up' publicly in supporting the principles in which we both believed."

Eisenhower added that he

"felt that the last thing the two strongest Western powers should do was to appear before the world as a combination of forces to compel adherence to their announced views, especially when these views concerned existing or former relationships between a mother country and a colony."[9]

The policy expressed in these statements was a return from the safe basis of the Atlantic Alliance formed by the Atlantic Community of countries for their defense from the onslaught of Stalin's imperialism to the Wilsonian vision of the world. In the Wilsonian concept America is not one nation among many others, with allies, partners, and rivals among whom compromises of principle must be made, separate spheres of influences have to be recognized in order to make mutual assistance and thereby alliance possible. It was a return from the all-pervading, primary importance of the Atlantic Alliance to the Wilsonian ideology, eloquently voiced by Cordell Hull in his home-coming statement after the Four-Power Moscow Conference promising us a world where "there will no longer be need for spheres of influence, for alliances, for balance of power, or any other special arrangements by which, in the unhappy past, the nations strove to safeguard their security or to promote their interests."[10]

In 1952, before the Eisenhower Administration entered office, it looked as if the Wilsonian ideology had faded away. Walter Lippmann expressed the hope that America had reached the mature realization of the fact that we have to adopt our special interests and difficulties to those of our allies, to harmonize our policies with theirs and present a joint front when we face the hostile opponents who threaten our free world. He expressed regret that the Atlantic Community and such proposals from both sides of the Ocean had been rejected because they were in conflict with the Wilsonian universal society.[10] But, so he hoped, this beautiful castle could not be fancied anymore in the air of the Nineteen Fifties.

He was mistaken. Eisenhower and Dulles brought back into United States policy the ideology in which—outside of those whom they branded the criminal outcasts, that is, Communist Russia and its allies, all states are equals. They live by the Rule of Law and they observe the self-evident principles of the universal doctrine of a peaceful world. In relation to the Communist enemy no possibility of a settlement is possible since their word must not be trusted;[11] they must be eliminated by victory in a crusade. Toward them compromise, accomodation of conflicting claims by diplomacy and give-and-take are not virtues but futile appeasements or moral treason. But towards all other countries the United States must not distinguish between its allies and others. They wanted the United States to act as impartial arbiter among nations, doing justice between them. But no statesman or government can possibly pass muster in this task. We turn for support to Bernard Shaw:

7

"There is only one condition on which a man can do justice between two litigants and that is that he have no interest in common with either of them. Whereas it is only having every interest in common with both of them that he can govern tolerably. The indispensable preliminary of Democracy is the representation of every interest. The indispensable preliminary of justice is the elimination of every interest. When we want an arbitrator we turn to a stranger; when we want a government a stranger is the only person we will not endure."[12]

The United States Government cannot be arbitrator among nations and has no power to settle conflicts as it would do in domestic politics. It has one possible stand and policy, that is, to use its power for its own interest.

American policy in the Southeast Asian crisis of 1954 was the earliest large scale demonstration of the new Eisenhower-Dulles policy.

2

Before World War II "Indochina" was the geographical designation for a group of French protectorates; after World War II Eastern Indochina became a group of three "Associated States": Vietnam, Laos and Cambodia. During the war the Japanese army conquered almost the entire area and remained in complete control until 1945, when—after Chinese and Anglo-Indian forces had recaptured most of it— the French moved back in. Had the French succeeded in reestablishing their authority or creating a peaceful new regime, neither the United States nor Britain would have become directly involved. But nationalistic aspirations for independence, with Communist overtones, and the loosening by war and Japanese occupation of the old cultural and economic ties with France, led to a guerrilla war between France and a substantial segment of the population controlled by a gifted Communist politician, Ho Chi Minh.

In the infancy of his organization, Ho Chi Minh was certainly not merely captain of an advance outpost of the Russian Communists. At that time he had a large segment of anti-Communist, leftist elements in his camp. He dissolved the Vietnamese Communist Party and would have

9

probably much preferred to become the head of a truly independent Vietnam instead of proconsul-viceroy in a Chinese satellite dependency which was until 1956 his political fate. There is little doubt that though he is a true Communist, his first loyalty is to Vietnam, as a patriotic Vietnamese.†

From 1946 until 1950, the struggle between the French army and the Ho Chi Minh guerrillas was a large scale colonial campaign of pacification against rebels with hardly more than local significance. But, in 1950, the operation changed into a confrontation of the Free World and Chinese-Russian Communist power. This change was brought about by events outside of Indochina. In January 1949, Mao Tse Tung's army occupied Peking. In the middle of that year Nanking and Shanghai fell to the Reds and, in December, Chinese Communist forces reached the Indochina border. As a result of these developments it was hardly surprising that in January 1950 Ho Chi Minh hurriedly recognized Communist China and received in exchange diplomatic recognition of the Democratic Republic of Vietnam, a state without territory, population and political administration, represented by Ho Chi Minh as Head of Government who—after victory—would determine its administrative and political elements within Indochina. A few days later Moscow also recognized Ho's Government. This turn of events in the political situation also foreshadowed a change in the military operations. Vo Nguyen Giap, the Commander-in-Chief of the Vietminh forces, who was to become the conqueror of Dien Bien Phu, let it be known that instead of the harassing guerrilla operations pursued until then, he was preparing

---

† "Ho Chi Minh himself was well known as an ardent Vietnamese Nationalist, Nguyen Ai Quoc (Nguyen the Patriot), some years before joining the French Socialist Party. Albert Sarraut, one-time Radical Socialist Prime Minister, noted before the French National Assembly in 1946, that 'the object of [Ho's] entire life' was 'the independence of his country, the reason that he has fought for forty years with a personal disinterestedness that we have the fairness to recognize." (O. E. Clubb, *The United States and the Sino-Soviet Bloc in Southeast Asia*, The Brookings Institution, 1962, p. 9).

an offensive attack for the conquest of Indochina in its entirety.

France was not blind to the dangerous consequences of the new situation. In view of later developments it is of interest and importance to note here that the problem confronting the country was brought into the open by, among others, a former member of the deGaulle cabinet, Pierre Mendès-France, in speeches made in the Assemblée Nationale on October 19th and November 22nd, 1950. He proffered two alternative solutions of the Indochina crisis, both equally unpleasant. The first would be, to undertake an all-out fight with no quarter given and with maximum effort expended. This would require tripling of the fighting forces in Indochina immediately to nip in the bud the developing strength of Ho Chi Minh. To achieve this the country would have to curtail investment for the postwar build-up of its economy, to raise taxes substantially, to increase the length of military service, to decrease its armed strength in Europe and in North Africa and to face the rearmament of Germany by the United States as a substitute for the diminished French military presence in Europe. The other solution would be a political settlement granting complete independence to Indochina, with recognition of Ho Chi Minh as its head.

It is not entirely surprising that the French Government evaded both alternatives. Since the war in Korea against the Communist power-block was in full swing the second alternative would have meant a dangerous break of Free World solidarity and in relation to the United States entail a serious risk of agonizing reappraisal, years before John Foster Dulles' threat. On the other hand, the sacrifices required for an all-out war effort might have delivered the electorate to its own domestic Communists. Yet, some diplomatic maneuvering toward a settlement would have been possible while Ho Chi Minh had difficulties with his die-hard pro-China Communists, with the anti-communist elements in his camp, and with the build-up of his army. This, combined with exploitation of the superiority in equipment and organizational strength of the French troops might have brought about a political settlement, reconciliation with Ho Chi Minh and might have influenced him to build Indochina into an independent leftist socialist state. But French policy chose the worse of two evils, and combined political intransigence with half-hearted military action. This drove Ho Chi Minh, who was badly in need of military equipment, into a satellite relationship with China and Russia.

Thus, what had been a colonial military operation—even though of substantial importance—grew into a major war sinking France deeper and deeper into the mire, with little hope of maintaining or reestablishing the colonial status. Yet the war could not possibly be simply discontinued and abandoned. The expeditionary force and its valuable arsenal had to be rescued. National prestige and self-confidence badly shaken by the defeat and surrender of 1940, the future life of the French settlers in Indochina, and the economic and cultural institutions developed in eighty years of colonial connection, all had to be taken into consideration. The General Staff, representing the military establishment, would not give up the struggle and demanded that no sacrifice be denied the war effort. On the other hand, the Government could not close its eyes to the fact that it faced the hostility of the great majority of the Vietnamese[1], that Ho Chi Minh was receiving wholesale help from China and that the costs of the war were an excessive strain on France's resources. All of these precluded military victory for the French: complete defeat of Ho was beyond France's power. Thus, the political aims of the military effort had to be restricted to settlement, partition, face-saving, rescue of the expeditionary force, and saving the local camp-followers and partisans of the French from the threat of massacre.

This was of course French reflection on the situation. For the NATO allies of France, for the United States, Britain, Australia, New Zealand and all other members of the Free World, however, the battle for Indochina had become part of the global duel between the Free World and the two imperialist Communist powers. A communiqué issued by the State Department, following a conference on Indochina with a French delegation on June 18, 1952, stated that the struggle in which the forces of the French Union were

> "engaged against the forces of Communist aggression in Indochina is an integral part of the world-wide resistance by the Free Nations to Communist attempts at conquest and subversion [though] France has the primary role there."[2]

A NATO resolution adopted unanimously on December 17, 1952 recognized that French resistance to the Chinese-supported Vietnamese rebels was essential to the defense of NATO, of Western Europe, and of the Free World generally and "deserves the continued support from the NATO governments."[3] Sixteen months later the Australian Minister for Foreign Affairs said that

> "the world was under a great debt to France for her sacrifices in Indochina."[4]

Eden showed without reservation his recognition of the French position.

> "Our campaign against the communist guerillas in Malaya, then in critical phase, gave us a close interest in the Indochina vortex.[†] It affected our Asian partners in the Commonwealth, particularly India quite as much."[5]

Vice President Richard Nixon in a speech reporting to the nation upon his return from a journey that had taken him to a large number of Asiatic countries, gave full credit to France for its war effort defending the Free World.

[†] As we see, Eden correctly foresaw the underlying basic connection of the situation in Vietnam with that in Malaysia. At that time, and ever since, the strategic purpose of the two operations by the United States in Indochina and by Britain in Malaysia is identical, to build an indigenous and independent power structure in Southeast Asia before the last white soldiers sailed for home. The collapse of either operation would leave the other so isolated that it would have to be abandoned. (*Economist*, June 27, 1964).

"Indochina is vitally important . . . The day the French will leave Indochina, the Communists will take over . . . The Free World owes a debt of gratitude to the French and to the forces of the Associated States for the great sacrifices they are making in the cause of freedom against Communist aggression.[6]

Eisenhower had been mindful of the problem before he became President:

"If Indochina fell," he wrote, "not only Thailand but Burma and Malaya would be threatened with added risks for East Pakistan, South Asia and Indochina as well."[7] "There is no question about the extent and nature of the sacrifices of the French fighting this war," said Under-Secretary of State Bedell Smith in a television interview. "They have been at it now for almost eight years."[8]

In spite of this unanimous recognition of the true nature of the war in Indochina the pretense that Indochina was not the responsibility of the United States, that, in spite of the recognized global importance of the war, the United States had no moral and political obligation there, was maintained throughout the 1953-54 period of the crisis until the end of the Geneva Conference. Eisenhower did not want the war in Indochina to "be shifted from the French shoulders to ours."[9] He maintained that the United States "had not been belligerent in the war."[10] This was made, however, somewhat self-contradictory by the strongest possible pressure brought to bear upon France to surrender completely its special position by granting unrestricted independence to the three Associated States. Consequently, it was not surprising that as soon as this American demand had been acceded to for the sake of the American financial support France was no longer primarily interested in defending Indochina against the intrusion of Chinese Communist power. French public opinion and the government felt it an imposition to be obligated to do the fighting single-handed for the general benefit of its allies.

14

Cited were the casualties suffered up to 1952, reaching about 50,000 killed and over 100,000 wounded. They expected to be—indeed insisted upon being—relieved of the burden of a fight in the global interest of the anti-Communist coalition, — a fight that simply by chance antecedents had been saddled upon them. The flag of freedom became much too heavy for France to hold up alone.†

This short sketch of the Indochina situation at the point where my narration takes its starting point should serve the purpose of acquainting the reader with the background of the diplomatic history which is the subject of this study.††

The review of the American-British conflict created by the Indochina crisis will begin with the Berlin Conference held in February 1954 by the foreign ministers of the United States, Britain, France, and the Soviet Union. That meeting was supposed to advance the unification of Germany and to agree on the terms of an Austrian peace treaty. Nothing was accomplished on either problem but Molotov used the Conference to make a formal proposal, forecast by him several times before, for another conference to be attended also by Communist China and to have a single agenda item: how to lessen international tensions generally. It was obvious to all three Western Foreign Ministers that this proposal was made only for one purpose: to bring China into the

---

† "La charge que la France assume pour la défense de l'indépendence des Etats Associés et pour la cause commune des peuples libres est trop lourde pour elle seule." (Joseph Laniel, speech in l'Assemblée Nationale, June 28, 1953; quoted in his Memoirs, *Le Drame Indochinois*, p. 9).

†† The main sources of the narrative in the text of the Indochina situation are: Bernard B. Fall, *The Two Vietnams*, 1963, pp. 81-129, a major work of undisputed authority, and Lacouture-Devillers, *La Fin d'une Guerre*, 1960, pp. 27-35. The latter is said by B. Fall, op. cit. p. 465, to be "beyond a doubt one of the finest pieces of diplomatic history recently written anywhere." Jean Lacouture is the Editor-in-Chief of the Foreign Department of Le Monde and Philippe Devillers is Professor at the Collège Libre des Sciences Sociales. Another author, Robert Scigliano [*South Vietnam, Nation Under Stress*, 1963, p. 196] calls Lacouture and Deviller's book "the most detailed account of the closing phase of the (French) Indochina war." Much of this background material will reappear in later parts of this study in more detailed form.

"Great Power Club." Yet, to Eden, anxious to save Indo-china without military involvement, it had appeal.

> "I like this much better than a debate at the U.N. . . .
> At least, we should be dealing with principals and not
> with nations anxious to talk but unwilling to bear much
> burden."[11]

Eden first attempted to persuade Molotov that the pro-posed conference should be restricted to the Far East, in-cluding Korea, where the armistice negotiations were hope-lessly bogged down. He thought that for Eisenhower and Dulles a settlement in Korea was so important that the United States could be lured into the same conference room with Communist China if there was a chance that peace in Korea might be achieved. On the other hand, United States recognition of China to that degree would represent for Molotov a substantial diplomatic achievement. Eden, thus seeing a glimmer of hope for success, set to work to obtain the consent of Dulles and Molotov to include Indochina on the agenda of what became the 1954 Geneva Conference.

Of the two, Molotov was the lesser problem. His opposi-tion was not caused by a point of principle; he probably just did not want Russia to be involved in a local Chinese venture whether this consisted of expansion to the south of China's defense perimeter as a minimum, or a trust by China for control of the South Sea as an optimum aim. Also, he perhaps did not dislike the idea of easing France out of Indochina or of alleviating her burden there. There is a report that he intimated to the French his willingness to help in their efforts at disentanglement from Indochina. He might also have considered the inclusion of Indochina on the agenda of the proposed Conference a welcome embarrass-ment to the United States, or a wedge, creating a conflict within the Western alliance.[12]

But for Dulles the agreement to negotiate a settlement of the Indochina situation touched sensitive nerves. With-out the Korean bait, Dulles would probably never have agreed to have Indochina on the Geneva agenda. It was also in conflict with a number of Eisenhower's preoccupations. Settlement meant concessions; and any concession yielding as much as an inch to Communist rule would be inconsistent with the 1952 Republican campaign pledge to abandon the "immoral containment policy" of the Truman-Acheson era and to commence the roll-back of Communism. Settlement with Communist China would appear to be, in fact would be, a victory for the "ungovernment," for a non-recognized ruler of the Chinese empire and a point scored by the opponent of our ally, Chang Kai-shek. This being so, Dulles did his best to thwart Eden's scheme by discouraging the French.[13]

Dulles used an arsenal of arguments. To put faith in agreements with Communists was naive; should Indochina be on the agenda of Geneva, the Chinese would step up the battle drive, through direct or indirect increase of their aid to Ho Chi Minh, in order to administer a knock-out blow or to achieve a greatly advanced military position enabling them to dictate terms. If, on the other hand, no negotiation were to take place and all-out fighting were undertaken by France, America would be willing to make formal and full commitment to provide for the fighting French army as much military equipment as it could possibly use, to pay all financial costs and to train the Vietnamese army with American technicians.

Georges Bidault, the French Foreign Minister, however, could not be alienated from the Eden policy, no matter how convincing Dulles' arguments against a conference on Indochina with Chinese and Vietminh participation might have been. Bidault had to contend with two important political groups in Paris. These demanded from his government for the termination of the war in Indochina more radical and more immediate action than his plan envisaged. A parliamentary group led by Mendès-France favored direct negotiation with Ho Chi Minh without participation of the powers on either side of the global battlefront. Another group represented by several members of the Cabinet itself, and by its Vice President, Paul Reynaud, was in agreement with Bidault about the advantage of an internationalized conference but was willing to concede to the three Associated States complete independence including the right to secede from the French Union. This was the point in regard to which Bidault, supported by Premier Laniel, was in sharp disagreement with the Reynaud policy.

On October 28, 1953, a majority vote of confidence was given to the Laniel government under the condition only that it would spare no effort to bring about general pacification in Southeast Asia keeping, however, a political hold upon the three Indochina states within the French Union. Laniel indicated that neither direct negotiation with Ho nor armistice would necessarily be avoided should they expedite the main purpose.[14] On November 12, to reinforce his government's position, he went even further. He made it known that France was willing, in order to end the fighting, to consent to a Korea-type settlement without total victory and the unconditional surrender of Ho Chi Minh.[15] Thus, Bidault knew he must bring back from Berlin evidence of his willingness and determination to negotiate and achieve peace. Otherwise his government would face defeat and France would have to seek solution of the crisis by concessions which he, Bidault, strongly opposed. He "felt that if the Laniel Government was to survive, he had to bring back at least a tentative pledge to discuss Indochina. . . .[16]

This eventuality was alarming to both Eden and Dulles. A different government in power might not have been willing to continue the Indochina campaign as vigorously as the Laniel Administration was doing. Also, no successor would stand firmly by the European Defense Community (E.D.C.), the pet project of the United States and Britain for the unified defense of Europe. Thus, the trumps were all in Eden's hand and Dulles had to yield.

This is the background of the agreement of the four powers: the Geneva Conference, to convene on April 26,

18

1954, became the incidental result of the Berlin meeting. Yet, Dulles' consent to allow the Indochina situation to be bargained with Red China created a furor among the extremists supporting America's China policy. Vehement attacks were made by Republican political leaders against this concession to France and Britain. They called the Berlin Conference a second Yalta on the Far East, and Dulles himself a Municheer.[17] In order to make palatable to such extremists his consent to Red China's presence at Geneva, Dulles made the less than diplomatic statement at his press conference on February 24, 1954 that the

> "Chinese Communist regime will not come to Geneva to be honored by us but rather to account before the bar of world opinion."[18]

To appease the partisans of anti-Chinese crusade Walter S. McConaughy, Director of the Office of Chinese Affairs in the Department of State, repeated the same presentation:

> "The Chinese Communist regime will be present (at the Geneva Conference) only because of its aggressor role, and it will be called upon to give an accounting for its aggression . . . Far from dealing with it as a great Power, we do not even deal with it as a legitimate government."[19]

The authority and the political position of the Chinese delegation at Geneva did not vindicate this expectation. The Chinese Prime Minister received, on his arrival, more general attention and was shown greater respect by the press than any other head of delegation. He chose as his residence the largest, most handsome private villa available in Geneva, "Grand Mont Fleuri," and had it decorated with priceless and spectacular Chinese furniture, rugs, and porcelains, all antique museum pieces for "the bar of world opinion."[20] It is generally admitted that "at the Geneva Conference on Korea and Indochina in 1954 Chou En-lai emerged as one of the strongest voices in Asia."[21]

The agreement to make Indochina a subject of negotiations was a major diplomatic victory for Eden.

> "It was essential that the French should hold their position militarily, in order that their bargaining position should not be weakened. But I did not consider it to be in the best interest of France [we may also add 'and Britain also'] that the scale of the fighting should be increased, or that she should be encouraged to expand her straitened resources in trying to force a military decision."[22]

On the other hand, American interest in inspiring France towards maximum effort on the battlefront was such that Dulles found it necessary to do what he had promised should no negotiation be agreed to—to make formal the commitment of the United States to maintain American material aid at the highest level that the French forces could usefully apply. This commitment was confirmed by a Presidential cable sent to Berlin.[23] The State Department's attitude, however, was not wholly favorable. On February 8 Eden reports

> . . . "our [British] Ambassador was told at the State Department that the U.S. Government were perturbed by the fact that the French were aiming not to win the war, but to get into a position from which they could negotiate."[24]

But Eden, without British military or financial contribution, had achieved the desired result: maximum French fighting effort, sufficient to enhance bargaining position, and full United States support of it.

Dulles was not the only one who blamed the decision to enter into negotiation with Ho Chi Minh and Communist China for ominous consequences. Henri Navarre, the Commanding General of the French Expeditionary Force in Indochina relates that the French Government agreed to the Geneva Conference without his consultation. He asserts that it was imprudent and thoughtless to enter in negotiation with Ho Chi Minh with no regard to the military situation in Vietnam at a time when he had already made his strategic dispositions, including the plan of a major battle at Dien Bien Phu. He seems to believe firmly that the Vietminh Command would never have dared to commit and risk its entire organized mobile battle strength in a major military engagement against such a powerful fortress as Dien Bien Phu was known to be had they not had as reinsurance the alternative of a settlement at the Geneva Conference. He believes also that Ho Chi Minh would not have obtained from China the massive, concentrated aid in military material and supporting personnel with commanders and technical troops for that one, isolated operation, which risked direct United States intervention if the convocation of the Geneva Conference had not served as reasonable protection against such risks. "The fate of Dien Bien Phu became sealed on the day when the decision in regard to the Conference at Geneva was made," writes Navarre.[25]

Navarre's denouncement of the Government in Paris is not convincing. He made the decision to take position at Dien Bien Phu about the middle of November and executed the operation between November 20 and December 10th. At that time he must have known already about the debate in the Assemblée Nationale in October 1953 and the firm commitment of Premier Laniel to enter into negotiations, made on November 12. Both had preceded Navarre's ominous Dien Bien Phu decision. It would seem that knowing these circumstances it was his responsibility to seek information about the undisclosed intentions of Laniel and the possibilities of negotiations with or without a conference, and to take them into consideration in determining his strategy.

3

To make understandable the history of the events in March and April 1954—following the Berlin conference but antedating that of Geneva—we must retrace our steps back to the second half of 1953.

In the middle of 1953, there was hardly any responsible French political group which, by that time, had not become aware of the necessity of adapting policy to the bitter fact that Ho Chi Minh was not just a little rebel who with slightly more effort, patience, and steadfastness, or perhaps by minor concessions, could be appeased, won over, or eliminated. Ho Chi Minh, by that time, was recognized as the leader of a strongly nationalistic group of Vietnamese intent on gaining complete independence for their country. They connected their struggle with the future plan of a communist regime, partly because Ho Chi Minh was a convinced communist, partly because the campaign for independence could not be made and would not succeed without the aid of Communist China. From 1950, Ho Chi Minh had no other choice but to accept a double satellite relationship to Moscow and Peking.[1] By this concession, Ho turned his war into a confrontation of France, fighting for the maintenance in one

form or other of its political power, against a strong nationalistic group representing the majority of the population[2]
and with the strong support of a neighboring Communist
government. Ho's powerful Chinese ally possessed an army
and organization which had just won a war against its own
ancien régime and acquired glory by success on another
front, asserting its power in Korea against the coalition of
the Free World, led by its most powerful enemy, the United
States.

The Joseph Laniel Government, with George Bidault as
Foreign Minister, was brought into power by the Indochina
crisis. The same predicament rendered necessary a change in
the Indochinese command position also. General Henri
Navarre, former Chief of Staff of Marshal Juin and later
Commanding General in Central Europe got the appointment. These two changes in leadership produced two new
lines of action in regard to the war in Indochina. One was a
military plan to bring about a position of strength. The
second was a new political policy for the support of the military plan and for the termination of the war itself.

The military plan was developed by the new Commander-
in-Chief. Its essence was to restrict, until the fall of 1954,
military activity in the northern half of Vietnam to defensive
operations and to complete elimination of pockets of infiltration in the southern area of Vietnam, in Laos, and (though
Communist presence was hardly noticeable there) in Cambodia. During this interim period a substantial Vietnamese
army would be organized and trained. With that army in
existence, the anti-communist front could be entrusted to
Vietnamese helped by French support in whatever way
such support would be needed; until that time it would be
the war of France, with some Vietnamese help. During
this twelve-to-fourteen-month intervening period, French
strength, with increasing Vietnamese participation, would
be able to keep the military situation under control, subject
to three conditions. First, immediate reinforcements were to
be sent from France to fill gaps which threatened the suc-

cess of the plan. Second, full equipment must be brought to Indochina for the new Vietnamese army and for a new mobile French task-unit to become the military backbone of a new, active battle-front ready for action for the fall of 1954. Third, the United States was to give formal and public assurance that direct Chinese intervention that might defeat the Navarre Plan during the interim period ending in the fall of 1954 would be met head-on by direct military measures. In the new situation to be created by the realization of these conditions, France could postpone until the fall of 1954 the political settlement that otherwise would have to be tackled without delay. A fall campaign in 1954 would make Ho Chi Minh realize that a reasonable settlement creating a non-Communist, or at least Titoist independent regime, would be the best solution for his country and would persuade him to acquiesce in that solution.

The execution of the Navarre plan was set on foot without delay. Preparations for the dispatch of the required manpower began and the first contingents were soon on their way overseas. As France had neither the financial nor industrial strength for the fulfillment of the second condition, the Navarre Plan was submitted to the United States Government with a request to supply what was lacking. It was not at all difficult to gain the patronage and backing of the new Eisenhower Administration. The personal dynamism of Navarre and the energy and logic of his plan had appeal to Washington. Creation of a Vietnamese army and gradual reduction of the exclusively French character of the operation suited Eisenhower's and Dulles' "anticolonialistic" tenets. Dulles in September 1953 made it public that the United States "agreed with the French Government to help carry out the Navarre plan," that the United States undertook to contribute "most of the military end-items and to finance most of the monetary cost of the program, particularly in relation to training, equipping and maintaining local forces." The contribution within the Mutual Security pro-

gram was increased from 400 million to 750 million dollars.†
The volume of military end-items was also greatly increased.[3]
At the same time the United States issued repeated warnings that overt Chinese intervention would bring direct
American action in the war on the French side. This was
several times confirmed and repeated by the State Department in Washington, and by President Eisenhower himself.††

We turn now to the new political policy. Its first line of
action was to lend reality to the promises of independence
held out several times before and to create in the mind of
the Vietnamese leaders the conviction that their army, envisaged by the Plan Navarre, would indeed be theirs and
would be the power base of their political self-determination. To this end, the Laniel Government in a declaration
drafted by Paul Renaud, *Vice Premier du Conseil de la République* and made public on the fifth day of its investiture,
July 3, 1953, made it known that the independence of the
Associated States would be brought to completion, and invited all three to join the government in negotiating the
terms and making it a reality.[4] In keeping with this declaration the Government of Cambodia, where practically no
fighting was going on, was in essence turned over to its king
and army early in the fall of 1953, and in October 1953 a
Treaty of Independence with Laos was signed.

As soon as independence had been conceded to the three
Associated States it became obvious that from the viewpoint
of France it was absurd to carry the entire burden of the war
alone to victory. There was almost universal agreement that
a settlement—saving the Expeditionary Force, insuring its
undisturbed exit with its equipment, the personal and economic security of non-Communist Vietnamese, and the pres-

---

† Funds voted or promised were not necessarily those which were
actually delivered but their political effects were important all the same.

†† [The] "administration has no intention of evading its pledges in the
area providing the French performance measures up to the promises made
by them as basis for requesting our increased help." (Eisenhower, *Mandate
For Change*, p. 344).

ervation of French culture and economic interests—would be sufficient to make the end of the war for France desirable.[5] Anything beyond this would be important for the Free World. But for France to carry on alone, even with the advantages of American financial help, would lead to a burden disproportionate to its interests.

We have reached now the point where we can revert to the period following the Berlin Conference. Had the Navarre Plan been more or less faithfully observed and its course kept on the line leading to the Geneva Conference with no radical change in the military situation, the shadow of a debacle for the Free World would not have appeared and the diplomatic crisis between America and Britain in the summer of 1954 might have been avoided. But history took a different course. Between November 20 and December 1 1953 General Navarre, instead of abiding by his plan, took up a position with crack troops at Dien Bien Phu, 200 miles from the center of military operations in Hanoi, and on December 3, decided to engage the Viet-Minh with a substantial part of his forces in a decisive battle. It is outside of the scope of this study to set forth the military and political considerations which had prompted this sudden deviation of General Navarre, or to discuss the controversy between him and Premier Laniel and its military and political repercussions both before and after the debacle of the fortress.[6] It should suffice to record, with the wisdom of hindsight, that this decision in combination with the circumstances which prevailed in France sealed the fate of the French war in Indochina.

Yet, even without fully anticipating the oncoming catastrophy, the French Government had ominous forebodings. Minister of Defense, René Pleven and several military experts went to Indochina to reconnoiter the situation. Advice and opinions of great military leaders were sought. But so great was the optimism of the fortress' defenders, of their local Commander, and of General Navarre that nobody would take the responsibility to countermand Navarre's decision while evacuation was still possible. "Whatever the reasons, the occupation of Dien Bien Phu caused little notice at the time, except to soldiers" writes Esienhower.[7] He continues: "I instructed both the State and Defense Departments to communicate to their French counterparts my concern."†

It is easy to find fault with Navarre's decision if one ignores his dilemma. The Vietminh army was moving towards Laos. The French Government, on October 28, 1953, in a solemn treaty undertook to defend it against Communist attack. Without a stronghold blocking communist reinforcements and military material, Laos could not be made safe. Dien Bien Phu served that purpose and served it well. Navarre and all his subordinate generals, including Colonel de Castries, the officer selected for command position at Dien Bien Phu, were convinced that the known strength of the Vietminh could not possibly endanger the fortress. If lack of foresight can be attributed to General Navarre at all, it must be proven by evidence that he ought to have known that Ho Chi Minh could and would throw in the battle larger and stronger forces against Dien Bien Phu than those employed in the regular course of Vietnam warfare until then. Whichever way Navarre would have moved, the risks were increasing every year, every month. The source of danger was the insufficiency of France's war effort to defeat Ho Chi Minh.

Intelligence about the worsening of the military situation around Dien Bien Phu reached Washington in two stages. The first was the result of an urgent French request for transport and battle planes and for 400 mechanics for maintenance and repair work. American enquiries about the urgency disclosed that the previous optimism in regard to the absolute safety of Dien Bien Phu no longer existed. Access to the fortress had become, on account of successful Vietminh manoeuvres, limited and certain positions import-

† Admiral Radford's view seems to have been different. (Eisenhower op. cit. p. 340.)

ant for the operation of the Navarre Plan were endangered. Those groups on the American military and political scene to whom the loss of any part of Indochina implied a danger to the entire Southeast Asia area began agitation for intervention. The "defaitist" atmosphere of French parliamentary debates and the political concessions to its opposition by the Laniel Government committing it to a settlement were no secrets. On the other hand, a group of senators of the Democratic party voiced opposition against any military involvement and objected to the employment of any American military personnel, even if only mechanics. But both groups of alarmists were appeased by optimistic assurances of the Eisenhower Administration. Secretary of Defense Charles Wilson insisted as late as February 9 and March 23, that military victory of the French-Vietnamese forces was possible and probable.[8] "Victory," he said, "would be more difficult should the Chinese intervene but there was no reason to assume that America would have to increase its participation in the campaign." President Eisenhower responded to the partisan danger-signals of Democratic politicians by a strongly worded statement denying that military interventon in Southeast Asia was contemplated, that he would consider tragic any such undertaking and that, in order to avoid it, the United States was giving substantial aid to the French and the Vietnamese. And last but not least, he would not let America become involved in the Indochina war without previous Congressional consultation.[9]

The second signal of approaching catastrophy was prompted by information reaching Paris about continuing American confidence that as a result of the Navarre Plan the war in Indochina could and would end in victory. The Laniel Government felt that it was dutybound to dispel that unfounded optimism, all the more since the reconnoitering emissaries returning from Indochina made it known in no uncertain terms and without any qualification, that the war could not be won, that victory by France was beyond reach. Under these circumstances the French Cabinet, on March

11 decided to send General Ely to Washington. He had been invited earlier by Admiral Radford for informative conferences in regard to the situation in Indochina. He was to convey three messages. First, he was to relay to the American administration the fact that military victory could not be expected and that the conference strategy in Geneva must be based on this. Second, he was to say that the United States, in order to eliminate the danger of direct Chinese intervention, must undertake a formal, publicized obligation to intervene directly should China appear over Dien Bien Phu in the air, thereby making impossible the use of airplanes for its supply. Third, he was to inquire what steps the United States would take should China, without overt intervention, support the siege of Dien Bien Phu by increased measures that would endanger its defense.

This account has reached now the dawn of the dramatic crisis which in the following four months enveloped the Alliance and the Free World. The beginning was the attack by the Viet-Minh on March 13, a surprise attack that reduced the Dien Bien Phu fortress to an almost indefensible state. The attack's surprise strength consisted mainly in its artillery support which destroyed the outlying elevated defense positions, made aircraft landings impossible, and enabled the besieging forces to direct, without air support, their artillery on any of the strongholds of the defense position.

As of March 15 Navarre and all his officers in command positions *knew* that unless overwhelming outside forces would intervene, the battle was lost, that Dien Bien Phu was under sentence of death.[9a] In this situation General Navarre sent an urgent SOS signal to Paris for massive American air support, all possible equipment for transportation by parachute of supplies, and bombardment of the besieging Viet-Minh by American aircraft. This message with all that it implied reached Paris at the time when General Ely was about to depart for Washington on the mission that had been entrusted to him by the French Cabinet on March

11. Meanwhile, however, the main original purpose of his mission—to obtain formal and public assurance against overt Chinese air intervention in the Dien Bien Phu battle—became, on account of the change in the military situation on March 13, practically pointless. The Viet-Minh did not need the air support anymore. In view of the optimism of the Eisenhower Administration, his first task now was to convey the truth about the Dien Bien Phu position and the possibility of the defeat of the Navarre plan with such color of pessimism as to prompt Washington to satisfy the new request of Navarre for immediate and massive air support. On the other hand, he was to keep alive enough optimism in Washington to make the increased semi-direct intervention by greatly increased military supplies and further auxiliary military personnel appear to be still worthwhile. Finally, he had to convey the message that France was not willing to fight to a victory, that the public statements reassuring the opposition on this score were not pretense, that they expressed the strongly held conviction of his government and its military advisors.†

Admiral Radford sent his special plane to New York to take Ely to Washington without delay. The Admiral met him at the airport and asked him to dinner. There Ely found Vice-President Richard Nixon, Allen Dulles and the Chief of Staff of the Army, General Mathew Ridgway. As soon as Ely had relayed to his hosts Navarre's requests Radford personally gave orders in the presence of Ely and the others for the immediate shipment from the bases in the Philippines of everything that might be useful in the Indochina campaign. The French General was also assured that direct intervention by China would be met head on by the United States.

---

† The narration of General Ely's mission and negotiations which, outside of one insignificant reference to it, are unreported in Eisenhower's *Mandate For Change*, is based mainly on Ely's Memoirs, *L'Indochine Dans La Tourmente*, pp. 59-81. Additional information completing and qualifying it are based on Lacouture-Devillers, *La Fin d'une Guerre*, pp. 73-77 and Joseph Laniel, *Le Drame Indochinois*, pp. 83-84.

These first exchanges took place during the week-end. On Monday Ely was received by President Eisenhower in the company of Admiral Radford. The President was greatly concerned about Dien Bien Phu. Ely could not fail to notice what extraordinary importance the President attributed to the Dien Bien Phu battle, how concerned he was about it. In Ely's presence he gave orders to the Admiral to do everything to save the besieged fortress, to satisfy with priority all requests that the French might make. General Ely had the impression that these instructions were not qualified by any restriction. Quoting for the sake of accuracy General Ely's words in the French original also, the instruction was "sans paraitre y mettre la moindre limite . . . c'était pour moi un point important que, d'ailleurs l'amiral lui-même devait me rappeler à plusieurs reprises."[10]

This feature of the President's order was the basis of a surprising communication by Radford to Ely on the day that was added, at Radford's request, to the planned period of the General's Washington stay. On that day the Admiral stated to General Ely that if the French Government requested direct military intervention, the President's unrestricted instruction *opened the possibility of such direct* intervention of American air force for the saving of Dien Bien Phu. According to Radford, this would not appear as a direct act of war, but would be a one run, one hit aid act by aerial forces based in Manila.[11] †

---

† The French text of General Ely at the quoting of Radford's statement might not have intended to go as far as my English translation. It says: "Radford m'avait affirmé avec *une certaine insistence**, que . . . les Etats Unis seraient *prêts à examiner la possibilité* de faire intervenir. . . ." My interpretation, however, is supported by other references: a) General Ely's own impression that Radford's initiative was more than a theoretical possibility appears in his sentence following the Radford quotation: "C'était là une proposition dont l'importance ne pouvait m'échapper et il convenait d'en bien peser la porté." b) We find on the same page: "Les instructions du Président Eisenhower à son administration étaient, je le savais, de tout faire pour nous aider à sauver le camp retranché." That the President's order could not concern delivery of *materials only*, is made probable by the fact that as far as military end-items were concerned, Radford did not need Presidential instruction. He fulfilled Navarre's request two days before Ely's meeting with Eisenhower. c) Ely points out that the

The theory behind the Radford-Ely project was not as bellicose as it might at first appear. In Ely's mind, at least, it had logic and was not in conflict with the peace-seeking policy of his Government. The Vietminh success at Dien Bien Phu was about to defeat the Navarre plan. This might and probably would crash the hope of peaceful settlement upon reasonable terms. It appeared to him and (according to his report) to the French Government, which agreed to the plan of one powerful bombarding intervention by Amercan planes, to be quite safe and would not bring into the battle Chinese aircrafts or result in stepped-up and more direct Chinese intervention. Following the bombardment and the reestablishment of the battle situation at the previous balance, a French official statement to the effect that France would abide by its determination to come to terms in Geneva would have eliminated the danger of escalation into global conflict. This is the reason that the same French Government which—as we shall see presently—refused to join, before Geneva, a coalition and a Southeast Asia Defense Pact consented to the bombardment project.

Whatever was the extent and the resoluteness of Admiral

---

intervention proposed by Radford would have been a strictly limited move, not an act of war. It would be made as an increased measure of the American aid already in operation. Ely adds that the proposition was the natural conclusion reached by the two negotiators as corollary of their discussion. In fact, so he writes, its initiative might have come in the first place from himself. How could he, General Ely, put the intervention in terms of American "possibility" d) My interpretation that the air action was not considered by Radford as "examination of a possibility only" is confirmed by Lacouture-Devillers. On account of President Eisenhower's instruction to do "everything" for the aid of the French forces in the Dien Bien Phu battle, the American Chief of Staff—in view of the unexpected increase of Chinese support by artillery and D.C.A. believed that as a ripost, American aid could be carried somewhat further, that is into a tactical, aerial, though limited, operation, limited in time also. The Admiral insisted that the intervention could take place without Chinese provocation merely to help, and perhaps to save, the fortress' defenders. It would not make the United States a participant in the war and it would not be a prelude to further intervention. (Op. cit. p. 73. English translation by the author). Lacouture-Devillers' knowledge about this incident is not based on General Ely's information. Their book preceded that of Ely and they do not mention the General as their source.

Radford's proposition that French request for direct intervention would be fulfilled, the two chiefs recognized that the final decision was of a political nature and required agreement between the two governments. The Admiral assured Ely that it would have his all-out support and hinted that he expected to obtain Eisenhower's approval without difficulty. Therefore, he held out the promise that preparation for the execution of the operation would be ordered by him immediately. But he had doubts about the French decision. He questioned whether Ely's government would consent to American presence over the battlefield, though General Ely did not share this skepticism. The meetings of the two military leaders ended on the key of harmonious anticipation of an important military achievement.

Prior to this phase of Ely's negotiations the General met the Secretary of State. Admiral Radford was present at this conference also. Outside of this one conference General Ely had no real occasion to convey to the American Administration the message of French determination to restrict the Indochinese military operations to such time limit and such measure of success which will serve as basis for settlement. President Eisenhower and Admiral Radford were not too much interested in that more remote problem. Their concern was focused on Dien Bien Phu, and as secondary goal, on the creation of a local, Vietnamese army and achieving the independence of the Associated States. Thus, Ely's first occasion to give emphasis to this particular message of his mission was the conference with Dulles. The effect was not much more than a flash in the pan. The Secretary of State was not interested; he did not even express an opinion. Neither did Dulles discuss with Ely the military situation, the new crisis and particularly Dien Bien Phu. His insouciance in these respects was demonstrated by his absence from the conference with the President though he must have known that General Ely's mission was, in essence, of a diplomatic nature. Instead of this he propounded extensively his thesis about the general protection of Southeast Asia and the necessity of a pact among all states who wanted to prevent communist domination of Southeast Asia. His premise was that direct and open intervention of the United States, if such were necessary, must be preceded by an agreement in principle at least about such a pact among the European and Asian countries interested.†

The lack of interest, manifested towards the main preoccupation of the French Government and French public opinion in regard to their Indochina problem, made it clear to General Ely that the Eisenhower Administration was not eager, was probably not even willing, to "settle." Dulles and Radford both spoke about victory, no concessions, position of strength, and did not even let themselves be drawn into a discussion about how, at Geneva, a rapid termination of the war would be reached.[12] They showed no inclination to consider the possibility that the six hundred million Chinese should be followed by millions of Vietnamese into the orbit of the Kremlin.[13] For the documentation of the unwillingness to listen and to take note of disagreeable facts, two statements of the Secretary of State should be remembered. On March 22, ten days after the debacle that, in the opinion of the French commanders, had practically sealed the fate of Dien Bien Phu and defeated the Navarre plan, he issued an official statement that he saw no reason for the abandonment of the Navarre plan and that, in a year, its success would be achieved. Even victory would be attained by it.[14] On April 5, after General Ely had informed him personally and all his associates of the desperate deterioration of the military situation, he still maintained that "nothing had happened to change the basic estimate of relative military power for 1955."[15]

They gave more credence to the equally unduly optimistic statement of Bidault made by him in March 1954 (though

---

† Here appears for the first time the preoccupation of Dulles with a Southeast Asia Defense Pact that will play such a substantial role during the diplomatic crisis of 1954. (Ely, op. cit. p. 73).

before the disastrous defeat at Dien Bien Phu on March 13) promising victory and capitulation of Ho Chi Minh,[16] than to the reports about the debates in the Assemblée Nationale, and all other manifestations of French public opinion which demonstrated French resignation to withdrawal and ending the fight at the price of substantial concessions. This failure of Ely's mission, however, was so strongly overshadowed at that time, even in his mind, by the intense attention to the battle of Dien Bien Phu that the disagreement on this more remote point between Washington and Paris received but scant attention. Yet, this superficial and ostrich-like response of Washington became the source of all the misunderstandings that developed later in the season between the United States and its allies. General Ely's memoirs show that he saw clearly the disagreement but failed to drive the point home. He too was more interested in the immediate danger of Ucalegon's house that was already burning.

Ely, upon his return to Paris, let Defense Minister Pleven in forthwith on Radford's spectacular overture.† The French Government, as Admiral Radford had anticipated, neither embraced with enthusiasm the proposition nor did it make a hasty decision. They despatched a special military envoy to Vietnam to ascertain whether the bombardment proposed by the Admiral would achieve the rescue of Dien Bien Phu. The envoy's affirmative report, brought back from Saigon, was accompanied by a formal cable-request of Navarre to bring the American air force into immediate action. Only when all this had been done and the repercussions from the political and military viewpoint had been carefully considered did the French War Cabinet decide that the official request should be made and transmitted through the American Ambassador to Washington. This was done by Premier Laniel personally at about midnight, on Sunday, April 4. Simultaneously, General Ely cabled the same message to Admiral Radford.[17]

---

† "Extraordinaire ouverture" are Ely's words in French. (Lacouture-Devillers, op. cit. p. 73).

The French Government and, of course, General Ely expected immediate military action.[18] Instead of the affirmative deed, the answer was the rejecting word: NO. Dulles delivered it to the French Ambassador in Washington on April 6.[18b]

Until April 3, the intervention plan of Radford was on its way to materialization. During Ely's presence in Washington and in the days after his departure a genuine panic shook the atmosphere there. The previous optimism greatly contributed to the strength of the reversion to pessimism. Domestic political considerations too must have played considerable role. No trainbearer of the Republican Party could have been impervious to the possible public reaction to a roll-back in reverse, losing Southeast Asia to Communism. No doubt, Admiral Radford was not inactive either. He must have divulged Ely's pessimistic information about the military situation to Vice President Nixon, to the right-wing of the Republican Party, to the State Department officers in charge of Far Eastern affairs, Walter Robertson, Assistant Secretary of State, and Douglas MacArthur II, the nephew of the General, in the higher ranks of the echelon to whom communist take-over in Indochina was cause for terror. One must include among the determinants the conclusions of a National Security Meeting on March 6, recommending that all possible measures should be taken to prevent communist conquest of that area,[19] and the reasonable concern about the countries neighboring Indochina which, since the end of the war, had not yet been able to set their newly independent houses in order and were therefore exposed not only to danger from outside but to threats to their internal security.

This alarm was behind the "fundamental policy decision," reported "on highest authority" by James Reston in the *New York Times* of March 30. The decision which President Eisenhower later called "momentous" meant the resolve to execute—as soon as France should ask for it—the aerial bombardment for the raising of the siege of Dien Bien Phu. Its political presentation was entrusted to the Secretary of State.

The assignment was not an easy task. Dulles had to reconcile the faithful execution of the presidential commission with his own long-term preoccupations and his own design for the treatment of the Indochina crisis. He had to build a bridge between the new policy of giving the ripost of an American military blow in case of indirect Chinese aggression with previous pronouncements pledging direct American military action only in the case of overt and *direct* Chinese intervention. Yet, the speech was the occasion also to kill the Ely-Radford plan of intervention and introduce his own general foreign policy line.

The Secretary of State fullfilled his task in the grand manner of a master. He made the address announcing the fundamental and momentous decision of the President on March 29 before an important gathering in the Overseas Press Club of America. The event was highly dramatized. The key sentences were leaked to the press before delivery. The text was also communicated, before delivery, to the British and French Ambassadors and to Congressional leaders. It was disclosed and consequently confirmed by Eisenhower that the President had approved every word of it.

Dulles in his address[20] set forth that

> "under the conditions of today the imposition on Southeast Asia of the political system of Communist Russia and its Chinese communist ally, by *whatever means,** would be a grave threat to the whole Free World community and . . . should not be passively accepted but should be met by *united action.** This might involve serious risks but these risks are far less than would face us a few years from now if we are not resolute today."

In order to fulfill the President's promise to General Ely, he added:

> "The chances of peace are usually bettered by letting a potential aggressor know in advance where his aggression could lead him. I hope that the statements which I make here tonight will serve the cause of peace."

Reston, again "on highest authority," disclosed that according to the official view, while the United States guaranteed Korea against aggression, Southeast Asia was to hold much more importance for the Free World.[21]

> "A complete communist conquest of Indochina would have had far graver consequences for the West than a Red victory in Korea,"

reports Sherman Adams as Eisenhower's and Dulles' opinion.[22] Dulles himself also expressed his opinion that by the conquest of Indochina, Red China and Russia expected to dominate all of Southeast Asia.

> "This would carry a grave threat to the Philippines, Australia, and New Zealand. . . . The entire west Pacific area, including the so-called 'offshore island chain' would be strategically endangered."

He also quoted President Eisenhower as saying: "the area is of transcendent importance."

Dulles' speech, according to the *New York Times* of March 31, had the twofold purpose of warning Communist China that the West was not going to buy peace with concessions and also of discouraging France in its hopes that peace would be gained by negotiations. In an editorial of the same day, the newspaper said that

> "Dulles was plain as words would allow in insisting that the United States look upon this struggle as vital to its interests and will not stand passively by."

There are two new moves imbedded in this speech. The first one was put in the words that imposition of communism "by whatever means," might bring about direct American action.† The second move was the linking of the Radford plan with his own policy by introducing in the key sentence of the speech the words "united action." In the discussions between the Admiral and Ely no such idea had ever even

---

† The full significance of the words "whatever means" was explained by Dulles in his testimony at the Committee on Foreign Affairs of the House of Representatives, on April 5. (See p. 54).

been mentioned. Neither Ely's memoirs, nor those of Laniel, neither the day-by-day, blow-by-blow report of Chalmers M. Roberts, "based both on the scanty public record and on private information gathered in London, Paris, at the Geneva Conference and in Washington from American and Allied officials,"[23] nor the exceedingly precise, specific and exhaustive narration of the Lacouture-Devillers' book admits the possibility that anything but unaided solitary United States intervention was contemplated. Prior to Dulles' speech we find no hint or insistence that the United States would not act without participation of allies or partners. Without the words "united action," Dulles' pronouncement would have been a powerful introduction to action on or after April 6 as soon as the French Government had made the request for it. The qualification that the action to be taken must be "united" produced the vehicle on which Dulles' opposition against the Radford-Ely plan rode to success.

An incident that involved former Vice President Richard M. Nixon in this chapter of the Indochina crisis confirms by inference my interpretation of Dulles' move for "united action." On April 16, Nixon in an address before the American Society of Newspaper Editors, made the assertion that

> "if to avoid further Communist expansion in Asia and Indochina we must take the risk now by putting our boys in, I think the Executive has to take the politically unpopular decision to do it."

This is the text in Eisenhower's version,[24] but according to the text in the *New York Times* the Vice President went beyond this:

> "For one, the problem (in Indochina) is not one of materials and wasn't four month ago. More men are needed and the question is where to get them. They will not come from France, for France is tired of the war, as we were tired of Korea. . . . But the Vietnamese lack the ability to conduct a war by themselves or govern themselves. If the French withdraw Indochina would become Communist dominated within a month. The

United States as leader of the Free World cannot afford further retreat in Asia. It is hoped that the United States will not have to send troops there, but if this Government cannot avoid it, the Administration must face up to the situation and despatch forces."[24a]

As this greatly disturbed Dulles' mollifying diplomacy the State Department issued a statement claiming that Nixon's speech[25] "enunciated no new policy," that it was in full agreement with Dulles' March 29 speech. This was true in regard to one point: Nixon's statement was not new policy. On the contrary, it was the old policy of the Radford-Ely agreement. But it certainly was not identical with Dulles' "united action" thesis. It specified that the Administration would have to send American soldiers into battle. In that regard the State Department's statement was misleading.

But the repercussions of the Nixon speech were not quieted by the attempt of the State Department to explain it away. Nixon was damned in Congress for "whooping it up for war." So, two days later, Nixon "greatly disturbed about some of the reactions to his recent controversial speech on the possibility of the United States' intervention in the Indochina war," gave a new explanation. "While he did not anticipate that the French would quit in Indochina, he thought the United States would have to replace them if necessary to prevent a Communist conquest of Southeast Asia."[26]

On April 20, the Vice President in another speech in Cincinnati was at it again. The essence of his speech there was that the United States would do everything to avoid war but "we have a test of that policy in Indochina. This is just not a civil war, it is a war of aggression by the Communist conspiracy against all the free nations . . . The aim of the United States is to hold Indochina without war involving the United States, if we can. We have learned that if you are weak and indecisive, you invite war. You don't keep the

41

Communists out of an area by telling them you won't do anything to save it."[27]

This confusing incident must have been caused by somebody's slip to keep Nixon posted about the repeated changes of direction of the Indochina policy. It is obvious that the Vice President did not know when he made his speech on April 16 that the Radford-Ely plan of solitary action had been abandoned and did not know that—as we shall see presently—even the immediate bellicose intervention by united action had been put off. This background of the vicissitudes of hesitant policy-making is confirmed by a revealing intelligence in Sherman Adams' memoirs: He narrates that Eisenhower called Nixon on the telephone and "told him not to be upset. Trying to cheer him up, the President reassured him that the uproar over his comment had been all to the good because it awakened the country to the seriousness of the situation."[28]†

This Nixon incident has, however, significance beyond the picture of confusion and indecision that it discloses. It makes it almost uncontradictable that the Radford-Ely intervention was conceived as a purely American operation. Vice President Nixon presented it on April 16 in the form in which it had been originally planned. It was Dulles who remade it into an operation that would be part of a "united action."

Before the repercussions of the "united action" insert in Dulles speech can be narrated, we reach the point where the conflict between the Radford intervention and Dulles' policy must be set forth. We must revert to the Berlin Conference. American consent there to negotiations towards a settlement of the Indochina conflict were, for Dulles, not for the purpose of abatement of differences and adjustment of con-

---

† Vice President Nixon in a private communication confirmed that though Dulles favored military intervention, he was forced to abandon the plan because Britain and other allies disagreed. On the other hand, Nixon himself advocated military action regardless of allied support. According to him, he expressed in his speech of April 16 the policy that he personally championed. Therefore, in his opinion, his statement was not the result of a misunderstanding. This is contradicted by the disclosures quoted in the text.

flicting interests, but rather to gain time. By creating independent Indochinese states, by eliminating the political handicap of French colonialism, by building a well-equipped Vietnamese army and by the continued fighting of the French Expeditionary Force, the communist forces captained by Ho Chi Minh, the Moscow-trained agent of International Communism, would be rolled back. Dulles opposed the British-French consent to the Geneva Conference and, supported by Eisenhower, put up strong resistance to it.[29] Ultimately, they ceased opposition but had no intention whatever of helping it to advance its purpose, the peaceful solution of the local Vietnamese problem. For them it was but a localized appearance of one head of the Hydra of communism that must not be permitted to increase further the power of the main body. But, over and above his own anti-communist phobia, Dulles had a personal motive in favoring strong resistance to any concession to Ho Chi Minh. The dominant elements of the Republican party, which after twenty years of exile came back to power with Eisenhower had on their shield anticommunism as *verbum regens*. Even Dulles, after Berlin, was under attack for letting our allies engage in negotiation with Communist China, and to boot, seat the United States at the same conference table. Thus, the Secretary of State could not be entirely rational and personally unaffected. He would not have liked to enlarge the target of the attack directed against himself.

Taking all this into consideration and anticipating here the matters that this study will detail about the relation of American diplomacy to the Geneva Conference, it does not sound credible that Dulles objected to the military intervention planned by Radford because it was a bellicose, aggressive move against Communism. It is tempting to venture a more probable answer to why he did not give it his wholehearted support. Ely's report sounds as if Dulles had been in the sulks. He had one meeting only with Ely and was absent from all other conferences. He did not show any interest in the developing plan of immediate military intervention in spite of its possibly wide international repercussions. During his meeting with Ely he was reticent. He maintained a nonchalant detachment towards Ely's exposé of the French Government's resolve to restrict its policy to the achievement of a political solution, to disregard military achievements, victory, prestige considerations, but rather to seek the end of the war above any other consideration.[30]

Dulles was not averse to the extension of America's participation in the war in Indochina *per se,* but his plan connected it, according to Ely's report, with three principles of general nature. First, the intervention must have as a basis a political understanding, a pact among the countries which have southeast Asian interests; such a political basis would make it possible for the United States to undertake a *stronger,* more far-reaching intervention. Second, he pointed out forcibly, that once the United States was a participant, it must achieve *total* victory. Third, before the United States could make its entry, all traces of colonialism must be eliminated.

These three theses of Dulles differed from the Ely-Radford plan of action in several respects. The Chief of Staff had a short-term operation in mind: the restoration of the balance of the military situation that had been tottering since the artillery attack on March 13. The Ely-Radford plan did not demand total elimination of all traces of French political position. Their intervention plan would have reactivated the Navarre plan, enabling France to reach a good settlement at Geneva which might have saved some political advantages for France. This, in turn, would make it worthwhile for the French to moderate the urge for peace at any price and to stay with full conviction in the fight. Thirdly, the Radford intervention would not have taken away from the French supreme and overall command. It would have been one restricted military operation. The Dulles plan would have internationalized the entire campaign and would have given the United States the right to make the ultimate decisions. Dulles' demand for a political pact before Geneva might have killed the Geneva Conference on Indochina before it began. A pact, threatening China with attack should further aid be given to the Vietminh, would have hurt Chinese prestige much more than an aerial attack restricted to Vietminh positions. This is the reason that the same French Government that agreed to the Radford Plan, refused, as we shall see presently, to join the Dulles-advocated coalition, a general Southeast Asia defense pact, or even a joint declaration approving its principles before the end of the Geneva Conference.

If this review correctly sets forth the characteristic features of the two American lines of proposed action the conclusion is warranted that Dulles' antagonism to the Radford plan was rooted not in caution—that is, the civilian, diplomatic aversion to the risks of a bold, aggressive military move. Rather, he opposed it because it was much too modest. Instead of aiming at total victory, it envisaged a temporary military result that would enhance the chances of a settlement by concessions. He opposed it because it was a short-term operation, certainly not part of an anti-communist crusade. He opposed it because it would accomplish nothing against French colonialism. Finally, the Radford intervention might be represented as American support of European colonialism, a demonstration of American imperialism that would endanger the claim of the United States to moral leadership of the non-Communist world to gain the support and partisanship of the emerging new powers of Asia and Africa.

While the proponents of nonintervention, both within and outside the United States, as well as the partisans of a Radford type of aerial action restricted themselves to diplomacy, conferences, concessions, and short-term ideas, the architect of American foreign policy, John Foster Dulles, subordinated the Indochina diplomacy, including military operations, to the principles of an overall foreign policy that begins where diplomacy ends. Whether his chosen policy was good or bad, right or wrong, whether he applied good or bad diplomacy for its realization, are other questions. But there is no doubt that his diplomacy in regard to the crisis in Indochina was grounded in a long-term foreign policy line and decision. He did not think merely in terms of local solutions in Indo-china, even in Asia as a whole. His planning embraced the global confrontation with the enemy, International Com-munism. His policy covered the entire field of the Crusade, the roll-back of Communism that must be achieved by a fighting coalition of allied European and Asian countries. This would make his victorious country the political and moral leader of the world. His policy would make the United States of America after its victory, the great, respected leader of the entire world community, among not only the more advanced European allies but among those peoples whom Dulles viewed as the emerging powers, the Arabs, the Africans, the South Americans, Hindus, and others.

For the achievement of this policy the Dulles diplomacy would use threats, limited military intervention and the face-saving possibilities of international conferences. But over and above such means of diplomacy and their manoeuvers Dulles insisted on a coalition, a large group of countries, as-sociated with the United States on the basis of a pact that would remove the imperialist color from its power position and would acquire and maintain moral leadership for the United States.

General Ely seems to have sensed that his mission did not find full sympathy with the Secretary of State. When this was noticed by Radford, he made it known to Ely that the President's position might differ in some degree from that of Dulles.[31] This much seems to be clear: that before Ely's return to France the President was in full agreement with Radford. Insofar as divergence of views did exist between Dulles and Radford, the President was on Radford's side.

But Foster Dulles was not easily dethroned. He achieved the comeback by manoeuvers which could not fail to bring the President to his side. Generals Ridgeway and Twining warned the President that, exactly as in Korea, mere air and naval action would not be sufficient, would have to be backed up by ground troops, and that eight full divisions would be needed for decisive action and that those divisions were not available.[32] The President had a distaste for using force, and Dulles' arguments against participation in a colonial warfare of France found him sympathetic. These influences, however, would have probably not overcome the President's almost emotional resolve to save the heroic defenders of Dien Bien Phu and thereby restore with one strike the military balance of power which would ultimately lead to peace, and which would end bloodshed and the financial burden of the Indochina war on American resources. The Presiden't change of mind was caused by two effects of the "united action" idea.

The first one was its international repercussion. Though Dulles did not elaborate the "united action" idea and did not say anything about its implications, reference to it, coupled with the call to arms, drove envoys of allied countries in a hurry to the State Department to discover what the two words had meant to say. There would probably have been no objection to the idea of a plan of coalition but there seems to have been serious resentment against a public announcement, almost on their behalf, without consultation and consent. Complaints were voiced that it had become

"the habit of the United States Administration to make unilateral statements about issues of world importance and then expect full support from London"[33]

It was reported from London that

"Great Britain would like to know just what Secretary of State Dulles meant when he said that the West would meet with 'united action'* the imposition of the Communist system in Southeast Asia. A Foreign Office spokesman said the government would seek clarification of points raised by Mr. Dulles."[34]

Announcement of united action without previous consultation of Britain and France and our other allies in-

47

terested in Southeast Asiatic problems was caused by an obsolescent image of the United States' relation to members of the Atlantic Community. There was a period, prior to 1945, when the United States could withhold its aid and support from the Western European countries, Britain or France whenever isolationist tendency was the prevalent atmosphere of the American political scene or grant it to them subject to conditions unilaterally set on this side of the Atlantic Ocean. Dulles did not seem to have been aware in 1954 of the great change that had occured in this respect. In the new power relationship—the United States facing a powerful hostile rival, the Soviet Power—

> "our problem has become, so it appears to us, not whether we will join the allies, but whether the allies will stay with us."[35]

An authoritative French publication[36] reported that at least five ambassadors (not counting the British and the French) called on Dulles with this inquiry and another source lists them as the Ambassadors of Canada, Italy, India, New Zealand and the Philippines.

At this juncture Eden sent the British Ambassador to the State Department with the following message:

> "We fully share the United States' desire to see Indochina preserved from communism and agree that, so long as there is any hope of success, the French should be urged to maintain their present effort. But after earnest study of military and political factors we feel it would be unrealistic not to face the possibility that the conditions for a favorable solution in Indochina may no longer exist. Failure to consider this possibility now is likely to increase the difficulty of reaching tripartite agreement should we be forced at Geneva to accept a policy of compromise."

The Ambassador introduced in his conversation with Dulles and Under-Secretary Bedell Smith the British plan to solve the Indochina crisis by partition. The response was wholly negative. The United States had, of course, already studied partition as a solution but had concluded that it would result in Communist domination of Southeast Asia and had, therefore, rejected it. Dulles also told the Ambassador that China must be compelled to stop aid to the Vietminh and that this should be done by a threat of *military* intervention proclaimed by several countries. Should the threat not be heeded, it would be followed by naval and air action against the China coast.[36b]

The address of Dulles did not commit any of the allies to intervention. But their immediate reaction against the use of force in retaliation for indirect Chinese aid and its possible effect on Russian policy in relation to them had no doubt some restraining effect on the President's thinking. But in all probability the appeal to the Constitution—to the principle that, in regard to measures which may engage America in any kind of war, the authority and consent of Congress must be obtained—decided the issue. Eisenhower expressed often his inhibitions in this respect.

> "Eisenhower did not want to repeat the mistake he believed that Truman had made in 1950 in sending air and naval forces to South Korea without consulting Congress."[37]

Thus the radical change came on April 3. On that day, Dulles, with the President's knowledge, assembled in the Department of State eight Congressional leaders—five senators and three congressmen—representing both parties. Admiral Radford, Under-Secretary of Defense Roger Keys, and Navy Secretary Robert B. Anderson attended the conference. Admiral Radford submitted his plan for intervention to relieve Dien Bien Phu. He set forth the military details, the considerations that led him to believe that a limited single bombardment would not necessarily put the country to war. The legislators disagreed. They were unanimous that the intervention must not be made unless the United States was acting not alone, but as a member of a genuine coalition, supported by the army and political power of its allies, with Britain and France among them at the top of the scale.

This demand that the United States should intervene only if a genuine coalition joined the action, only if other armies would participate in the warfare, connects Dulles' united action idea with the refusal to comply with the French request for immediate military action. Dulles could not argue convincingly against the congressional demand that was in full agreement with his own idea. The legislators, in essence, joined his camp, became his associates.

This consultation with Congress wiped the slate clean. On April 3, the Radford-Ely project lost the support of President Eisenhower. From that day the reins were again in the hands of Dulles. The direction was from then on not towards the Navarre plan, nor to aid to the British-French project which would pursue settlement and peace through success at Geneva. Whatever interim diplomatic measures might be employed, the ultimate goal of the Dulles diplomacy would be the realization of his victory policy. Thus the answer to the French request based on the Radford-Ely plan had to be *NO*. Dulles wanted intervention but of a different kind, a farsighted comprehensive, long-range operation.

4

On April 4 Dulles must have already known what would be, in all probability, the French Government's decision about the proposed aerial intervention. The response of the field commanders in Saigon to the American rescue operation must have reached the Department of State from its listening posts in Vietnam and Paris. Thus as soon as the Radford-Ely plan of aerial intervention came a cropper in Washington, Dulles went into action at full speed. The threatening defeat at Dien Bien Phu and the danger of a settlement with substantial concessions at Geneva demanded urgency.

As a good Secretary, true to his thesis about the proprieties of the relationship between cabinet members and the President,† he let Eisenhower make the opening shot. But it was also good strategy, with special regard to the previous slight difference of opinion between him and Eisenhower, to make his coalition plans appear as Eisenhower's own proposal. This could be expected to help Dulles' scheme

---

† Dulles' planned deference in his relation to the President is described fully by Richard Goold Adams, The Time of Power, pp. 69-71; Roscoe Drummond-Gaston Coblentz, *Duel At The Brink*, pp. 21-22.

to receive the blessing of approval of Congress and consent of the allies.

Thus, on April 4, a personal letter of Eisenhower was dispatched to Churchill.†† The letter was insistent. As *captatio benevolentiae,* it dealt with the French situation as the joint concern of Britain and the United States, as two special allies who have to handle it as their combined operation. The letter appealed to their special comradeship in world affairs.† Finally, the letter invoked the Churchillian sense of history. Eisenhower set forth his conviction that "there was no negotiated solution of the Indochina problem" and that the only satisfactory answer to the grave threat by Russia and its Chinese ally was "united action" with teeth in it, by a strong coalition

> "willing to join the fight if necessary—though I [Eisenhower] do not envisage the need of any appreciable ground forces on your or our part . . ."

Eisenhower enumerated the prospective members of the coalition—United States, Great Britain, France, the three Associated States of Indochina, Australia, New Zealand, Thailand and the Philippines—and stated that "the United States Government would expect to play its full part in such a coalition . . ." He ended his solemn entreaty by recalling past failures to heed Churchill's prophetic warnings.

> "We failed to halt Hirohito, Mussolini and Hitler by not acting in unity and in time. That marked the beginning of many years of stark tragedy and desperate peril. May it not be that our nations have learned something from that lesson?"[1]

Simultaneously, possibly one or two days later, the State Department sent to the British and French governments a formal proposal, embodying in language of diplomacy the tangible features of the Eisenhower letter.[2] It recommended

---

† This appeal to the special relationship between Britain and the United States sounds somewhat hollow after the refusal to maintain such bond of kinship when Churchill at the Bermuda Conference of 1953 suggested it.

†† See Appendix I, p. 231.

that the United States, France, Britain, Australia, New Zealand, Thailand, the Philippines and the three Associated States of Indochina should issue, before the Geneva Conference, a solemn declaration under Article 51 of the United Nations Charter, in which they would state their readiness to act in self-defense against the aggression committed by China by its intervention in the Indochina war. This threat would be followed by naval and air action against the China coast and by active intervention in Indochina itself. The states participating in this action would *simultaneously* begin organizing the collective defense of South Asia for any subsequent situation.

On April 5 Dulles, in his testimony before the Committee on Foreign Affairs of the House of Representatives, presenting for committee approval the Mutual Security Act of 1954, gave the fullest possible exposition of his new Indochina policy.[3] He set forth a number of new elements which made new policy necessary. He alleged as fact that the Communist campaign aimed at the domination of all Southeast Asia, threatening Malaya, Thailand, Indonesia, the Philippines, Australia and New Zealand. He brought out that the Communists were making a supreme effort, expending recklessly their military assets to break the fighting spirit of the French before the Geneva Conference.

> "That scheme must be frustrated. The way is to prove that when the Communists use their manpower in massive, suicidal assaults designed to break a single will, the result is the rallying of many wills that, together, are unbreakable. . . . That is the judgment of this administration. . . . I hope that it will be shared by the other nations concerned. . . . The imposition on Southeast Asia of the political system of Communist Russia and its Chinese Communist ally would be a grave threat to many. It should not be passively accepted but met by unity of will and and, if need be, by unity of action."†

---

† These last words are almost literally identical with Eisenhower's words used in the letter to Churchill.

Continuing the enumeration of new elements, the Secretary of State brought out that the size of Chinese aid and the proven presence of Chinese military personnel under the command of a Chinese General Ly Chen-Hou made Chinese participation in the war a direct and overt operation, "a very ominous" event. In his opinion the Chinese were "skirting very close to doing the kind of thing against which President Eisenhower gave the warnings," i.e., that the Chinese must not exploit the truce in Korea for intervention in Indochina. In this connection Dulles referred to a speech he had made in St. Louis on September 2, 1953, in which he said that "if the Chinese sent their Red armies into Indochina that would be apt to produce reactions which might not be confined to Indochina."

Finally, Dulles put in high relief a part of his speech made on March 29.

> "I did something in the speech of (March 29) which is something rather *new*.* I [Dulles] said there that this conquest [of Indochina] *'by whatever means'*
> I used the term *'by whatever means'* . . . and that the United States concern should not be mitigated by the fact that the means are perhaps technically evasive."

One more point needs be recorded from Dulles' statement. When one of the Congressmen, correctly, pointed out that the March 29 speech did not exclude the possibility of United States action "individually" or "alone," Dulles corrected this interpretation.

> "The threat," he said, "is a grave threat to many countries and our judgment is that it should be recognized as such by them and I [Dulles] would hesitate to ask for action by the United States alone."

This extensive presentation of Dulles' testimony serves to highlight the newness and aggressive militancy of the policy adopted by Eisenhower and Dulles in preference to the Radford plan. The testimony was more articulate, more explicit than the speech; it makes the conclusions already set forth evident and well grounded.

On April 7, both Eisenhower and Dulles were at work keeping the flames of excitement, the forewarnings and the forebodings of ominous possibilities in operation. Their obvious purpose was to prepare public opinion at home to the dangerous nature of the world situation and keep the psychological warfare in high gear. On that day Dulles in another address[4] to the Republican Women's Centennial Conference, reiterated his previous warnings:

> "The potential danger [in Indochina] is very, very great and needs to be soberly appraised with a view of seeing whether a united will can be created."

Eisenhower in his press conference on April 7 picked up where Dulles left off. Speaking slowly and deliberately,[5] he said that the possible consequences of the loss of Southeast Asia were incalculable to the Free World. He set forth his "domino theory." The tumble of one piece is necessarily followed by the fall of a whole series of neighboring ones. Similarly, weak and shaky states exposed to Communist conquest collapse in groups if any one of them falls victim to its onslaught. Thus, in the sequence of events, if Indochina were to fall, it would be followed by the likely fall of Burma, Thailand, the whole Indochinese peninsula and Indonesia, and the consequent loss of more people to dictatorship. There were also, he said, strategic considerations. Further losses would mean that the so-called defensive island chain of Japan, Formosa and the Philippines would be affected and, furthermore, Australia and New Zealand would be involved. The Communist domination of Southeast Asia would mean that Japan would have as its only trading area, China, and the other Communist countries.

> "But this problem could not be handled by one country alone. There must be "a concert of readiness to react *in whatever way** it was necessary."[6]

To a question whether there was a chance of reaching a negotiated settlement at Geneva, Eisenhower said that he did not think so—at least not one which the Free World could consider adequate. In summary, he said the Indochina problem was of the utmost importance.

According to the London Times,

> "Dulles with the President's support, appears now to have moved beyond the concept of retaliation. He has suggested that a Communist victory, even if achieved with Vietnam forces alone, is not to be tolerated."[7]

In answer to the bellicose formal proposal reported by Eden (supra p. 53) the French Government made its decision on April 6, the British on April 7. The two governments were in agreement that no action should be taken before the possibilities of negotiated settlement had been exhausted. They would not agree to any step, any act of diplomacy or anything else, which might interfere with the negotiations that were to take place in Geneva. Premier Laniel, on April 9, assured the Assemblée Nationale in Paris that his government would not make any commitments that might curb its freedom of action in Geneva. These refusals, their promptness and resoluteness not only against bellicose acts and threats but against any kind of joint diplomatic statements, the endorsement of this refusal in England and in France by public opinion, by legislators and by the Commonwealth countries (especially Australia) could not fail to impress Washington. The *London Times* characterized the response in Washington to these manifestations of disagreement as a "shock."[8] Eisenhower found this contrary to good sense. He made light of the attitude which

> "puts such heavy reliance on the value of negotiations with the Communists . . . Any preparations made in advance of the Geneva Conference for united action, the British felt, would be unacceptable, apparently for fear of irritating the Communists."

He rationalized the British stand with the disparaging remark that Britain was a "small island," its power was created and maintained by diplomacy, negotiation and changing configurations in alliance. (What misreading of history and the power of Great Britain whose fleet protected the safety of the United States for a century.) Eisenhower continued:

> "To put much faith in the process of negotiation" may be true in principle," but in its application to dealings with Communists I considered it unrealistic. To my knowledge the fact that Communists were to participate in any international conference never implied that they would either make concessions or keep promises."[9]

Under the disappointing impact of the British and French rejection of his new aggressive line of action Dulles realized that it would be better diplomacy to make a partial withdrawal by dropping from his plan, at least temporarily, the threat of immediate military intervention against the semi-overt, though technically concealed, Chinese participation. He decided that, for the time being, it would be of advantage to create first the second coalition, the defense-pact for the protection of Southeast Asia. He became aware of the fact that even for the achievement of this less ambitious step stronger and more direct pressure was necessary than the Eisenhower letter to Churchill or the State Department diplomacy. His personal intervention and persuasive power might achieve success where the previous attempts had failed. Eisenhower agreed: Dulles must go to London and Paris.

Before we turn to the ominous pilgrimage of Dulles to bring home Britain's and France's consent to diplomatic intervention it is worthwhile to point out that the fundamental decision by Eisenhower and Dulles to change the position of the United States from a helpful ally supporting France in its effort to beat the Communist rebels into a leader of a coalition meeting head on the aggressive onslaught of International Communism, was not a frenzy of adventurous saber-rattling. Neither was it dictated, as inimical interpreters of political life construed and explained it—by domestic politicking and currying the favor of extremist Asia-firsters or members of the China Lobby only. It was the truly logical and rational corollary of the Eisenhower and Dulles diagnosis of the Indochina crisis. They sincerely believed, first, that:

France could not be trusted to be willing and able to fight to the finish and achieve victory, backed only with financial and material support.

Second, they believed that partial loss of Indochina by partition and settlement would soon bring about the complete loss of that country because Communists never respect international agreements and use them invariably as stepping stones for further aggression.

Third, they believed that consent to the loss of Indochina —implying enslavement of thirty to forty million people —was unethical and would endanger the moral authority of the leaders of the Free World and would lead to the voluntary defection of other weak or hesitant peoples and their governments.

Fourth, they believed that even without such political consequences, under the domino theory of international politics, a large number of countries in a shaky economic, financial, and political situation would be conquered easily by the Soviet and Communist China.

And fifth, they believed that to prevent isolation and loss of strategic bases, the powers of the Free World would have to stand up soon anyway and face the increasing danger of the deteriorating situation; if they delayed doing so they would gain nothing but endanger and risk everything while "the loss can be prevented without extending the Indochina war if the free nations having vital interests in the area unite in their determination to preserve peace and freedom in that area."[10]

Summing up, the decision to turn to direct military action was the rational and sensible inference from the assumption which Eisenhower and Dulles held to be true and commanding. It was not merely "brinkmanship." This will be clearly shown by the step-by-step development of American policy before and during the Geneva Conference. Thus, history must evaluate and judge this American policy decision in the light of its determinants and not *a posteriori* interpretations. But understanding and setting the new Southeast Asia policy in its proper framework does not absolve it from its grievous shortsightedness. History cannot judge results by the motives or intentions which prompted them. It was rooted in dogmatic obsession with the immutability of communism's drive for expansion and with the impossibility of even a temporary coexistence and accommodation by which the Communist Powers might abide. It was rooted in lack of confidence in the recuperative vitality of Europe and Free Uncommitted Asia. To Eisenhower and Dulles there was no half-way house between total victory and total defeat. They judged every international action by a strict code of law and morals that demands rewards for good actions, and punishment for bad ones. Their sudden militancy and demand for immediate action in Indochina neglected the possibility of erosion in the Communist camp of internal controversies of their own. Last but not least, their dogmatic domino theory obscured from them the possibility that the fall of one piece, one bastion, one country does not necessarily mean destruction of all others if the others have the time to strengthen their own, independent base. They did not foresee the spectacular recovery of Western Europe and Japan, the new vigor of the Philippines, or the self-assertion of the European satellites. They shut their eyes to the sources of conflict between Russia and China, and China and India, with its balance of terror. It is certainly surprising that Eisenhower as late as 1963, at a time when these earthshaking changes were clearly ascertainable, printed in his *Mandate For Change* the dogmas and obsessions which directed his thinking in 1954.

The chances of success of the Dulles mission to Europe could not have been less promising. Eisenhower and Dulles knew that Britain, more especially Eden, was dead set that no move should be made which might disturb the chances of a settlement. Eden never left any doubt that he attributed great importance to doing nothing in Southeast Asia unless

India and other neutralist Far Eastern nations were consulted. He felt that these states dreaded the extension of the Indochina campaign into a general war—with direct and open participation of America, Britain and China—and that therefore, they might be persuaded to support from the sidelines the efforts towards a settlement. India, indeed, did not look with favor on non-Asian interference in the Indochina situation, and did not appraise Ho Chi Minh's campaign as an offensive move by Communist China. To India, Ho was fighting against colonialism, for independence, and for freedom. Thus, India's presence at the conference table would be tantamount to making intervention impossible.

Dulles had another reason to abhor the thought of India joining the coalition or being consulted in the preparatory phase of the combination. He anticipated that such an occurrence would immediately create a clamor back home in Congress to include also Chiang Kai-shek, who with his army—so the argument ran—might make military intervention possible without engaging substantial American ground forces in the fight. This idea might have been behind that sentence of Eisenhower's letter to Churchill in which he hinted that, probably, no strong participation by American and British ground forces would become necessary. In fact, General Stewart, chief of military aid operations, did publish his plan to send Chiang's army units to Indochina.[11]

In brief, the opposing diplomatic battle lines were clearly drawn. America wanted a coalition of Eisenhower's choosing to make threatening moves and then to intervene militarily in Indochina. This would be done before the Geneva Conference. It would be for the purpose of rekindling the French will to win, and, correspondingly, to raise apprehensions in the enemy camp. The British wanted no action before the Geneva Conference. They wanted to keep the opponents guessing and they wanted to nurture India, Pakistan and Ceylon as eventual helpers to promote their strong interest in keeping the fighting localized. Therefore, though to all outside observers the Dulles mission must have appeared from the beginning doomed to failure, to Eisenhower the alternative course—that of a negotiated settlement— was "too serious in its broad strategic implications to be acceptable."[12]

Shortly after reaching England, Dulles reported back to the President

> "*with some optimism** . . . that he had accomplished much toward dispelling British reluctance to say or do anything *before** Geneva,"

and that

> "the official communiqué issued that day indicated a large measure of acceptance of our [American] view of the danger and necessity for united action."[13]

But the joint announcement after the talks—repeated by Eden word for word next day in the House of Commons— stated

> ". . . We [the United States and Britain] are ready to take part, with the other countries principally concerned, in an *examination of the possibility** of establishing a collective defense within the framework of the United Nations Charter to assure the peace, security and freedom of Southeast Asia and the Western Pacific."[14]

It will be recalled that Eden and Dulles did not disagree that a Southeast Asian defense agreement might be a desirable objective. The conflict between them related to three other issues: (a) whether, in addition to a general defense organization, there should be the immediate formation of a coalition, "with teeth in it," which would threaten intervention in Indochina; (b) whether the defense organization should be formed *before* the Geneva Conference; and (c) what should be the organization's membership.

The language of the communiqué would have to have been greatly stretched if one were to construe it to mean that Eden was prepared to consider these three points. Besides, the statement of Eden in the House of Commons and the interpretation of the communiqué by the Labor Party which remained uncontradicted by Eden should have eliminated the possibility of any doubts.† Eden at this time said that the desirability of a collective defense organization would be greatly influenced by what happened at Geneva. Finally, if there had been any gap left for misunderstanding, it should have been closed by the communiqué issued by the French Government following Dulles' meeting with them after his London visit:

> "No effort should be spared to make the Geneva Conference a success . . . the joint proposed defense arrangement would not follow the pattern of NATO and, in any case, would be profoundly conditioned by the *outcome of the conference.*"*[15]

In spite of this, as soon as Dulles was back in Washington, he issued—within three days of the conclusion of the London talks—invitations to the Ambassadors of nine countries (Britain, France, Australia, New Zealand, Thailand, the Philippines and the three Associated States of Indochina) to convene on April 20 in Washington to set up a working group to study the collective defense of Southeast Asia. It is no exaggeration to interpret Dulles' move as an attempt to brush off his defeat in London, to go ahead with his own plan, hoping that Eden would not brave open defiance of a *fait accompli* and would indeed acquiesce. Undoubtely, Dulles thought that the Southeast Asia defense organization would serve as a base which still might make possible *immediate united action.*[16]

Eden's reaction was immediate and sharp: the British Ambassador was instructed not to attend the meeting. The instruction cabled to the Ambassador included this sentence:

---

† Eden, answering Aneurin Bevan, denied "that there [was] any definite commitment to take certain action in certain circumstances. That is not so. We are ready to take part with other countries, principally concerned, in an examination of the possibility of creating collective defense. . . . What I was committed to was an examination. We could not possibly have gone further. . . . The outcome of that examination will at least be greatly influenced by what happens at Geneva. . . . All the Commonwealth governments, including India, had been informed of the proposals and would be consulted as the matter developed." (*London Times*, April 14, 1954).

"Americans may think the time past when they need consider the feelings and difficulties of their allies. It is the conviction that this tendency becomes more pronounced every week that is creating mounting difficulties for anyone in this country who wants to maintain close Anglo-American relations. We, at least, have constantly to bear in mind all our Commonwealth partners even if the United States does not like some of them. . ."[17]

The same reproach was also voiced by others:

"The Laborites are convinced that this country [Britain] is being treated as a rather unimportant junior partner by the Eisenhower Administration."[18]

"During 1953 and the first half of 1954, according to one study, the British Government was placed on the defensive before Parliament on eleven different occassions because the United States Government announced policies or proposals intimately involving Britain without full prior consultation."[19]

Eden also reported at this time that there had been a warning by the State Department that should India be invited or consulted, Chiang Kai-shek would immediately be given equal treatment.

It was too late to cancel the meeting altogether, as it had already been publicized. Thus, Dulles had to convert it into an inconsequential briefing of the Ambassadors on the coming negotiations at Geneva. The fiasco of the "diplomacy by *fait accompli*" was one of the best preserved secrets of Washington. No newspaper or commentator reported the original purpose for which the meeting had been arranged.

Eisenhower and Dulles both had something to say about the abortive meeting. The former called this incident a "misunderstanding" but added that it was also a repudiation by Britain of a

"*firm** agreement for the Ambassadors of nine countries to meet in Washington to discuss unified action."[20]

Dulles explained the embarrassing event by the guess that

Nehru, who was out of sympathy with assisting the French, had brought pressure to bear on Eden to act as he did. We now have overwhelming evidence that no pressure by Nehru on Eden was necessary to prompt his instructions to the Ambassador to abstain from attending. Why did Dulles bring Nehru into the picture? According to an article in *Le Monde* (April 13th) Dulles' personal prestige and his reputation as a politician and diplomat were in the balance. Should he suffer defeat his foes and adversaries would use it for his destruction. Reference to outside pressure and intervention might have helped to explain away his error in appraising and reporting the result of his démarche in London and Paris.

But Dulles had another explanation for what Eisenhower called a "misunderstanding." He did not misunderstand anything; what he reported was the full truth. It was Eden alone who might have misunderstood. He had no doubt that it was specifically understood in London among Churchill, Eden and himself that conferences should begin without delay. Yet, even in this explanation, he admits one basic disagreement. When Sir Winston suggested that a defense system for Southeast Asia be the objective of the conference he brushed this aside, saying in answer that "there is no time for 'system'."[21] He wanted action.

Dulles' personal standing was unquestionably greatly affected by this incident. It must have been a bitter test for him to be the target of a Republican legislator shouting "you're either a liar or Eden is a double-crosser."[22] We can read in a Washington report that the Secretary had to face the most serious criticism of his career for having demanded united action from America's allies "before finding out in advance whether he had the support of the Congress, the French and the British."[23] This incident was the first major frustration Dulles had encountered as Secretary of State, and for several days he was at a loss to invent a substitute for his plan or rather, a disguise to conceal the defeat. It is generally believed, and most political commentators and biographers of Dulles report, that there had existed between Anthony Eden and Dulles a personal antipathy, perhaps even feud, before Dulles became Secretary of State. This was at least on Eden's side not true. It is a fact that before Eisenhower returned to the United States for his presidential campaign, Eden had expressed the hope to him that, should Eisenhower be elected, he would choose someone other than Dulles, as Secretary of State.[24] This suggestion of Eden was not caused by his personal feelings. Eden's opinion was influenced by Herbert (now Lord) Morrison, the Foreign Secretary of the Labor Government preceding him in office. According to Morrison Dulles did not abide by certain promises he made to him personally, connected with the Japanese peace-treaty negotiations. It was Morrison who had told Eden before Eden made this objection against Dulles that he, Dulles, was not a trustworthy person. Yet there had been other skirmishes between the two before the Indochina crisis. But even without such previous personal antagonism, it would be only human for Dulles to have retained a feeling of resentment from these events that might well have influenced his mind two years later in the Suez crisis. Then the United States led the campaign against Eden's policy which ultimately brought about his political downfall.

Dulles might have been the victim of convictions much too strongly held. He does not seem, for instance, to have had any hesitation about his interpretation of the London Conference. Eden noted on April 24, at a meeting in Paris, in the presence of the French Minister of Foreign Affairs, that some of Dulles' remarks clearly implied that the London communiqué of April 13 had in some way committed the United Kingdom to armed action in Indochina.

> "[Eden] interrupted to point out that this was not so and Bidault at once agreed."[25]

Dulles on April 30, during a conference in Geneva with Eden, insisted that "he had come back to Washington from London with an understanding that both countries were agreed that he should start to set up conferences in Washington to discuss an alliance with the nations involved, and the British Government had seen fit to repudiate this understanding without offering an alternative."†26

This reference to an "alternative" program sounds as if it were out of context but Eden's book gives a clue to its meaning. In Geneva, when Eden once again cut dead an attempt of Dulles to make a move toward action without waiting for the result of the Geneva Conference, he (Dulles) asked Eden whether there was not something "we could do to help the French." This sounds almost like an entreaty to do anything if only a promise of moral support or perhaps preliminary talks.27 As we shall see, Dulles' question did produce a modification in the British position; Churchill and Eden agreed to military and technical staff talks.

---

† Dulles, in his speech before the World Affairs Council, on June 11 1954, repeated the same description of the April 10-13 conferences. "I went to Europe on this mission (for united defense of Southeast Asia) and it seemed that there was agreement on our proposal. But when we moved to translate that proposal into reality some of the parties held back because they had concluded that any steps to create a united defense should await the result of the Geneva Conference." (*Department of State Bulletin*, June 28, 1954, p. 972).

5

While the wounds inflicted by the "misunderstanding" were still raw, the two opponents, Dulles and Eden, met at a NATO meeting in Paris on April 22, 1954. Both were on their way to the controversial Geneva Conference. Dulles used this incidental get-together to renew the attempt to obtain British consent to an immediate nine-power conference, the project which had been scuttled only a few days before. Again Dulles met the same adamant refusal. The next day, however, the drama of Dien Bien Phu took a new turn and gave Dulles a new opportunity to reopen the campaign. Dulles received a warning from the French Government that the commander of their forces in Indochina, General Henri Navarre, had radioed an SOS message for massive American air force support; should this not come within seventy-two hours, the heroes of the fortress, all exhausted and mostly wounded, would have to surrender.

With this telegram in hand, Dulles saw a chance to revert to his original twin scheme of immediate military action to be followed by the aggressive coalition. So, he insisted on an immediate decision. He brought into the conference General Alfred M. Gruenther, Supreme Allied Commander in

Europe, to support his view that the collapse of Dien Dien Phu would be followed by an inevitable debacle in Indochina and possibly by a crisis in France resulting in the installation of a neutralist government. But, Dulles said, if Eden were able to stand with him, he was prepared to recommend that the President ask Congress for "war powers" to move armed forces into battle. At the end of this meeting, in the late hours of the night, Eden asked for a day of deliberation and for reassurance that no action would be taken without consultation with him.

At the next day's meeting, on April 24, Dulles and the United States Chief of Staff, Admiral Radford, were in complete agreement about the urgency of the Dulles plan of action. They presented their opinion that

> "there was no chance of keeping the French in the fight unless they knew that we [the United States] would do what we can within the President's constitutional powers to join them in the fight . . . It would not be enough if we were to assure them that we would join them in the event of the fall of Dien Bien Phu in defending the rest of Indochina. Unless we participated in an air strike, the battle then going on for the fortress itself would be their 'last battle.'"

Radford was specific that when the fortress fell

> "the whole military situation would get out of control within a few days."[1]

Eden questioned both aspects of the American thesis: he asserted that it was an error to assume the French collapse and he doubted if air intervention by the United States and Britain could decisively affect Dien Bien Phu's fate. He had a number of critical questions: Had the Americans considered how Communist China would react? Would British-American intervention not bring into operation the Russo-Chinese alliance? In answer Radford said he was confident that bombing of Chinese airfields would foreclose Chinese intervention. Bidault had now been brought into the conference to answer the question: Would France continue fighting after the fall of Dien Bien Phu? His response was hesitant but he agreed to Dulles' proposal that promise of United States intervention at Dien Bien Phu be made formal and definite by an official letter of Dulles. In the face of this pressure for an immediate and portentous decision, Eden decided on personal consultation with his Government. He flew to England to report that Dulles would be satisfied with British participation, even if quite insubstantial and should a token British participation be promised and given, Eisenhower would get Congressional approval and the United States would act immediately.

Eden drove to Churchill's residence directly from the airport for a midnight conference on April 24. There, according to Eden, Churchill summed up Dulles' proposal:

> "What we are being asked to do is to assist in misleading the (United States) Congress into approving a military operation which would be in itself ineffective, and might well bring the world to the verge of a major war."[2]

The essence of Eden's report to Churchill and the British Cabinet was that Britain should firmly refuse participation in an immediate military intervention. Neither should Britain undertake in advance of the Geneva Conference any commitment to military or any other action in the event of the failure of that conference. The commitment Britain should undertake would be restricted to willingness to guarantee the settlement if any should be reached at Geneva, to setting up a collective defense of Southeast Asia to make the guarantee effective, and to study—together with the United States—measures for the defense of Thailand and the rest of that area in the event all or part of Indochina were lost. The following day, April 25 (Sunday), the British Cabinet met at 11 a.m. and unanimously approved Eden's recommendations.[3] Eisenhower had no desire at this time to force the issue. He went so far as to roundly deny in his press conference on April 29 that there had been an American proposal to intervene by a massive air attack of carrier-based war planes. That he in fact knew fully of Dulles' action and proposal is attested to by his own statement.

> "The Churchill Government on April 25, Sunday, decided once and for all that unified action must wait until all possibility of settlement by negotiation had been tried and failed. This ended for the time being *our efforts** for any satisfactory method of allied *intervention.** I was disappointed . . ."⁴

But Dulles would not have been his true self had he given up his plan because of one setback. He changed course abruptly and pursued another avenue of approach to the same goal. He now tried his hand with the French, and with them he held a trump card. Dien Bien Phu had now become for the French nation as well as for the Free World a symbol of French *gloire*. Thus, the Laniel-Bidault Government was in panic that the fall of this fortress might precipitate in France an outburst of violent resentment not only against the Government that had exposed France to such defeat but also against the allies who had deserted the heroes of that fortress and let them perish. The French statesmen had genuine fears that France's new government might go neutralist.

The negotiations between Dulles and the French took place after the departure of Eden for London on the night of April 24. The slight hope of saving the fortress bent French policy to agree to any condition Dulles demanded and produced immediate results. Thus, among other conditions, Bidault acceded even to Dulles' demand that the Americans be allowed to take over the strategic command in Indochina, a concession up till then and again, after the loss of Dien Bien Phu, energetically resisted by the French.⁵

On the same Sunday, April 25, the day of Dulles' negotiations with the French and the day of the first Cabinet meeting in London, French Ambassador René Massigli called on Eden during the afternoon. He informed him that Dulles, in a letter to the French Government, had proposed that an immediate declaration be made by a coalition—in which

Britain would also be a member—"proclaiming their common will to check the expansion of communism in Southeast Asia" and to use "eventual military means for this purpose." Dulles had also reiterated his prior plan: if the British participated, Eisenhower would seek Congressional approval for intervention and United States naval aircraft would go into action before the expiration of the seventy-two hour deadline of General Navarre. The letter urged the French Government to persuade the British to agree to this course.[6a] According to an article in *Life*,[6b]† it took Dulles several days to invent a substitute plan after the British repudiation of the united front and the ambassadorial conference proposed for April 20th. This must have been a plan to do via France what had failed by a direct method.

Eden reports that he was surprised at the American tactic of approaching the British Government on a major issue by way of the French. This surprise shows how far he was from sensing the true extent of Dulles' resentment caused by the incident of the "misunderstanding" of April 13 and by the consequent defeat of his policy of immediate intervention. Challenged by this action of Dulles, the British Cabinet met for the second time on that same April 25, Sunday afternoon, and decided to reject this American proposal as well.[7]

The following day, on April 26, Churchill made a statement on his Government's Indochina policy:

"The Government are not prepared to give any undertaking about United Kingdom military action in Indochina in advance of the results of Geneva. We have not entered into any new political or military commitment."[8]

The Government spokesman in the House of Lords, the Marquis of Reading, repeated the same:

"We have gone no further than agreeing with the United

† Dulles took full responsibility for the interview by confirming the substance of what *Life* had reported. (Sh. Adams, op. cit. p. 120).

71

States to go together into an examination [of the situation] with other countries concerned."[9]

Neither Churchill nor the Marquis of Reading explained why—without any challenge or parliamentary prompting— these two pronouncements were made. The following day, on April 27, however, when Attlee as the leader of the Opposition, asked for a statement as to whether there was a change in British Indochina policy, Churchill stuck not only to the policy but even to the words he had used on the previous occasion, yet adding:

> "No decisions were taken in advance of the conference at Geneva. . . . Nothing should be said here today which would render more difficult the momentous discussions and vital contacts which are now in progress. The episode of Dien Bien Phu creates a violent tension in minds at a time when calm judgment is most needed. . . . We have the fullest confidence in the wisdom of the course we have agreed Eden should follow in circumstances so largely governed by the unknown."[10]

The Churchill statements were received with official irritation in Washington.

Eden's sudden return to London and two successive Cabinet meetings on Sunday could not pass unnoticed. For the most part the press was unable to guess the import of events on April 25 but the *London Times* came fairly close to the facts:

> "Mr. Eden's unexpected return for talks with the Prime Minister and the sudden summoning of Cabinet ministers and Chiefs of Staff to Downing Street show that the Cabinet required an urgent review of policy before the Geneva Conference opens today. . . . It would certainly be a mistake if the Western powers under the impact of military news were to neglect the chances of a political solution if one is at all within reach . .."[11]

The *Christian Science Monitor*, a week later, hinted at critical decisions of the British Cabinet without being able to set forth fully the issues. Thus, the dramatic details of the crisis of that Sunday remained undisclosed until May 2 when Stewart and Joseph Alsop narrated them in full detail.[12] At that time the story remained both uncontradicted and unconfirmed, but in 1960 it received confirmation by Eden himself in his Memoirs. The Alsops also maintained that after the British Cabinet at its second meeting had rejected the American proposal, President Eisenhower made one more futile attempt to persuade the bi-partisan Senate leaders to consent to intervention without British participation. This, however, is not confirmed by Eden or any other source.

In spite of Britain's firm decision against participating in an armed intervention or any other action before the final outcome of the Geneva Conference, no sooner were Dulles and Eden present in the same city, Geneva, that Dulles revived the diplomatic battle. Twice during the first five days of the Conference, before Indochina was reached on the agenda—when in spite of entreaties by Eden and Bidault he flew back to Washington—Dulles tried to argue Eden into immediate united British-American action. Each time his course of reasoning took its start from Eden's consent to consider and bring about a general Southeast Asia defense pact *after* the end of the Geneva Conference. Dulles argued that were such a step taken immediately it would have a beneficial effect on France's fighting spirit. He appealed to British interest in keeping France in the fight, both because of Malaya and the importance of getting tolerable terms at the conference table. What else, except immediate negotiations for a pact—even if defensive only—could Eden suggest to hearten the French and show that preparations against all eventualities had been made? Eden did not budge; the answer was *always no*.[13]

6

THE MILITARY AND FINANCIAL POWER OF THE UNITED
States was much too important to the Western alliance generally and for Britain especially to ignore United States animosity. Thus, the two statesmen, Churchill and Eden, were
hard at work at the end of April to devise a face-saving step
that would help Eisenhower and Dulles to silence the domestic criticism of their policy without affecting British policy at
Geneva and its coordination with India and the other Commonwealth countries of Asia. The result was an eight-point
memorandum delivered to Dulles in Geneva on April 30.
In seven points the memorandum reiterated the British
policy as it was already known, but its eighth point suggested

> "immediate and secret joint examination of the political
> and military problem in creating a collective defense for
> Southeast Asia, namely, (a) nature and purpose, (b)
> membership and (c) commitments."[1]

Thus, while no conference would be called of those powers
which might ultimately become members of a Southeast
Asia pact, the United States and Britain would begin
bilateral discussions about the pact's scope and membership.

75

Also, military problems might be examined without waiting for the result at Geneva.

This half-hearted concession on the part of the British, meant as a gesture of conciliation, ultimately caused more trouble than good. The reason for this unexpected effect was that Eisenhower sought to exploit the British offer in order to prove, first, that Dulles had been right from the beginning; second, that Britain had agreed to a Southeast Asian defense agreement *before* the Geneva Conference was concluded; and finally, that it was untrue that the United States had planned united action with powers which in fact were not united. This left the British no alternative but to discount this inflated interpretation of their offer.

The first news report of the "concession" appeared in the *London Times* on May 5, and advanced the possibility that "staff talks" on the situation in Indochina might be held in Singapore or Washington. These staff talks would be a

> "precautionary step of technical nature and would not imply any change or development of policy."[2]

The *Herald Tribune* reported that Britain and France had had for some time an arrangement for the exchange of information about their military problems in Indochina and Malaya, and that, since May 1953, the United States, Australia and New Zealand had participated in these talks. It was these staff talks that would now be actively pursued. It was London's hope, this same source stated, that the staff meetings would

> "help to restore Anglo-American unity and produce joint policy."[3]

This report was fully confirmed by Eden himself on June 23 in the House of Commons. As a five-power staff agency already existed it was decided

> "that a military study should be made of all possible situations which might arise in Southeast Asia on the various possible assumptions about the success or failure of the conference, but *without any commitment of the*

*five powers.** This was the best contribution towards organizing united action."⁴

No sooner had the news of the possible staff talks leaked out, than the world was told by Eisenhower on May 5 that plans were proceeding for the realization of a Southeast Asia security arrangement that was publicly suggested by Dulles on March 29. He said also that

> "most of the free nations of the area and others directly concerned have shown affirmative interest and conversations were actively proceeding . . . There is a general sense of urgency. The fact that such an organization is in process of formation could have an important bearing on what happens at Geneva during the Indochina phase of the Geneva conference. The countries of that area are now thinking in constructive terms which include the indispensable concept of collective security. Progress in this matter has been considerable and I am convinced that further progress will continue to be made."⁵

At the time when this statement was made it was impossible for anyone to ascertain what were the new developments which justified this optimistic interpretation. It might seem to be the staff meetings initiated by Churchill and Eden or the attempt of Dulles to organize the united action of a coalition, with Australia and New Zealand as leaders, without British participation. Now, with Eisenhower's memoirs before us, we know that it concerned the staff talks, interpreted broadly and extensively as a change of British policy and adhering to the plan to form a Five Power coalition.

> "The British for the first time showed their willingness to try to do something *before** the end of the Geneva Conference. . . . Accordingly, I said that any reply to Eden (along with my acceptance of his proposal) should make clear that a Five Power Staff Agency along with other nations [that was not proposed by Eden] was not to the United States a fully satisfactory substitute for a broad political coalition. . . ."⁶

He put his personal authority behind the Dulles version of the "misunderstanding" by saying, with reference to the Dulles speech made on March 29, that "our principal allies were advised in advance."[7]

The British Labor Party was irritated by Eisenhower's statement and a report in the *London Times* that there was a closing of ranks on the Western side, that

> "plans are being made for meetings to be held in Washington to consider the political and economic aspect of the situation *after the settlement** . . . Nothing is being said of planning in case no settlement is reached."[8]

The Government was pressed for clarification. Selwyn Lloyd, representing the Foreign Office in Eden's absence, answered the inquiry.

> "No agreement has been reached to hold formal discussion for establishing a Southeast Asia pact. Britain refused to accede to American desires that such discussions be held now."[9]

When the Laborites pointed to the conflict between this statement and that of Eisenhower, Selwyn Lloyd made his statement more explicit.

> "The President was referring to informal and exploratory conversations between us and I referred to formal discussions by representatives of a number of states."

He elaborated this by saying, "we refuse to go beyond military staff talks which do *not** involve immediate commitment."[10] Embarrassing comparisons were made in all newspapers between the statements of Eisenhower and those of Selwyn Lloyd. These, naturally, did not help the unity that the staff talk "concession" had meant to foster. Dulles added to the confusion by denying that talks might be carried on in Singapore. British sources insisted on Singapore talks; American leaks spoke of talks in Washington.[11]

The negative aspect of the staff talks received renewed exposition on May 13 when the New Zealand Minister of External Affairs stated that they "would not begin until the course of the Geneva Conference became clearer and might not start until the Conference was finished."[12]

Four days later Churchill said in the House of Commons that no conference would be held and no pact negotiated before the end of the Geneva Conference and that the proposed military staff talks did not involve commitments.[13] Nine days later Churchill repeated the same interpretation:

"Great Britain's policy remains unchanged, as frequently stated . . . The military staff talks are directed to immediate practical issues and are quite distinct from the question of a collective defense organization. They involve no specific commitments."[14]

The *Herald Tribune's* comment on this was that the United States was modifying its previous plan to proceed immediately with creation of a Southeast Asia defense pact.[15]

The staff consultations ended on June 9. They remained, as they had been conceived from the beginning, a non-political, technical military channel for exchange of information about the strategic problems of the guerrilla war in Southeast Asia.[16] A report of these talks has never been published.

Thus, the scheme for staff talks, advanced as a conciliatory measure by Britain, widened, rather than closed, the rift between the United States and Britain.[17]

7

Eden's obdurate opposition on all these occasions had made clear to Dulles that no reasonable likelihood existed of luring Britain into immediate united action. So the Secretary rearranged his hand and produced two substitute plans aimed at realization of his policy without British participation. Both he and Eisenhower still hoped, however, that if either of these plans were successful, alliance-conscious Britain might yet return to the fold.

The first substitute plan was that a coalition should be formed with Australia and New Zealand as principal members. Immediately after the failure of the second meeting with Eden on May 2 (Sunday), Dulles invited Richard Casey and Clifton Webb, the Foreign Secretaries of Australia and New Zealand, into consultation.[1] The meeting was called on the basis of the third paragraph of the ANZUS Treaty (Mutual Security Treaty of Australia, New Zealand and the United States):

> "Any signatory can call a meeting if its territorial integrity, political independence or security is threatened."

Dulles' idea was to use the treaty to obtain participation in the Indochina coalition of the two Commonwealth members without having to gain Britain's support, since the Anzus Treaty did not include Britain.

President Eisenhower's press conference statement of May 5 might have referred—in addition to the Staff Meetings—to this consultation also in saying that

> "plans are proceeding for the realization of a Southeast Asia security arrangement."

and that

> "most of the free nations of the area and others directly concerned have shown affirmative interest."

Be that as it may, another statement made two weeks later, at his press conference on May 19, reported progress of coalition plans, saying that with Australia, New Zealand and several Asian countries (Pakistan, Burma and Ceylon) an effective Southeast Asia pact could be built *without the support of Britain**, even if it was not as satisfactory as he would like.[2] During the month of May Eisenhower and Dulles were working hard on Australia and New Zealand to persuade them to join a Southeast Asia group without Britain.[3] Eisenhower was led to believe that

> "both Australia and New Zealand were ready to listen to any proposal the United States Government might make to them for collective action for entering the Indochina war."[4]

But even now, curiously, Eisenhower had some reservations about going into Indochina with Australia and New Zealand, but without Britain. He commented that

> "I would have been most unhappy to urge collective action with other members of the Commonwealth without sturdy Britain as a participant."[5]

> "This would inevitably tend to weaken our normally

close and highly valued relationship with the British."[6]

Meanwhile the *Herald Tribune* reported that the tightening of the screws on the Churchill Government was being observed in London with anger and dismay.[7]

All of this fully publicized activity was stillborn. The Australian Prime Minister, Robert G. Menzies, as early as April 28, had published a statement saying that it was completely untrue that his Government had decided to support American policy in Indochina.[8] But Eisenhower, repeating in essence Dulles' performance after the April 12-13 conference in London, believed

> "that Australia and New Zealand had *withdrawn from their original position** favorable to united action."[9]

There is much information (in addition to the Menzies speech of April 28) to indicate the improbability that Australia and New Zealand ever consented to united action without British participation. The Prime Minister of New Zealand on May 4 denied that the ANZUS Treaty would be used as a basis for a Southeast Asia defense organization.[10] From Geneva it was reported on May 17 that

> "Americans have to face the fact that even if the Geneva Conference fails, neither Britain nor any other member of the Commonwealth are prepared to participate in united action in Vietnam."[11]

Churchill said in the House of Commons on May 17 that

> "there is of course very intimate consultation with Canada, Australia and New Zealand."[12]

Clifton Webb, New Zealand Minister of External Affairs, on May 21, after a full hour conference with Dulles, published a statement that he could not "conceive of a satisfactory alliance in Southeast Asia which did not include Britain."[13]

Three months later the Australians were still moved to refer to this phase of the diplomatic history of the Indochina crisis. The Australian Minister of External Affairs, R. G.

Casey, on August 10, denied that his Government had *ever* considered intervention before the end of the Geneva Conference.

> "When intervention [in Indochina] was being talked of in April, the Australian Government's view was that it would put those who might intervene in the wrong with world public opinion, particularly in Asia, it would probably embroil them with Communist China and with those who participated in the Geneva Conference and was most unlikely to prevent the fall of Dien Bien Phu."[14]

The Australian Government had agreed with the United Kingdom that calling a formal political conference on collective defense of Southeast Asia should be postponed until after the settlement at Geneva because it might give the Communists a pretext for terminating the Geneva negotiations, and, besides, the two Governments wanted an opportunity to explain to the Asian countries the objectives of the Southeast Asian pact. Asian countries were always suspicious that proposals for new international organizations might be a subtle way of reimposing outside domination over them.[15]

Dulles' second substitute plan for circumventing Britain's opposition was directed towards France and was a direct outgrowth of his previous attempt on April 25 to use the special trump card he held in his hand—Dien Bien Phu. The symbolic importance of the fortress made the French willing to consent to conditions which otherwise would have seemed deplorable to them. To keep up France's resistance against substantial concessions in Geneva Dulles, before he returned to Washington on May 3, assured Bidault that the

> "United States will do everything in its power to support France during the Conference,—and if it fails, afterwards also. But it will be quite difficult to achieve a peaceful settlement unless alternative plans are ready, should the Communist proposals not make an honorable solution possible. The United States is ready to do its share and

will contribute to the development of such an alternate solution."[16]

The main thrust for a special agreement with France was made in the middle of May. The negotiations took place in Paris between Ambassador Dillon and Prime Minister Laniel, and in Washington between Dulles and French Ambassador Bonnet.[17] Little was reported on these negotiations, however. Dulles cancelled his press conference and the *Herald Tribune* reported that he had ordered a blackout of news during negotiations with France.[18] The most likely reason was that on account of the negotiations with France he had decided that silence was the best policy at the moment.[19]

Eisenhower felt that an agreement with France was necessary. With an obvious reference to Great Britain, he said that

> "even if others were reluctant to act, we could not afford to sit on the sidelines and do nothing. I felt that a prompt French decision to abandon their claim to exclusive direction of the fighting . . . should come soon, and that they should seek instead a coalition of power to carry the burden. . . . Therefore we decided to inform Ambassador Dillon in Paris of the preconditions under which I *might* [emphasis by Eisenhower†] ask Congress for authority to use the armed forces of the United States."[20]

The conditions, or more politely, the proposal that was made to the French, asked that the United States, Australia

---

† In the more than 600 pages of the Eisenhower memoirs, containing about 250,000 words, there are altogether three italicized words. One of them is the "might" in this quotation. This special emphasis makes, as it were, the assertion that at no time was firm decision made or expressed to intervene in Indochina by direct American military operations. In a press conference in January 1960, Eisenhower made a positive declaration to this effect. Outside of his own and Dulles' statements (see infra 104) this is contradicted by French Prime Minister Laniel's report about Eisenhower's message delivered to him in the middle of May (Laniel, op. cit. 107), by Sherman Adams (op. cit. 122) and Assistant Secretary of State, W. S. Robertson, (*Department of State Bulletin,* August 23, 1954, p. 261).

and New Zealand be invited by France to participate; that France acquiesce in granting complete independence to the Associated States; that France promise to keep its army in the fight; that the United States assist the French "principally" by air and sea "as supplements, not substitutes"; that the United States take over the training of native troops, and that, last but not least, "a command structure for united action" be worked out, meaning that a full, or at least influential command position over the fighting forces be given the Americans.[21] Eisenhower added to these conditions his understanding that Thailand and the Philippines would participate in the campaign at once, with Australia and New Zealand probably following after the Australian election, and that the United Kingdom would eventually "either participate or acquiesce."[22] But President Eisenhower in his press conference of May 19 said

> "the United States is thinking of proceeding with the Southeast Asia defense treaty without Great Britain."

This, then, was Eisenhower's offer to the French which United States intelligence estimated involved a fifty-fifty chance of bringing on the Chinese force. Eisenhower's comment on this piece of information was that

> "this, of course, is the type of danger that sometimes must be faced, and we are prepared, if necessary, to meet it."[23]

In Eden's *Full Circle* (pp. 133-134), we have access to his version of this incident.

> "On May 15th I was surprised to find reports in the Swiss morning papers about French-American secret discussions for United States military intervention in Indochina."

The then head of the United States Delegation at Geneva, Bedell Smith, when questioned by Eden, flatly denied any knowledge of this. The same day a member of the French Delegation let Eden see a confidential American document which proposed American military intervention, even if

Britain did not participate but was "acquiescent." Next day the *Herald Tribune* printed the full story of French-American secret negotiations, making it possible for Eden, without referring to the confidential disclosure made by the French delegation, to lodge a protest with Bedell Smith against such unfair and unfriendly tactics.[24] Bedell Smith, Eden later disclosed,

> "exploded with indignation against Washington's inability to keep any discussion secret, [admitting] that it was intolerable that we [the British Government] should get information of this kind from a newspaper and that of course we should have been told."[25]

but Smith assured Eden that if the French had agreed to United States intervention, Britain would have been immediately informed. Also, Bedell Smith played down the importance of the American military intervention. He asserted that American assistance to the French would consist only of troop training, a statement squarely contradicted by what Eisenhower reports. (Supra 85-86)[26] On May 17, the *London Times* reported that Eden and Bedell Smith had "a full and frank discussion."[27] "It was well known during the entire course of the Conference that Eden and Bedell Smith had maintained harmonious personal relationship even at times when the American Delegation's diplomacy was not entirely friendly to Eden's policy.

The negotiations with France were not broken off by France even after the fall of Dien Bien Phu on May 7. On May 19 the United Press could still report agreement between France and the United States for united action but still, of course, without Britain.[28] But a few days later the *London Times* received information that

> "some of the American conditions for a special American-French campaign could only with difficulty, if at all, be accepted in Paris."[29]

Two of the American conditions were especially distasteful to the French Government. The first was the insistence that France should grant complete independence to the Indochinese Associated States. French sentiment towards this demand was voiced by Prime Minister Laniel on April 10 when he stated in the Assemblée Nationale that France, for all her deep moral and physical weariness with the Indochinese war, approached the Geneva Conference determined, no less than Britain and the United States, to preserve from Communist control this precious key to Southeast Asia. Indochina, Laniel continued, was an integral part of the French Union and French troops had fought for seven years to retain it. But France was not concerned only that Indochina should remain French. It was also concerned lest the internationalization of the dispute either by its referral to the United Nations or by accepting decisive outside assistance through a proposal such as Dulles and Eisenhower had in mind, would result in Indochina being lost to the French Union. To overlook this cardinal factor would make recent French policy appear ridiculous. If military victory had been the sole French requirement, the dispute might have been internationalized years before, for the French had been unable to put down the Vietminh insurrection by themselves. They believed, however, that for Peking as well as for Paris, the negotiations might represent the last and best chance to preserve something out of seven years' struggle and that it was better to negotiate than to risk losing all by an extension of the war. Laniel's plea, commented the *London Times* on April 10, should have carried weight, but it was obvious that the Prime Minister was defending a lost cause.[30] Before May 7, in order to avoid the Dien Bien Phu disaster, this objection would certainly have been given up, but as soon as the Dien Bien Phu emergency ended, it re-appeared as an important French concern.

The other and much stronger objection to Eisenhower's conditions was raised against American command concerned with the training of a Vietnamese army and with the military operations themselves. For Eisenhower this was a condition *sine qua non*.

"I would never agree to send our ground troops as mere reinforcements for French units, to be used only as they saw fit."[31]

For the French on the other hand, wrote J. J. Servan-Schreiber in *Le Monde*, internationalization would in its end effect enmesh France in unforeseeable commitments. It would kill all chances of a settlement within a reasonable time. It would, at best, lead to a Korean-type settlement at some later date (then why not now?) or what is much worse, to an endless war, allied to Chiang Kai-shek and Syngman Rhee, over which France would not have ultimate control. Internationalization, Servan-Schreiber continued, would engage France in a large-scale American-Chinese war. France wanted to save her army; internationalization would prevent her from doing so.[32]

Internationalization by large-scale American participation was looked at with misgiving by the French. They knew that as soon as a sizeable American force participated in the fighting the United States would demand at least participation if not take-over of the command position. Ambassador Dillon was told in Paris that though they wanted American participation beyond naval and air forces, they would not like to have more than one or two divisions.

> "General Ely may have felt that one or two divisions of United States ground troops would be sufficient to prove good faith but not large enough to create any threat to the French over-all command."[33]

Feelings against American interference went so far that the French command barred American officers who were in Vietnam for assisting training operations from advising native forces in battle.[34]

There was another and a more serious reason for Ely's insistence. The *London Times* ventured that

> "if enlargements and broadening of the war would have to be faced, the French Government would have to go to the Parliament to request the means with which to prolong and enlarge the war. A sizeable section

of the present government, Parliament and people would refuse this and would rather opt for direct abandonment of Indochina and withdrawal of the expeditionary force."[35]

The French broke off negotiations with the United States as of May 19. On May 20, the *London Times* reported that Maurice Schuman, the French Under-Secretary of Foreign Affairs, saw the British and Australian Ambassadors to clear up any doubts or anxiety about the discussions between France and the United States. On May 22, Eden, in a report to Churchill published in the *New York Times* on May 23, stressed the existence of complete understanding with the French Government and on the same day made a public statement that there was not a shadow of misunderstanding between him and the French delegation: they were still bound by their pledge to bring about a settlement at Geneva.[36] Dulles himself in his press conference on May 25 denied that the United States had received a request from the French Government for intervention. All that had happened was that conversations had been held to explore the conditions under which such intervention could be considered possible. Bidault, on May 31, told Eden that in case no agreement were reached in Geneva, American help was contemplated to the extent of three divisions, but that these informal understandings were to remain distant rumblings meant only to help the Conference.[37]

In spite of these developments, one more attempt was made by President Eisenhower to win over France into united action with the United States. On June 19, he wrote a letter to M. Coty, President of France.

"The United States was ready to plan new discussions about the united defense of Indochina."

The proposals for such defense

"were on our part a momentous and grave decision . . . Nothing here has happened to change the attitude thus expressed even if time and events created a new situation."

He emphasized that the pledge of support embodied in his message to Laniel on April 16 was available to his successor. According to the *London Times*, the purpose of this message was to warn

> "that while the conditions for United States participation in a united defense have not changed yet, they will not remain unchanged for ever, and that therefore France must act quickly if United States help were desired. The offer would not remain valid forever."[38]

The new French Government of Mendès-France, formed on June 20, interrupted and swept aside all these negotiations. Mendès-France would not let himself be diverted from the one and only important purpose: to achieve a cease-fire, an armistice and a settlement. In consequence of this absolutely negative stand, Washington, on July 9, informed the French Government that it would no longer continue the training of Vietnamese troops by American technicians as it had been doing. This declaration of complete disinterest marked the end of United States influence on the policy of France in the last days of the Indochina crisis just before the Geneva Agreements were arrived at. The French Ambassador in Washington had every reason to warn Mendès-France, which Mendès-France in turn reported to the Assemblée Nationale on July 25, that the rift between the two countries was becoming daily more serious.[39]

While this chronicle has implied that French actions sprang in the main from a clearly defined policy, there are indications, gleaned from the speeches of statesmen and reports of reliable observers, that the situation might have been other than it appeared. In a constantly deteriorating military situation, Bidault had to maneuver between the Scylla of French domestic politics and the Charybdis of Geneva. He also had to navigate between his conviction that the continuation of the Indochina war held little interest for France and his hope that full-scale United States intervention might rescue some advantage for France; between the desire of France to remain her own mistress in Indochina—by refusing or at least restraining American intervention—and to maintain Chinese concern that China might have to fight the United States. In the background loomed, furthermore, the issue of ratification of the European Defense Community by France, urged by Dulles and resented by Russia.

For the historian, therefore, it is no easy task to find the prime line of French strategy. Nonetheless, it is more than probable that the policy of the Laniel-Bidault Government changed after the fall of Dien Bien Phu on May 7 and that from that time its strongest direction signal pointed towards a settlement at Geneva.

In spite of the indifferent reaction of all three candidates (Australia, New Zealand and France) for united action, the Secretary, as late as June 4, still seems to have entertained hopes for changing their policy. This is documented by his testimony to the Foreign Relations Committee of The Senate in which he did not yet admit defeat.

> "This effort," he said, "to organize collective defense is still going on and the United States has been maintaining close contact in that matter with Thailand, the Philippines, Australia and New Zealand as well as with France and the Associated States." "Nothing is definite?", asked the Chairman. "That is correct," was Dulles' answer.[40]

Four days later, however, Dulles at last admitted publicly the failure to gain the support of Australia, New Zealand or France for the coalition and for united action. In his press conference on June 8, he expressed his regret that

> "the proposal for Southeast Asia alliance has not won sufficient acceptance to justify going to Congress."[41]

As a last resort, there remained the hope that the Geneva Conference would fail and that Britain, France and the ANZUS powers would have to come back to the United States begging for protection from Communist onslaught.

Thus, henceforth, it became a rational course of action to obstruct and hamper the Geneva Conference by procedural and other steps hoping that Eden's sensitive diplomatic gambit would be disturbed thereby and that Communist China and the Vietminh would, by intransigence, "help" Dulles' game.

These obstructions were obvious to the Conference participants. Eden diagnosed "American impatience" as one of the chief obstacles to success of the Conference.[42] In mid-June it was reported that American officials were hoping that Molotov's increased toughness would provide a basis for the break-off of the Conference.[43] Dulles himself had left the Conference on May 3 despite the insistence of Eden and Bidault that he stay until negotiations reached the Indochina agenda item in order to demonstrate American interest.[44] And even when Dulles was still in Geneva he never acknowledged the Chinese Prime Minister's presence.

The initial sessions of the Conference were public and were characterized by inconclusive wranglings and no progress. But on May 13 the Conference went into restricted session in which some modest progress was achieved. After only two restricted sessions, however, the American delegation proposed that public sessions be resumed. "It has taken us three weeks to get into secret session," Eden narrated,

> "and now we were to go out in two days. We must, I thought, give the experiment a full and fair trial. M. Bidault commented simply that a proposal such as the Americans had put forward would immediately bring his Government down. It was decided that the restricted sessions should continue."[45]

At the end of May, on the twenty-ninth, Eden's tentative text for bringing about staff meetings on a cease-fire had been agreed to by the Russians, French and the Chinese. "Very far-reaching American reservations were made" to it, however, and Bedell Smith, the head of the American Delegation wanted these reservations made public.[46] This started off a chain reaction; each delegation wanted its reservations publicized and the Chinese Prime Minister jokingly suggested that each of them should do so through a press conference. It took long arguments to persuade Smith to abandon his request. Eden said that

> "Bedell Smith's action indicated that Washington must once again be losing patience with our negotiations. He had given me no prior notice, which was unlike him, and so had presumably received new instructions. As I reported to London at the time, the Americans seemed deeply apprehensive of reaching any agreement, however innocuous, with the Communists."[47]

Whenever the Conference got into a temporary deadlock and Eden tried to find a way out, strong criticism appeared in the American press against him. He was referred to as "Municheer," an appellation in sharp contrast to the congratulations bestowed upon him by Commonwealth and neutral governments for the "great job" he was doing.[48] Also, the *Times* reported,

> "stories reaching Washington from Geneva all tell of a bitterly disillusioned American Delegation asking why Churchill and Eden, who opposed Munich in 1938, cannot understand the need for immediate action now."[49]

Another indication of United States impatience came on a different point—the withdrawal of Communist forces from Laos and Cambodia. Mr. Robertson, temporarily the head of the United States Delegation, "launched a violent and wholly unexpected attack on the Chinese proposals" at the restricted session on June 18, though these had seemed acceptable to the French and to Bedell Smith also when he had first seen them.[50] Robertson's action was probably the result of a telegram from President Eisenhower—which Bedell Smith showed to Eden—advising Smith "to do everything in his power to bring the conference to an end as rapidly as possible, on the grounds that the Communists were only spinning things out to suit their military purposes."[51]

All these events refer to the last days of the first phase of the Geneva Conference which ended on June 20 with the agreement that military staff committees would arrange the separation of the intertwined battle lines and the complete withdrawal of the Communists from Laos and Cambodia. It was also decided that after twenty-one days, if the work of the committees was sufficiently advanced, the heads of delegations would return. While these agreements signified progress towards success, wishful thinking prompted Dulles to make public statements asserting that the possibilities of Geneva had been exhausted and no satisfactory solution was in sight.[52] During a stop-over in Paris on his way to London, Eden met the new Prime Minister, Pierre Mendès-France. He told Eden that he was not optimistic about Geneva "in view of the difficulties presented by the American and Vietnamese attitudes";[53] both, it was now known, opposed any agreement that would concede partition or anything else to the Vietminh.

The final and last obstructive act of the American Delegation was, of course, their refusal to sign any of the Agreements or the Final Declaration. The most they would do was to issue a separate Declaration taking note of what had been decided and undertake not to disturb the settlement. Eden feared that this might lead to serious difficulties, for the Chinese had indicated that they would insist upon signature by all the delegations. Fortunately for the outcome of the Conference, this last obstacle was hurdled through the efforts of Eden, helped—according to his own report—by Molotov whose motives were set forth in the context of the Conference in Berlin.[54]

The blame for this negative, unproductive, almost destructive policy should not be put entirely on Dulles. His diplomacy and negotiating position were paralyzed. President Eisenhower was unwilling to draw upon himself the wrath of the extremist, anti-Chinese Republican senators by straightforward support of the British-French policy of settlement. Neither could he clear his mind of the cant of the anti-communist crusade that obsessed him and Dulles. Both impulses worked against active, vigorous participation and leadership in Geneva, and a settlement that was anything but unconditional surrender of the victorious Vietminh. On the other hand, Dulles could not even pursue straightforwardly a bellicose policy line either, since Eisenhower would not enter the military conflict by direct participation except by united action in which nobody was willing to join us.

8

From the beginning of May, until Churchill's and Eden's trip to Washington on June 24, mutual reproach and resentment increased alarmingly between Britain and the United States. The American Administration resented Britain's obstruction of American Indochina policy which had not only foiled United States plans of action against Communist China—the enemy whom at that time some spokesmen of the Eisenhower Administration still hoped to destroy completely—but had also disturbed their domestic political preoccupations. They resented the British refusal to agree to united action as fighting members of a coalition (April 13), the repudiation of the alleged consent to an immediate defense organization (April 20) and (on April 25) the refusal to participate in military intervention even if it were done only as token of moral support.

The British Government, on the other hand, was irritated by United States attempts to disrupt their Commonwealth ties with Australia, New Zealand and, still more, with India, Ceylon and Pakistan. Burma, also, was a consideration. They objected to the secrecy of United States negotiations with France to realize their militant plans. Their main ob-

97

jection, however, was to the United States campaign to frustrate their sensitive diplomatic activity which they believed to require conciliatory gestures toward Russia and Communist China, encouragement and support of French aims, and cultivation of the sympathy of Commonwealth partners. This diplomacy was directed to a single goal: to end the fighting and to gain time for the consolidation of the South Asian pro-Western or neutral belt resisting Communist expansion.

The consequence of American hostility was the demotion of the British alliance in United States foreign policy to a secondary relationship. This degradation was a one-sided American move, shocking and surprising to the Churchill Government and to a great many, perhaps the majority, of the leaders of American political thinking. The vibrations of these feelings reached the surface of awareness following the eventful Sunday of April 25. From London it was reported that there was "official irritation" in Washington.[1] In the latter capital the Majority Leader of the Senate, Mr. Knowland, called Britain an "undependable ally."[2] Back in London, on May 4, the reaction of the State Department to the diplomatic events of April was diagnosed as unconstructive futile quarrelling about who was to blame.[3] On the same day, Lippmann called our alliance "shaken" and David Lawrence suggested that the United States should look for allies in Asia, stronger ones than Britain or France. The *Herald Tribune*, in an editorial of May 5, said that the tendency on this side of the Atlantic was

> . . ."to weigh lightly the harm of disparaging words about Britain and France. . . . The first task of Dulles is to make certain that nothing is said or done now that might damage irretrievably the Western Alliance."[4]

Marguerite Higgins forecast that the return of Dulles from Geneva would be used for a "thorough-going military-political re-appraisal of United States relations with its European allies."[5] Lippmann on May 6, referring to the overwhelming influence of Senator Knowland who knew "one solution only"—the unconditional surrender of Vietminh—said, with the truly astounding foresight of a prudent man,

> "there is a notion in what might be described as highly irresponsible responsible quarters that while it would be better to have allies than not to have them, it would be feasible for the United States *alone to take over the war in Indochina and to win it. This is a most dangerous fantasy.* . . ."[6]

It was reliably reported to the British Embassy in Washington that

> "Dulles had declared his conviction that American policy in the Middle East as well as in Asia had been badly handicapped by a tendency to support British and French "colonial" views."[7]

He was reported to have spoken of his determination to talk bluntly about the Middle East and of his aim to "shift policies."[7] Another observer reported that

> "in the State Department harsh things are being said about Eden. Words reached the Foreign Office that Dulles had made disparaging remarks about Eden . . . that he lacked moral stature. . . . Eden made his Locarno speech in the House of Commons, proposing that Communist China join with the non-Communist powers in a peace pact. . . . This was an affront to the Knowland group who objected even to the participation of India. . . . Eden, reviewing the Geneva Conference, never once mentioned Dulles. The indignation among Dulles' assistants was boundless. . . . The British accuse Dulles of inspiring criticism of British policy in the Middle and Far East with the theme of colonialism that he developed in his recent speeches."[8]

Eden was called in Washington "slippery" and "uncongenial." Hoover, the Under-Secretary of State, "could not stand him." One State Department official "asserted that he had never met a dumber man."[9] On the other hand, leaders of the Democratic Party, former President Truman, Speaker

Sam Rayburn, Senators Lehman, Theodore Green and Guy Gillette branded our Indochina policy "insulting toward our allies and friends" and "a diplomatic disaster." The strongest accusation, however, was made by President (then Senator) Johnson:

> "American foreign policy has never in all its history suffered such a stunning reversal. We have been caught bluffing by our enemies. Our allies and friends are frightened and wondering, as we do, where we are headed. We stand in clear danger of being left naked and alone in a hostile world.[10]

An editorial called the Anglo-American split one of the most serious in the relations between Britain and the United States.[11]

All these instances of contemporaneous comment from American sources were confirmed in his *Full Circle* by Eden. At a conference on May 1, in Geneva, with Dulles and Bedell Smith, Eden was subjected to a heated onslaught. Dulles thought that complete disarray existed, that Britain refused to back up the United States in any action in Indochina and that Eden had not given him even mere moral support. The statements made in that conference showed Eden that the Americans "were deeply aggrieved" by Eden's reaction—reported to the British on the following day, May 2—that it would be a grave mistake "to endorse a bad policy for the sake of unity," and that the British must refuse, pending the Geneva negotiations, not only to be drawn into the Indochina war, but even to promise moral support for measures of which they did not know the full scope.[12]

During much of this time the British Government avoided, as much as possible, open condemnation of the American maneuvers, although the Labor Party, in order to embarrass the Government, pressed many times for public pronouncements. On only four occasions, before the reconciliation trip to Washington undertaken by Churchill and Eden on June 24, were direct statements made by the Churchill Govern-

100

ment regarding the American actions which they considered injurious to the Geneva Conference. Each of these statements was *un*avoidable; each was as sparse, short, and resolute as human language permitted. "Nothing should be said here today," said Churchill on one of these occasions, "which would render more difficult the momentous discussions and vital contacts which are now in progress."[13] Another of these statements, that of Churchill on May 17, demonstrated the resoluteness of the British stand:

> "Our immediate task is to do everything we can to reach an agreed settlement at Geneva for the restoration of peace. Her Majesty's Government are resolved to do their utmost to achieve this aim."

He added:

> "Until the outcome of the Conference is known, final decisions cannot be taken regarding the establishment of a collective defense pact in Southeast Asia and the Western Pacific. The Government have not embarked on any negotiation involving commitment."[14]

The same reticence was demonstrated by Churchill when America, ignoring Britain, had pursued its attempts to arrange intervention: "Britain had nothing to do with the United States-France negotiations."[15] Churchill delivered this sentence on a flat neutral note which muted whatever emotions he might have felt at having to glean this information only from press reports. At the same time, British correspondents in Geneva reported how angry Eden was over the failure of the United States to inform him of the bilateral negotiations with France and that the United States had not taken the trouble to extend the courtesy of informing the British of these steps.[16] Yet, finally, open British censure of United States' procedure was bound to come. Churchill, in the House of Commons on May 20, stated categorically that "French-United States talks on Indochina were inconsistent with the spirit of the Western Alliance."[17]

A month later, on June 20 in Geneva, Britain, France, Russia and China reached agreement about further East-West talks to end the fighting in Indochina. In spite of the detached attitude of the American Delegation Eden continued to give continuous reports about his negotiations and plans to the American Delegation. It was reported that "because the United States Government wants to play little more than observer's role," Bedell Smith was returning to Washington.[18] Dulles, in his news conference of June 15th hinted hopefully that the Geneva negotiations might "be terminated or recessed or perhaps reduced to a lower level of negotiation."[19] He said this though the French and Vietminh military negotiations had already begun their conference to disentangle their armies and make the final settlement possible.

The growing chance of political settlement in Geneva did not give a turn for the best to the alliance relationship between Britain and the United States. One might even say that this ray of success had rather increased Washington's irritation. Thus, to Britain, reconciliation became more crucial than ever.

The conflict between the two Anglo-Saxon countries was on two levels. At the base there was disagreement on policies. Washington's view stemmed from Eisenhower's falling domino hypothesis. He compared Indochina to the first in a row of dominoes which when knocked over, made the fall of the last one a certainty.[20] Loss of any part of Indochina would result in losing all of it. This, in turn, would render all Southeast Asia indefensible from the offensives of international Communism with its monolithic structure, set upon the conquest of the world; each step forward, each success, no matter how small, would serve as the base for the next move. No genuine settlement could be arrived at, for the Communists would concede nothing unless it advanced their general purpose and made new conquests possible. Washington felt, therefore, that the United States would be in violation of its moral credo if it did not prevent the thrust of Communism into any area where Washington could act. For Eisenhower and Dulles the war in Indochina was part of the global crusade against Communism. Another special feature of American Indochina policy was an emotional frenzy against contact with Communist China. Any contact, it was thought, would somehow be changed, as though by magic, into a step towards recognition and United Nations membership. For the President and Secretary of State this possibility was a nightmare. For fear of Republican Party hostility, they could not relax the rigid stand in which the Chinese "terror" held them, no matter how advantageous it might appear to do so in a given situation.

On the policy level, also, it was impossible to disentangle true United States policy from the confused, conflicting and ever-changing statements claiming official status. It was intransigently indecisive. Thus, it was not surprising that former Prime Minister Attlee felt

> "that sometimes it is awfully difficult to understand just what the American line is between what members of the Government say and what Senators say and sometimes what Generals and Admirals say."[21]

Eisenhower, also, recognized the chaos that prevailed in his administration.

> "Statements by members of the State Department which seem to be at variance with statements by members of Defense can best be explained, perhaps, by their differing emphases. The United States policy is for peace but we are ready to fight for our rights and our liberty, if necessary. State voices this with an emphasis on 'We are for peace' while Defense underscores 'We are ready to fight.' "[22]

But Eisenhower went beyond this to explain the seemingly conflicting statements. Much later, at a press conference on January 13, 1960, he said that Dulles

> "could very well talk about possibilities and ask people about possibilities that might by them be considered as proposals when they were not meant that way at all. It was to put out an idea and study it."[23]

The State Department, the Defense Department and Dulles were not alone in issuing contradictory policy statements. Eisenhower himself made the assertion—at the same press conference in January, 1960, (repeating an earlier denial made in a press-conference on April 29, 1954)—that there never was a plan for American military intervention in Indochina. But could this be reconciled with his letter of April 4 to Churchill (supra p. 52); with Dulles' letter to Bidault proposing air attack within the seventy-two-hour deadline of General Navarre (supra p. 69); with Dulles' pressure for immediate armed action on April 25 (supra p. 70); or even with Eisenhower's message delivered to Prime Minister Laniel in the middle of May† (supra p. 90)? Assistant Secretary for Far Eastern Affairs, Walter S. Robertson, who during the "sit-down" uncooperative, non-participation period was the head of the American delegation in Geneva, a few days after the end of the conference made a statement saying the United States was "prepared to intervene (in Indochina) with our own military forces on certain conditions."[26] There exists reliable testimony that, on April 4th, 1954

> "at a Sunday night meeting in the upstairs study at the White House Eisenhower had agreed with Dulles and Radford on a plan to send American forces to Indochina under certain strict conditions" (that is, coalition with British and French participation, independence to the three Indochinese States.)[25]

They were at war "twixt will and will not."

Finally, the American line was certainly not strengthened by the domestic political situation which made it questionable whether the United States would indeed do what its avowed policy required: go into a full-scale fight with ground forces and face the Chinese who could be supported by the Soviets.

Eden confronted the United States with a line of action

---

† According to the Memoirs of Laniel, Ambassador Dillon's communication brought to his knowledge a "decision" not a vague possibility.

that then appeared as it does now to be simple, logical, unemotional and practical. For the containment of Communist imperialism there was almost unanimous British support; for a crusade against it—especially one to be launched in Indochina—there was none. British policy took into consideration that "the other side" had problems too, that the chance of a consolidation of a partial gain would be tempting for Ho Chi Minh, and that the Chinese had to reckon with a possible comeback by the French who were not really beaten yet. It recognized the strength of the military and political position of Ho Chi Minh which made his complete or partial conquest of Indochina inescapable unless a world war were to be risked. It did not close its eyes to the war weariness of France. It gave weight to the importance for Britain of the approval and support of its Asiatic Commonwealth partners, India and the others, to their desire to terminate the war in Indochina and to their antipathy to United States, British, Australian, and New Zealand intervention in the Indochina war which the Commonwealth partners and Burma regarded as a local conflict. All these factors precluded a military solution and ordained a political settlement. Therefore, from the moment when Eden discovered in Berlin that Molotov was not averse to coming to terms, he did not swerve or change course. He resisted pressure and persuasion; he was patient; he moved doggedly using all the tools of diplomacy to reach the desired result: a cease-fire, an armistice, concessions of form and substance, saving the maximum possible, and, last but not least, gaining time for consolidation of the non-Communist countries in Southeast Asia. He fulfilled what, according to Harold Nicholson,[26a] is the duty of a minister at an international conference "first to defend and further the interests of his own country and secondly to adjust those interests to the requirements of the community of nations."

All other participants of the Geneva Conference were engaged in diplomatic maneuvering solely for their own country's benefit. Nor was Britain a disinterested broker either. The safety of Malaya and the advantage of ending the Indochina war to India, Ceylon, Pakistan—members of the British Commonwealth—were of considerable value to the British political position. But, over and above these direct British interests, an impartial observer of the events at Geneva cannot avoid perceiving an additional role that Anthony Eden played. He gained the confidence of all participants; he was the spokesman of interests, concerns, personal and national inhibitions of all others; he

PROFESSOR EDEN'S BUSY DAY

appeased the participants, helped them eliminate rigidities and invented face-saving formulas.

So, to keep the Laniel-Bidault Government in office, he counteracted the United States pressure on the French Delegation to abandon the Conference. To gain and keep Molotov's support for pressing the Chinese and North Vietnam Delegations into a conciliatory mood, he hinted in official statements and permitted leaks to the effect that Britain would not continue peace-making efforts indefinitely and might respond to American calls for united action and to the internationalizing of the war in Indochina. To conciliate Chou En-lai, Eden became the first Western political leader to attempt to satisfy Chou's desire for recognition as leader of a great power with influence beyond the perimeter of his own country. At the same time his personal contacts with the Chinese Delegation became

> "a real contribution to peaceful coexistence, which is still our aim and object with every country."[27]

Eden was, of course, greatly helped by the fact that his hands, unlike those of Bidault and Dulles, were not tied by personal and domestic political considerations. He had the support in his Indochina policy of both parties of his country, of the uncommitted powers of Asia and of all Commonwealth countries with interest in the Southeast Asia situation.[28]

Those who accused Eden of appeasement and Municheering were crusaders up in arms against Communism. They knew only of victory and defeat and disdained diplomacy's persuasion and compromises. Eden's flexible and versatile use of all these methods of diplomacy, coupled occasionally with hints at the alternative policy of joining Dulles' threatening posture achieved diplomacy's raison d'être, avoidance of war, preservation of peace.

In one relationship only did Eden not maneuver towards a draw. This was with Dulles. Behind the Indochina problems there was always present their mutual distrust fostered by a general feeling of contempt, and specifically the memory of the April 13 events. Dulles was annoyed by Eden, and Eden clearly indicated in the House of Commons that he was angry with Dulles. The tincture of personal feelings in this relationship was in sharp contrast with the personal harmony between Bedell Smith and Eden, undisturbed by the conflicting policies of the two nations. To a reliable reporter who observed them during the few days which they spent in Geneva "the signs of unhappiness if not actual rancor and resentment between them was evident."[29] The memory of April 13 was an ever-present provocation to both: to Dulles, the blow by Eden to his plan of an immediate defense organization; to Eden, the insulting accusation by Dulles of faithlessness. Neither of them grew tired of repeating on every occasion his own thesis. Dulles, in an important policy speech on June 11—just before the reconciliation journey of the British statesmen to Washington—gave new publicity to the accusation made so often before that Eden had gone back on the agreement reached on April 13.

> "I went to Europe on this mission and it seems that there was agreement on our proposal. But when we moved to translate that proposal into reality, some of the parties held back."[30]

There were reports that Dulles in a personal cable to Eden accused him of having gone back on a firm agreement.[31] He persuaded everybody in the White House to believe that "the British changed their mind."[32] On the other hand, Eden, in his speech on June 23 on the eve of the departure to the Washington reconciliation conference, set forth again that there had been no agreement on the membership of the organization and that it had been specified that no action would be taken until after Geneva. Thus, he said later

> "when I learned that an influential gathering of a number of powers was to be held in Washington April 20th, it seemed to me that it would prejudge the question of membership at the outset, which it was important not to do. I said so and the meeting was transformed into one of the powers concerned with the Korean Conference."[33]

The frustration of Dulles' aims for the conference of the Ambassadors in Washington the Secretary persistently laid to Nehru's pressure on Eden. He said at a hearing before the Senate Foreign Relations Committee on June 4, that if the

British could veto American policy and the Indians could veto British policy and the Chinese could veto Indian policy and the Russians could veto Chinese policy, then it meant that the Russians held the final veto on anything the United States wanted to do.[34] An important weekly magazine in the United States asked:

"does the United Kingdom hold a veto over the United States? If so, then we are trapped by Communist policy."[35]

In answer, the *London Times* devoted a long editorial to the absurdity of such presentation of the political factors; it pointed out that it is not veto power that gives influence to one country over the policies of another.

"The curb is obviously the need to preserve alliances and partnership. India has never vetoed British policy but the British government have recognized that there can be no lasting settlement in Southeast Asia that has not the support of the independent Asian countries led by India. Talk of a veto is a 'misuse of words.' "[36]

American ire and fury were raised to an even higher pitch with Eden's report to the House of Commons, made June 23, on the eve of the departure for Washington. The divide between the two countries now yawned wide and deep. In this speech, Eden set forth his plan for the solution of the Indochina crisis. He forecast independence for Laos and Cambodia, and partition of Vietnam. He said that he was working for an international guarantee, a reciprocal arrangement such as Locarno in which both sides would take part, with guarantees by China and Russia on one hand, and the United States, France, Britain and perhaps India and other Asiatic countries on the other.

"That would be something entirely new in our international experience and something worthwhile trying to get. This would be entirely separate from a defensive alliance, such as NATO. Refraining from any precipitate move towards it, the necessary conditions would be created in which both systems would be brought into being.†

With obvious disparagement of Dulles' plan to create immediately, before the end of Geneva, a defense organization instead of a reciprocal guarantee, he said:

"The idea of a pact for Southeast Asia and the Pacific is not a new one. It is wrong to suppose that it suddenly sprang into life a few weeks ago, fully armed like Minerva from the head of Jupiter. Its relevance to current events must not be exaggerated. It could be a future safeguard but is not a present panacea."[37]

This speech was interpreted by one of the influential members of the Foreign Affairs Committee in the House of Representatives in Washington as a shocking suggestion that

"we become footsie-tootsie with the Communists in Southeast Asia."[38]

It is obvious that the Eden plan was in every single detail in conflict with the Dulles policy. Eden thought of the Southeast Asia general defense organization as a future safeguard without immediate relevance to the Indochina crisis, while Dulles, after his March 29 speech, thought the organization to be of utmost urgency and relevant to the battlefield situation. Dulles in a press conference statement on June 15 went so far as to interpret the Churchill-Eden visit as a reliable sign that now, at last, action would be taken on the Southeast Asian alliance project.

"There seems to be some indication that the British feel that the possibilities of Geneva have been exhausted and that the result is sufficiently barren so that alternatives should now be considered. If that is the way they feel when they come over here, I hope that it can lead to a closer meeting of minds which may permit the taking of some decisions."[39]

But Eden wanted a five-power guarantee covering the hoped-for settlement, while Dulles would not put his signa-

† Treaty of Mutual guaranty, signed at Locarno October 16, 1925.

ture on a paper where Chou En-lai's would be next to his, and wanted to build the safety of Southeast Asia on a NATO kind of organization of such anti-Communist states as would participate in a defensive agreement. Eden aimed at a Russian-Chinese guarantee for the anticipated independence of Laos and Cambodia and the peaceful integrity of free Vietnam, while Dulles looked at the map the other way around, viewing with abhorrence Britain and France as guarantors of Ho Chi Minh's country and its protection from attack. But regardless of the differences in policy and the sharpness of the personal antagonism this much was clear to Churchill: leaving the Anglo-American relationship in the hands of the two antagonists might endanger not only the Indochina settlement but other areas of British interest where support by the United States was essential. The game to be played at the American table needed him. He had to take over. Whatever sacrifice would have to be made would be better done under his personal emblem of authority, rather than by the Foreign Secretary, in anticipation of the storm that would inevitably be raised for purposes of party politics by British parliamentary opposition.

9

The two months following the failure of Dulles' *tour de force* in April brought the American-British alliance close to a breakup. To ward off this ominous estrangement, Churchill's personal intervention was required. Two years later, in the Suez crisis, Churchill was not available to maintain by his extraordinary prestige, speaking terms between the two Governments. The result was catastrophic: the United States joined its foes to defeat its friends. But for Churchill this disaster might have happened in 1954. In that year, too, President Eisenhower sensed the danger. These were, he writes,

> "anxious hours and days when the leaders of the Free World tried to find among themselves at least a temporary, workable unity when diverse intentions, plans and purposes caused chaos, misunderstanding and tragedy in that unfortunate land."[1]

Yet it was Churchill who signaled for a reunion, which at last took place on June 24-26.[2]

Two argonauts embarked on the journey on June 24 to

bring back in renewed splendor the golden fleece of the American alliance. Eisenhower recorded his satisfaction:

> "Now, with Winston and Eden coming to Washington we could talk out any Anglo-American differences."[3]

He recorded also that in a letter to him, Churchill seemed to have dissociated himself from Eden's disparagement of a NATO-like Southeast Asia treaty organization. Eisenhower was "delighted with this particular reaction to our earlier suggestion,"[4] and as the meeting with the English was about to take place, appeared to be in a receptive and conciliatory mood. Dulles in his news conference of June 15, with a great deal of wishful thinking, voiced his expectation that the British would concede the hopelessness and barrenness of Geneva and would at least come around to the American plan for the solution of the Indochina crisis by a Southeast Asian Defense Pact.[5]

Meanwhile, the press continued to fill the atmosphere with furor and alarm. *TIME Magazine*, for instance, wrote of Eden on July 1, that he "was busily courting the Communists," that his speech made sense only if Britain were indeed free to adopt a course of neutrality in a war between Russia and the United States.[6] The *London Times* correspondent in Washington cabled, on June 25:

> "It is generally agreed among those who believe that the future of the Free World depends on the intimacy of the relationship between its two leaders that the talks have not begun a minute too soon. Officially, the State Department remained coldly polite about Eden's speech [of June 23] but unofficially it was seething with emotions that have been variously described as shock, dismay, uneasiness, indignation and exasperation. Almost overnight Locarno has joined Munich and Yalta as an unmentionable word. Congressmen who had probably never heard of it a week ago and even now have only the dimmest idea of what it signifies, have denounced Eden's suggestions as a sell-out of the Free World, a blow to the United States."[7]

Leaders in Congress, such as Representative McCormack, expressed resentment that Eden criticized the President and Secretary of State and showed contempt of their policies. He voiced suspicion that Churchill and Eden had

"made a deal with France and Red China at Geneva. . . . Do they expect us to enter into a Locarno agreement, so called, which would mean at least a *de facto* recognition of Red China"?[8]

An editorial of the *London Times* on June 26 found the source of American alarm in her terror of being forced into recognizing the Peking regime.[9] Eden's plan was generally interpreted in Washington and in the press as meaning that the settlement in Indochina would involve the hitherto opposing sides in a measure of mutual trust, confidence in their reciprocal guarantees. Special significance was attributed to the time element. The five-power guarantee planned by Eden would be part and parcel of the basic agreement. On the other hand, Eden demoted the future Southeast Asian defense organization, the ranking project of the American peace scheme to a secondary role, and having no relevance to Geneva. This was in sharp contrast to the broadcast speech of Dulles on May 7, to the publicized decision of the United States National Security Council on May 6, and to Eisenhower's press conference statement on May 5 that such a pact and the organization to be created by it should have an important bearing on the work to be done in Geneva for peace in Indochina. In his testimony on June 4, to the Foreign Relations Committee of the Senate, Dulles returned again to this controversy.

"Certain of the countries felt that no concrete action should be taken towards organizing collective defense in that area or collective security arrangements until it was possible to foresee the result of the Geneva Conference. The United States felt that it would be possible to foresee the results which would be very largely unfortunate unless there was provided some united security arrangement for the area to bolster it up. The prospect for the Geneva negotiations would have been much better if some collective action had been organized in advance of the Conference or during its early days rather than to wait and see what happens. Without them the results of Geneva are not apt to be very good."[10]

The idea of a five-power guarantee clashed also with the reassurance given by Eisenhower to his Republican Party that the Geneva Conference was not a five-power meeting as the Soviet Union had tried to make it, and that it has not involved diplomatic recognition by the United States of the Chinese Communist aggressors.[11]

Thus there was plenty of material for exciting news reports about the crisis in the alliance. Churchill, to quiet the storm, made light of it: "I have come to talk over a few family matters and to make sure there are no misunderstandings."[12] But animosity in Washington was so great that several members of Congress objected even to this sentence. It was said that the British Prime Minister's statement would have most mischievous effects on people in Asia where the

> "single biggest handicap and liability which the United States has in Asia is that it generally is too closely allied with the European colonial powers. . . . The United States and Congress must disassociate themselves most emphatically from the notion that we have peculiar ties, or obligations or attachments to our Anglo-Saxon forebears."[13]

What was the score card after this confrontation? Overall agreement could not be reached. Eisenhower recognized this by a statement made in his news conference of June 30.[14] Churchill and Eden did not yield an inch on their main premise that there must not be, prior to concluding the Conference in Geneva, any publicized meeting to plan and proclaim an anti-Communist alliance in Southeast Asia. Nor did they commit themselves to any form of "united action" in the area before the results of Geneva were known.

On the positive side, Churchill and Eden obtained agreement to a partition of Vietnam. By way of concession, the British acquiesced in Eisenhower's and Dulles' determination that the United States should not sign an agreement that would imply its consent to the surrender of North Vietnam or would imply a guarantee of its integrity. Churchill and Eden also agreed to the acceleration of the NATO kind of defense organization which Eden, until then, had planned as a delayed follow-up step (not to be taken immediately after Geneva but only after long and thorough preparation) to make possible the participation of the three Commonwealth powers of Asia—India, Ceylon, Pakistan, and Indonesia and Burma.

No acceleration of a defense agreement for Southeast Asia was fast enough for Dulles. In his broadcast report to the nation on the Manila Treaty, made in September 1954, he returned to reproachful regret about the delay.

"This Manila Pact represents a considerable accomplishment. I would have been glad if it had come earlier. But it is definitely better now than never."[15]

The summit conference had drawn up in a seven-point memorandum the outlines of an acceptable settlement on Indochina, including among its terms a partition of Vietnam. The four statesmen were in full agreement on every detail but one—the heart of the matter.

"On one aspect only did our viewpoints differ. Churchill and Eden merely wished to state a *hope** that the French would settle for nothing less than our seven points: we wanted these as *minimal*.*"[16]

In order to screen from domestic critics in both countries the concessions made, the agreement avoided the conference formula. It called for a study group, with a preparatory agenda only. First, the group would work out a system of guarantees for inclusion in the final agreement, guarantees which could be subscribed to and underwritten by those countries which were to participate in the Conference to

117

establish the Southeast Asia defense organization. As to this point, Churchill, in his report to the House of Commons on July 12, expressed the hope that "other countries with interest in Southeast Asia might also subscribe to such an undertaking."[17] Second, the study group would examine how a collective defense organization for Southeast Asia should be formed, what countries should be members and what should be their obligations.

In regard to the system of guarantees by the countries participating in the Indochina Conference, there took place, according to Eden, a thoroughgoing discussion between him and Dulles.[18] It was in the course of their discussion that Eden made the concession to examine through the instrumentality of the study group *at once* the possibilities of a Southeast Asian general defense organization which would undertake specific commitments for military action in the event of renewed Communist aggression. Dulles cashed in on this. He also made Eden agree that the seven-point memorandum drawn up by the four statesmen would[19] be transmitted to the new French Premier, Pierre Mendès-France, before the Premier entered into final negotiations, as a summary of minimum terms which the United States and Britain would feel able to accept. Eden, at the end of the discussion

"was satisfied that the American Administration not only understood what the Locarno-type system of guarantees meant, but seemed to like the idea."[20]

Eden soon learned however—actually before he arrived home—that this guarantee plan not only was not liked by the Americans but had instantly received the kiss of death. On June 30 the House of Representatives adopted by unanimous resolution an amendment to the Foreign Aid bill declaring

"that no part of the [foreign aid] funds shall be used on behalf of governments which are committed by treaty to maintain Communist rule over any defined area in Asia."

The State Department let it be known that there was no objection to the House of Representatives' resolution.[21] This killed the idea of mutual guarantees by which Britain and France would have guaranteed North Vietnam in exchange for a guarantee by Russia and China regarding Laos, Cambodia and South Vietnam. In 1954 the two Atlantic allies could not possibly have renounced the aid funds which kept their foreign exchange budget in balance.

Yet, the Churchill-Eden visit to Washington achieved its main purpose, the smoothing over of the beclouded personal relationship of the Foreign Secretary and the Secretary of State, and the attainment of greater mutual understanding of their respective Indochina policies. Dulles did not even produce his three-page catalogue of grievances.[22] In fact, only a few months later, in October, 1954, Dulles is reported to have said at a meeting of the Cabinet:

"The United States has never been so respected nor had such good relations as now."[23]

The temporary reconciliation was greeted with satisfaction on both sides of the Atlantic. A London newspaper said

"An Anglo-American compromise on methods appears to have been reached and that calls for thankfulness."[24]

Churchill, in the opening sentence of his report to the Parliament, expressed the same feelings:

"The Washington talks have helped to get Anglo-American discussion of the problems of Southeast Asia back on to a realistic and constructive level—at least that is my hope."

He added that the visit by him and Eden

"was intended to clear up misunderstandings and not to aggravate by sharp expression any of the necessary and natural differences which exist between great free communities working together."[25]

119

By these statements, he gave recognition to the fact that—before the visit—the negotiations had been carried on unrealistically and unconstructively and that serious differences had existed. It is surprising, however, that Churchill on July 12 does not seem to have thought it unlikely, or indeed impossible, that the Geneva settlement would be guaranteed and underwritten by *all* the countries which participated in the Conference, and that he took no notice of the Congressional roadblock preventing such guarantees.

Nevertheless, Churchill made it clear that he fully agreed with Eden in regard to the participation in the Southeast Asia pact of the three Commonwealth powers in Asia and Burma, which Dulles so strongly opposed. He took great care to leave no doubt that Eden had his full support in everything that he had said on June 23 in the House of Commons.[26] Further, on his departure from Washington, much of his fifteen-minute statement was devoted to praise of Eden and his unfailing patience.[27] But in order to sweeten his words, he made a reassuring gesture toward the American anti-China extremists by saying:

> "To try to force the entry of Communist China into the United Nations would be to complicate the very grave affairs to be dealt with, and would be regarded as a most harsh and uncalled-for act of unfriendliness by the mighty people of the United States, to whom we all owe so much."[28]

As a result of the reconciliation the Americans took no active steps to block success in Geneva. But the grudging ill will, *aeternum servans sub pectore vulnus,* remained, manifesting itself in abstentious tactics. The main feature of this passive resistance was studied non-participation, through the absence from Geneva of American delegates of ministerial rank. Regardless of whether the Geneva Conference was a success or a failure, either Eden or Dulles was bound to be righteously indignant. Had the Conference failed, nobody could ever have persuaded Eden that the fiasco was not the result of the obstructionism of Dulles. On the other hand, success at Geneva would imply for the Secretary of State defeat of his pre-Geneva plans for intervention and the disproving of his general thesis that no agreement was ever possible with Communists. Of course, it would also entail a certain, even though limited, recognition of Communist China as a factor in world affairs.

Eden returned to Geneva on July 12. The French Prime Minister Mendès-France in his acceptance speech on June 20 committed himself to resign should settlement and agreement not be achieved within a month. There remained only eight days for his pledge to be fulfilled. During the absence of the principal delegates, the discussions in the military committees had made little progress. Yet conversations held by Eden with Molotov and Chou En-lai indicated to Eden that there was an even chance of success.

Meanwhile, on the same day, July 12, urgent messages from Churchill, Eden and Mendès-France reached Washington demanding Dulles' return to head the American delegation in person. The delegation, in his and Bedell Smith's absence, had been downgraded to an "observer" mission. Fear had already been expressed in the American press that United States absence would result in harsher conditions, that should the United States continue to play truant anything might happen.[29] On the other side of the Atlantic it was said that the position of Britain and France was considerably weakened by the coldness and suspicion evinced by the American Administration.[30] United States absence at this time could have been explained only by the still prevalent feeling of Dulles that success at Geneva would demonstrate the error of United States policy.

Apparently the comment in the press, the urgent entreaties from the British and French statesmen and a direct appeal from the British and French Ambassadors in Washington did have some effect on the President. Acting with military promptness he "called Defense Secretary Wilson, asked him to have a Constellation available and sent Dulles back to Europe" not to Geneva, but, as a compromise, to Paris.[31]

There, Dulles met Eden and Mendès-France. They assured him that the seven-point memorandum drawn up in Washington—the basis of the British-French stand and practically agreed to by Molotov—would be abided by and that his or Bedell Smith's appearance would not necessarily imply formal United States consent to the partition of Vietnam. Dulles had no excuse to refuse the support "by mere presence"; Bedell Smith went back to Geneva.

At 3:00 p.m. on July 21, Eden took the chair at the final plenary session at Geneva. After Mendès-France had paid warm tribute to Eden, whose personal contribution was the paramount factor of the success of the Conference, Eden made the closing statement which he later recounted:

> "We had now come to the end of our work which for a number of reasons had been both prolonged and intricate. The result of the Conference is not perfect but we had stopped an eight-year war and reduced international tension at a point of instant danger to world peace."[32]

The success of the Geneva Conference was due to the degrading of the Vietnam area from the hypothetical level of vital, primary importance given to it by the domino theory to its more realistic appreciation as secondary confrontation between the Free World and the Communist Powers. The rigidity of United States policy, however, in the years 1954-1960 upgraded Vietnam again to an area of primary importance .

10

THE GENEVA CONFERENCE ENDED WITH A SETTLEMENT GIV-
ing independence to Laos and Cambodia. It arranged the
withdrawal of Communist forces from the territory of these
states and from South Vietnam. It eliminated the bogus
Cambodian and Laotian groups which claimed to be gov-
ernments-in-exile and their previous recognition by their
Communist sponsors. It partitioned Vietnam into North and
South Vietnam, conceding North Vietnam to the rule of
Ho Chi Minh. It arranged for the unhampered withdrawal
of the French army units surrounded in North Vietnam and
the emigration to the south of many hundreds of thousands
of non-Communist Vietnamese, mostly Roman Catholics.
It set up an international commission to supervise the execution of the settlement, with Canada, India and Poland as
members.

Whether the settlement would in the long run be beneficial to the Free World could not be foreseen in 1954. But
—as an emergency operation—it was surprisingly good. Let
us recall American pessimism concerning France's will to
continue fighting; the risks of open full-scale war with the
Chinese; and the implications for Europe and the United

States of a war at the wrong place with eighty percent of the Vietnamese against us and, unlike the Korean war, without a Syngman Rhee lining up local support for the West.

At this writing, in 1965, the "run" has been sufficiently "long" to speak of general and permanent results. During the ten years since Geneva, Laos and Cambodia have developed into united, self-conscious independent entities. They may still adopt a Communist system of government—the danger of which has been acute since 1962—but they will not, without resistance, be part of a Chinese-controlled satellite empire. "With the truce in Indochina the march of Communism has been halted," admitted Eisenhower.[1] The Russo-Chinese falling-out is somewhat of an assurance that China will hardly undertake a large-scale imperialistic war for the conquest of Southeast Asia, and Russia will certainly not intervene there to bring about such an expansion of the Chinese empire. Finally, Malaya overcame the guerrilla threat which endangered it in 1954, with South Vietnam serving for ten years as its buffer state, and the soft belly of South Asia did not become a strategic Communist advance position endangering the Indian Ocean and the Pacific.

The Geneva settlement may be criticized, and the Eisenhower-Dulles resistance to it vindicated because Ho Chi Minh did not respect the agreements and has renewed the fight to conquer South Vietnam. Without going into a factual analysis of whether the conflicts and guerrilla activities since 1959-60 are Chinese-supported or not, this much can be said: had Ho Chi Minh been driven out of all Vietnam by united military action and had he suffered military defeat ten years ago, there is no convincing reason to believe that now, ten years later, he would not be pursuing the same guerrilla activities as in 1954. The guerrilla war of the nineteen sixties could have erupted irrespective of whether settlement or military victory had ended the war in 1954. In fact, it is probable that without the Geneva settlement the war would have begun sooner. After all, the South Vietnamese, their army and their leadership establishment have since developed a vested interest in maintaining their country's independence. The settlement in Geneva gained for the Free World at least two years, possibly ten, to consolidate, to strengthen its position in Southeast Asia. If ten years later the situation in Vietnam may not appear better than it was in 1954 it should not be attributed to the Geneva agreements but to the events that followed it.

This entire story of threatened United States military intervention would appear in a radically different light if it were thought of as a piece of psychological warfare, a cunning device to obtain a favorable settlement in a situation that otherwise was pretty weak, rather than as a genuine threat of war, to be followed, if unheeded, by immediate attack. In 1956, an article appeared in *LIFE Magazine* which is enlightening. We read that:

> "The Western Powers faced a conference with Russia and Red China to be held at Geneva. Dulles regarded this conference with extreme misgivings. Mendès-France evidently wanted to dump the load of the Indochina war at any cost. The threat of a Communist take-over throughout Southeast Asia was grave. But again the policy of boldness impressed the Communists. Dulles had seen to it that the Chinese and the Soviet Union knew that the United States was prepared to act decisively to prevent the fall of all Southeast Asia. It was also clear to the Communists that the French and the British, if they were pushed too far, would accept Dulles' suggestion for united action. Thus, instead of negotiating from the extreme and undisguised weakness of the French position, Mendès-France and Eden found themselves able to bargain from Dulles' strength . . . Dulles is convinced that the solution finally agreed to was acceptable because it eliminated the possibility of a domino effect in Southeast Asia. Half of Vietnam was lost to the Communists but Southern Vietnam, Laos and Cambodia were saved."[†2]

This "edge of the brink" story is preceded by another,

---

† Dulles confirmed the statements, attributed to him by LIFE Magazine, in his press conferences of January 11 and 17, 1956.

related to the Korean armistice. The same article repeated Dulles' claim, voiced several times before and after, that confidential whispers into Nehru's ear had reached the nerves of the Chinese and that that little touch had changed their negativism into a tractable state of mind and resulted in a final agreement.[3] An editorial in the *New York Times* in late April questioned this myth:

"It has become an article of faith," it wrote, "that the armistice was signed thanks to Dulles' shrewdness. But

"CARE TO ADD A NEW INSTALMENT, Mr SECRETARY?"

this *post hoc, propter hoc* argument may be fallacious. Nobody knows whether Nehru passed on the warning or whether, if it was passed on, it had any effect on Chinese policy."[4]

The *Christian Science Monitor* called the entire theory about the Korean armistice, "fallacy."[5] Sherman Adams, Eisenhower's confidential advisor, is among those who were skeptical about Dulles' contention.[6]

Dulles' assumption, the scepticism of the *New York Times*, the *Monitor*, Adams and many impartial observers, in regard to Korea, cannot be more than guesses. However, Dulles' theory that "brink-diplomacy" had saved the Indochina situation, that the saber-rattling of the United States Congress and the Department of State altered decisively the results of the Geneva Conference, is demonstrably incorrect.

The Chinese knew that Bidault was practically begging for the inclusion of Indochina on the agenda of Geneva. They knew that the "momentous decision" for direct action against China, publicized by the Dulles-Eisenhower-Nixon statements in March and April, had run into such loud opposition in the United States Congress, in the House of Commons, and by Eden, Menzies, and almost all NATO members, that Dulles soon after had to sound retreat and admit defeat. The distaste and resistance to sending American ground troops into the Vietnam jungle could not have been a secret. As spokesman for a democracy which had emphasized its general opposition to the use of force as an instrument of foreign policy, Dulles' threats frightened America's allies more than its enemies. As "brinkmanship" it was neither convincing nor plausible. "Molotov was fully aware of the political pressures on Bidault to achieve settlement,"[7] and that peace at almost any price was the Mendès-France program. The refusal of Australia and New Zealand to join United States military action, and the rejection by Britain of any aggressive step without consultation with India, Pakistan, Burma and Ceylon, were on public record. The absence of Dulles from Geneva and the hesitant return of Bedell Smith demonstrated that the negotiations were controlled by Eden and the French. In Korea the United States army was already present and might have been given by the President, without the necessity of anyone's assent or cooperation, the order to attack. In Indochina nothing but the atom bomb could have backed up Dulles' threats, and its use by Eisenhower without Congress' consent for its use was a very remote possibility.

But there are other convincing arguments against the credibility of the "brink" myth. Had the appeal to the sword been intended to build negotiating strength, is it credible that Churchill, Eden and Bidault would have publicly repudiated it? If Dulles trusted Nehru in the Korean situation, why did he not trust Nehru again with Eden as intermediary? If a settlement similar to the one which in fact was made had been the object of Dulles' policy, why did the United States refuse to sign the Agreements?

Without positive knowledge about the motives of the Chinese leaders, the "brink" hypothesis sounds incredible. Eisenhower does not even hint that the policy that he and Dulles pursued, namely threats of military action and use of arms, was not meant to be genuine and that what they aimed at was a good settlement to be gained by a bogus menace of united military action. Sherman Adams also doubts its truth.[8] Eisenhower did not describe the settlement as a victory by negotiation; it was for him a sad event bringing enslavement to millions because the allies refused to cooperate. We have, in addition to all this evidence against the credibility of the "brink" theory, direct testimony from one of the leading architects of our Southeast Asia policy. Assistant Secretary Walter Robertson, on reviewing our policy, said in a speech:

> "We made clear our readiness to continue massive support of France's military effort. We attempted to intervene with our own military forces on certain conditions. It might appear that these, our actions, were ineffectual. *For the purpose intended they were,** but it is probable that their effect was important, that without them an agreement even more unfavorable had been the result."[9]

The words to which emphasis is added admit that our acts were what they purported to be. They were not concealed acts of psychological warfare. We intended to execute our threats and plans. They were not part of a carefully devised "brinkmanship," but demonstrations of a policy of action.

If it was not American bellicosity that helped Britain and France reach a good settlement, then what was it? Without reviewing all the components which might have influenced the result, a few educated guesses can be ventured. According to the dramatic exposé of Prime Minister Mendès-France in the Assemblée Nationale on December 21, 1954, the mobilization of three full-size regular divisions and their publicized appearance in combat readiness at embarkation posts must have influenced the military leaders of Viet-minh.[10] A speech published in Hong Kong by Chen Yun, a high level Chinese party official, referred to conflicts between Chinese policy and Ho Chi Minh's war aims, specifically that Ho would need more material and financial where-withal than what China could afford to spare.[11] Ho Chi Minh had ambitions beyond the length of his Chinese reins. Molotov's siren song to the French in Berlin should be remembered in this connection. In 1954, the Chinese depended on Soviet resources as much as Ho did on Chinese. Molotov seems to have entertained the hope, or anticipated —which, in fact, did happen—that France, if relieved of the burden of the Indochinese crisis, might use her increased independence to upset the United States-British plan of a European Defense Community, a plan which displeased France because of her fear of E.D.C.'s German re-armament implications. Also, failure of the Geneva Conference might have entailed a costly military campaign to defeat the French Vietnamese army, pushed to the wall but not yet beaten. In addition, Soviet diplomacy had always been fond of moderate achievements based on concessions which served afterwards as new bases for further advances. And finally, chaos is not necessarily a desirable situation even for Communist dictators. In a nuclear and balkanized world even they dislike the possibility of a Sarajevo which might escalate into a conflict in the wrong place at the wrong time—wrong for them.

Summing up the history of United States policy before

the Geneva settlement, the Eisenhower Administration had a desirable objective—to save South Asia from conquest by the Communist bloc—but the Eisenhower-Dulles team rushed into a diplomatic action without clearing the ground first. We demanded from France that she fight to one end— the unconditional surrender of Ho Chi Minh. She refused. We wanted Britain and a number of other Western-oriented countries to form a fighting coalition with us. They declined. We tried to overcome their resistance by threats, by diplomatic maneuvers, by crash and shock devices. We failed. With the French in control of the military situation —commanding their own forces and the Vietnamese auxiliaries—we could not have taken over the fighting without their consent to its "internationalization." They demurred. We resented their policy of settlement and attempted to block it. We did not succeed.

We tied our hands by our obsessive abhorrence of the image of the United States as an imperialist power. When we could neither use our immobilized hands for striking nor for the handshake that closes a deal, we became passive spectators standing on the sidelines, demonstrating that we had no more than indirect and nominal influence over the decisions which—as we shall see presently—laid the foundations for the second Vietnam crisis in which we are now bogged down. Walter Lippmann described this immobility of policy in eloquent words:

> "From South Korea to South Vietnam we are inhibited from any policy, except to seek no solution and to remain frozen where we are. Considering the fact that we are by all odds the most powerful of the non-Communist countries, we look a lot like one of those pre-historic animals, which was all armor and teeth but had almost no brains."[12]

Talleyrand portrayed certain Great Powers at the Vienna Congress as "too frightened to fight, too stupid to agree." Would history characterize U.S. policy with Lippmann's or Talleyrand's words, or find a more favorable profile?

The first part of this story, the chronicle of the crisis of the British-American alliance of 1954, ends at this point. The settlement in Geneva, the armistice, and the end of fighting reduced the diplomatic crisis of the Alliance to an incident of history. As far as Britain was concerned, nothing was left over to disagree about, for Eden's policy had brought to completion a new edifice in Southeast Asia. The fighting was over; France's predicament in her pointless war was ended; the existence of three buffer states acted to contain China. And the countries in which Britain had substantial interest had gained a breathing space.

But what deep wounds ever close without a scar? Thus, the diplomatic battle narrated here could not be without influence on the political events in the decade that followed Geneva.

> "The unequal sharing of the Geneva burden placed severe strain on Anglo-American relations and particularly on the personal relations of Mr. Dulles and Mr. Eden, each regarding the other as making up his own rules for playing what was supposed to be a common game."[13]

Accordingly, the personal antagonism between Dulles and Eden continued to play a considerable role in the following two and one-half years—into the second half of 1956 —when Dulles' Suez policy dealt Britain a smashing blow and destroyed the political life of Anthony Eden.

11

THE BACKGROUND OF AMERICAN-BRITISH POLITICAL RELA-tionship connected with the Indochina crisis has been chronicled in the previous ten chapters. United States involvement in Indochina after the Geneva Conference will be taken up in the remaining chapters as diplomatic history. The focus will remain at the United States as it faced its al-lies. A review of this diplomatic relationship will serve to cast light on an important aspect of our foreign policy: our re-lationship to our allies in situations in which their interests and policies differ from ours.

Before we tackle the post-Geneva situation, however, we have to revert to the Geneva Agreements. Four peculiarities of that settlement were not described previously: First, no documents incorporating the Agreements were signed at the Geneva Conference save with regard to three military tran-sactions. These carried the signatures of a French Brigadier-General and Ta-Quang-Buu, the Vietminh Vice-Minister of National Defense; both of these gentlemen acted for their respective Commanders-in-Chief, who were not present in Geneva. Six unilateral declarations were made—two each by France, Laos and Cambodia—but none were signed.

These nine documents were complemented by a statement called the "Final Declaration of the Geneva Conference," which seemingly emanated from all *nine* participants of the Conference listed one by one. Yet two of the listed participants, the State of Vietnam—now generally called South Vietnam—and the United States were not members of the "club." They made separate statements which repudiated entirely or partly the thirteen paragraphs of the Final Declaration. Second, the Agreements were made possible under the pretense that they were of a non-political nature. Nevertheless, they did contain a political substance inherent in the military clauses ordering the cease-fire and the withdrawal and re-grouping of troops. Third, the settlement regarding Vietnam was made to appear as a temporary accommodation, while the final political arrangement was to be worked out two years later, based on the result of an election to be held in July, 1956. And fourth, at the time the settlement was made, it was an incomplete edifice, without a protective roof, that is, without any obligation by any participant toward any other.

The first peculiarity was the result of the fact that the Indochina war was a confrontation of the whole free world by the whole Communist world, and that *they*—the global combines—did not settle *their* conflict. They did, however, eliminate a local problem that might have brought them into the full-scale confrontation that neither of them wanted; both acquiesced in an accommodation. This procedure was reminiscent of similar adjustments, truce and *modus vivendi* in the Greek Civil War, the Soviet thrust into Iran, the Arab-Israel war of 1948, the Berlin blockade, the Korean conflict, and the East German uprising. At each of these instances, actual fighting was stopped at an early stage, or before the brink was passed.

This procedure repeats, furthermore, the history of the nineteenth century with its revolutionary and counter-revolutionary civil wars and interventions. Illustrative are the French intervention at Cadiz in Spain; the Russian expeditionary army which helped the Habsburgs suppress the Hungarian revolution in 1848; the activities of the Holy Alliance in Belgium, Poland, Switzerland, Denmark and Venice. China, also suffered an invasion that opened her door to foreign colonizers and influence; Italy achieved unity; and Rumania, Bulgaria and Serbia achieved independence without large-scale conflict. These and many other European and colonial conflicts—potential occasions for global or large-scale wars—were settled by compromise, bribery, moral argument, dynastic deals and sometimes by gunboats and the moderate use of bayonets. Yet, by avoiding rigidity over second-rank issues, peace on a global scale was in every case preserved. All these events were in a sense "assassinations of an archduke," yet they did not unleash a real war.

Similarly in 1954, in Indochina, the military arrangements were but the front behind which political equilibrium was created. Each side promised to behave towards Laos and Cambodia as though they were taboo, and each meant it. They promised to do the same towards the two halves of Vietnam but this they indeed did *not* mean. Each half of Vietnam was if left to its own resources, though in degree greatly different, unviable. Each without the support of its backers would probably have dropped into the out-stretched hand of the other group. Thus, both global groups must have had reservations, well-known to the other, about the military arrangements: each would do its utmost to make its own half viable, neither would follow a hands-off policy and each would make its part of Vietnam militarily strong enough to maintain the fragile balance.

At this point the first peculiarity of the settlement touches the second. Military agreements, if genuinely military, affect the past only. Had the fighting been renewed, the formulas and promises of the military arrangements would have lost all their significance. They do not affect the military operations which lie in the future. In contrast, the military documents of the Geneva Conference did very much affect the future. By creating a balance of local forces, the military arrangements of the Geneva Conference ushered into the world a new political structure. These arrangements were not put into such language as normally expresses the results of political give-and-take. All the same, they were the result of a political deal. One reason for this peculiarity was that some of the participants denied the very existence of others. To the United States, for instance, China, certainly not a secondary figure as a participant, was "non-existent." Vietminh—that is, the "Democratic Republic of Vietnam"—was also "non-existent" to the United States (as well as to the other Vietnam) and remained non-existent for twenty-six other countries which recognized South Vietnam in 1950 as the only Vietnam. For France, however, the Democratic Republic of Vietnam was somewhere between existence and non-existence during Geneva and afterwards. Eden, in his report to the House of Commons, on June 23, reported this oddity, as "the absence of normal diplomatic relations between a number of [participating] countries" as a circumstance quite unique in his experience which "I devoutly trust, never will be repeated."[1] This was the reason that Eden, serving as channel of communication between them, was treated by both sides as "Municheer." Yet it must be remembered that the settlement would never have been reached if as much as a single word had qualified it as "political" or "final."

Even had normal diplomatic relations existed between the participants at Geneva, it was clear to *all* participants that a genuinely final political settlement was unattainable. On May 12, the Vietnam Delegation introduced into the minutes of the Conference categorical opposition to any partition, direct or indirect, definite or provisional, *"de fait ou de droit."* The Vietnamese Chief of State, Bao Dai, went so far as to refuse to appear in Geneva or be represented at the Conference until the French Government would agree that no partition would be negotiated or agreed to, though everybody knew that the matter was being discussed and partition was, in all likelihood, unavoidable. He forced Bidault to confirm in writing on May 6 that

> "no final political status would be negotiated, that the truce would not predetermine the final situation."[2]

China, other than by armed intervention, could not have forced its protégé, Ho Chi Minh, to abandon himself or his area of military control to Bao Dai, France or the United States. The same was true the other way around, in regard to Bao Dai, Diem, Communist China and Ho Chi Minh. Thus, Article 6 of the Final Declaration with bashful hypocrisy pretended

> "that the essential purpose of the agreement relating to Vietnam is to settle military questions . . . and that the military demarcation line should not in any way be interpreted as constituting a political or territorial boundary."[3]

At this point the second peculiarity of the Geneva Agreements touches the third. It appears obvious that the unification of Vietnam—foreseen in Paragraph 7 of the Final Declaration and to be achieved by a referendum-type election in July, 1956, two years after Geneva—could not have been seriously contemplated. As pointed out above, neither of the opponents—the "Free" and the "Democratic" worlds, as they called themselves—would let its share of partitioned Vietnam fall to the other. Would Ho Chi Minh let his country slide into the area controlled by America? Would Diem be willing to disappear behind the bamboo curtain? Would Communist China allow Ho Chi Minh—even if Ho wanted—to align himself with the Free World? Or, for that matter, would the United States look with indifference on Diem making a deal with Ho Chi Minh, Mao-Tse-Tung or Chou En-lai? The answers to all these questions could only be *no*. Nevertheless, in the year preceding the election date of July, 1956, parties to the Geneva settlement went through the motions of showing interest in the elections. The Vietminh, Ho Chi Minh, the Soviet and Communist

China issued at regular intervals statements insisting on carrying out the elections. India—whose appointee was Chairman of the International Control Commission which would have supervised the election—wanted the Foreign Ministers of Britain and the Soviet Union to meet on the subject. The Soviets suggested that all Geneva participants convene again to enforce the election provisions or to discuss the problem with Britain. France and Britain were the two conference participants which insisted at Geneva on a long preparation period before the election—for, given time, they hoped the Vietnamese would pursue an election campaign which would take the form of building a viable and strong economy and well-organized administration in South Vietnam. They had hoped that the result would be in favor of the Free World. But by 1956 they were far from showing enthusiasm for the election. Conferences were in fact held between Andrei Gromyko of the Soviet Union and Lord Reading of Britain, but, as was expected by all, in July 1956 the two Vietnams joined the two Germanies, the two Koreas and the two Chinas as opponents on the battlefield of the cold war.

The fact that the election was never held was no surprise to the two Vietnams. Diem of South Vietnam, fully backed by the United States, would consent to an election, but only upon an unrealizable condition: abandonment in North Vietnam of the Communist dictatorship.[4] Ho Chi Minh had wanted the election immediately or soon after Geneva because at that time—so he rightly thought—Diem would have had no more than a "Chinaman's" chance of carrying even his own half of Vietnam. But Diem, and his United States sponsor, having refused to agree to the temporary partition, were committed neither to the promise of the election nor to its results, and it would have required a political earthquake to change their minds.

In 1954, the Chief United States delegate, Bedell Smith, in his closing statement to the Geneva Conference, had already forecast that the United States would not join in

138

an election arrangement to achieve unity unless the elections were "free" and supervised by the United Nations to ensure that they were conducted fairly. The Vietnamese Delegation filed a solemn protest against the Geneva Conference Agreements, arrived at between the French High Command and the Vietminh Commander-in-Chief; these agreements abandoned to the Communist Vietminh one-half of their state and fixed a date for a future election. In regard to Vietnam's protest, the United States Government made a special supporting statement reiterating

> "its traditional position that peoples are entitled to determine their own future and that [the United States] will not join in an arrangement [meaning the one that is in the Final Declaration] which would hinder this."[5]

It is the irony of history that the same two Governments at the Geneva Conference which would not agree in 1954 to an *interim* partition were the very same which objected in 1956 to the unification by election and, thus, made the partition temporarily *permanent*.

Ho Chi Minh, probably having no scruples about not respecting an election which might go against him did not need to plead reservations to the election. The United States, however, with moral precepts, uncompromising principles, allies, and an uncommitted third group of states watching its every step, could not simply refer to vital interests or any similar device for avoiding fulfillment of an obligation. Therefore, for America a good legal case had to be built for the refusal of the election.

Paragraph 7 of the Final Declaration demanded the establishment of

> "fundamental freedoms, guaranteed by democratic institutions established as a result of free general elections by secret ballot."[6]

Even if Ho Chi Minh had not headed a strictly controlled, dictatorial, Communist regime in North Vietnam and even if South Vietnam had not been ruled by a fanatical, anti-

Communist dictator, the possibility of free voting would have been incredible. Thus, the United States was in no way hampered from announcing that it would not force President Diem to subject his country to the fate of an election. Already, on August 30, 1955, Dulles asserted with unmistakable finality that free elections to unite North and South Vietnam were not possible.[7] He did this, though only two month earlier he had concurred with the French Government statement that "the promised elections in Vietnam should faithfully be carried out."[8] Assistant Secretary of State, Walter S. Robertson, issued the formal statement on June 1, 1956:

> "We believe in free elections and we support President Diem fully in his position that if elections are to be held, there first must be conditions which preclude intimidation or coercion of the electorate. Unless such conditions exist there can be no free choice."[9]

In addition to this appraisal of the political situation there was no legal basis for forcing the election on the Government of Vietnam. Since the Vietnam Delegation had protested against the Geneva Agreements in a formal statement filed on July 21, 1954, it could certainly not be said that the Diem Government consented or acquiesced in the plebiscite election in 1956. The protest was repeated in a message of the South Vietnam National Assembly, sent to the SEATO meeting in Karachi, held in March 1956. The message formally denounced the entire Geneva Agreement "signed against the will and in contempt of the interest of the Vietnamese people.[10] The United States was not alone in recognizing this; Britain and France were in agreement. French Foreign Minister Christian Pinneau, in a speech on February 3, 1956, though influenced by existing French interests in Communist North Vietnam, could only say that France did not have the "practical means" to oblige the parties to go through with the election. Though Britain did not declare its open support of Diem as the United States did, it agreed that the Diem Government was not bound in this respect by the Geneva settlement.[11] Even Moscow did not show more than token interest in the election. No doubt the awareness of the mutual resolve that the election result would be ignored by whomever was the loser was the main reason that neither party insisted on it, and only formal statements were made.

There was one more reason that dampened even Ho Chi Minh's earlier enthusiasm for election. The election date, 1956, determined in Geneva, was probably the most advantageous of all possible dates from Diem's point of view. By that time the massive American aid and Diem's strong, creative power produced out of the initial chaos a tolerably successful state of affairs and South Vietnam had not yet been disturbed and its roots gnawed by the guerrilla war that began in 1959. Finally, in 1956, no less an authority than General Vu Ngugem Giap, the victor of Dien Bien Phu, leading member of the Vietminh Communist Party and Vice President of the North Vietnam Government, admitted in a published statement that the agrarian reform in North Vietnam was a failure, that there was considerable animosity against the regime in the country and that new policies were needed.[12] Thus, Ho Chi Minh, firm in his resolve not to respect a decision if it should be against him and knowing the same was true of his adversary, was as hesitant to throw himself into a militant election campaign as was Diem of South Vietnam. The election issue had been dead from the beginning, or certainly became dead in 1956.

We have reached the fourth peculiarity of the Geneva settlement. Dulles needed a protective political shield against the expected extremist domestic opposition to *any* settlement. The refusal to associate the United States government with the agreement and to sign a formal document served that purpose. This was the last stumbling block on the road to the successful termination of the French phase of the Indochina war. Since the Chinese would not sign up without American signature, Eden and Molotov

141

persuaded both the Chinese and the Americans to consent to be listed in a Final Declaration as participants, together with the other seven, but it was understood that the Declaration would not be signed either by them or by anyone else. Eden comments on this queer attitude of Dulles by saying that since he (Dulles) "had been at least as responsible as ourselves for calling the Conference, this did not seem to me reasonable."[13] Eden ignores by this comment the point that for Dulles the Korean phase of the conference had strong attraction because he hoped to redeem Eisenhower's election promise to end the war there by some kind of an agreement in Geneva; but he hated the conference as far as Indochina was concerned—again because any concession in that regard was in conflict with other election pronunciamentos.†

These shennanigans *à double entente,* to be in Geneva, but with one foot outside the door and to participate in the conference with a concealed emergency exit—produced a document with participants, but without contracting parties, with declarations which remained unsigned by delegations. They spent three months together and parted company without shaking hands to signify an accord.

The sum total of the conference documents are: three military papers signed; a Final Declaration with nine listed participants, of whom two (United States and Vietnam) were dissenters; six unilateral statements (Cambodia, Laos and France, each with two); thirteen verbal addresses; and at last an exchange of letters by Pham Van Dong of Vietminh and Mendès-France.[14]

The Final Declaration is not a document *binding the participants towards each other.* Out of the thirteen paragraphs, nine (1, 2, 3, 4, 5, 6, 7, 10 and 11) put on record events,

---

† "Dulles' erratic boycott of the Indochina Conference at Geneva rated as the most bizarre performance of his Secretaryship. . . . Dulles' motive was painfully clear . . . He did not want the United States visibly associated with the proceedings. It would have been too galling an epilogue to the ennobling pronouncements of the Republican party platform." (Drummond-Coblenz, *Duel at the Brink,* p. 120).

agreements, and declarations of which *"the Conference took note."* Paragraph 8 interprets the military agreements. Paragraph 9 imposes certain duties on the authorities of the two zones of Vietnam, Laos, and Cambodia and finally, Paragraphs 12 and 13 impose duties on members of the Conference. But, as the "members of the Conference" had not signed this declaration, even if its dispositions did "commit" them, it is merely a collection, in merged form, of unilateral pronouncements without mutuality and inter-connection.

The South Vietnamese Delegation's first declaration, made by Tran Van Do, the Chief of Delegation, was a very short one. It promised to "make and to support every effort to re-establish a real and lasting peace" and not to use force to disturb the arrangements which would carry into effect the military agreements and their cease-fire provisions. In the second and much longer statement the Vietnamese delegation filed a protest against the armistice agreement, against all its dispositions, and specifically against the partition, even if temporary, and the arrangements regarding elections to be held in 1956.[15] This protest reserved for the Vietnam Government complete freedom of action, except the use of force, against all and any provisions of the Geneva agreement.

These statements of Vietnam have not played any role in further developments of events outside of the plebiscite of 1956. In that respect, however, they established the legal basis for South Vietnam to repudiate and defeat the unification that the election was supposed to bring about.

The separate declaration of the United States was introduced by Under-Secretary of State Bedell Smith with an oral statement that repeated and confirmed one made by him on July 18 in a restricted meeting. Though we have no access to the first statement made then, we have sufficient information about the Conference policy of Dulles to know that it must have determined that statement also. Asked during the first days of the Geneva Conference what course he would follow in regard to Indochina, "he replied that 'we just do not participate.' He said he would never sign an accord ceding territory to the Communists. He asserted that his name would never be found on such a document."[16] The July 18 statement must have served Dulles' objective of not having his or his Under-Secretary's signature appear on a document along with the unrecognized Government of Communist China, especially since it entailed sanctioning the passing of twelve to fourteen million Vietnamese and the northern half of Vietnam into the communist orbit.

Twice within twenty-four hours, on July 14 and 15, just before Bedell Smith returned to Geneva, statements of Dulles were published,[17] contending that he—Dulles—by his consent to the return of Bedell Smith had not departed "from the United States principles" which Dulles on July 14 had expressed to Eden and Mendès-France. In the statement made in Washington upon his return from Paris on July 15, 1954, he again put on record his concern that the participation of the American delegation must not prejudice "basic principles to which the United States must adhere if it is to be true to itself and if the captive and endangered peoples of the world are to feel that the United States really believes in liberty." These principles were solemnly pronounced in the joint declarations of Eisenhower and Churchill made in the presence of Dulles and Eden on June 29 at their reconciliation meeting in Washington (supra p. 117) as follows:

"We uphold the principle of self-government and will earnestly strive by every peaceful means to secure the independence of all countries whose peoples desire and are capable of sustaining an independent existence. We welcome the processes of development, where still needed, that lead toward that goal. As regards formerly sovereign states now in bondage, we will not be a party to any arrangement or treaty which would confirm or prolong their unwilling subordination. In the case of nations now divided against their will, we shall continue to seek to achieve unity through free elections supervised by the United Nations to insure they are conducted fairly."[18]

The separate declaration of the American delegation refers to the text quoted here by repeating part of it and calling it the "traditional position" of the United States.

If this is all that those principles were, their repeated ostentatious display seems overwrought and pretentious. There is hardly an international agreement or other document, either of the United Nations or elsewhere in the diplomatic community, which does not refer in one way or other to self-determination and self-government. These terms have become clichés of diplomacy, meaning different things to different devotees. Dulles' special insistence on them as considerations which would shape his policy in regard to the settlement of the crisis in Indochina would be hardly more than simple obedience to the biblical command: "These things I will that thou affirm constantly." In present day international relations their significance in specific situations would never be undisputable and clear.

There are considerations, however, which color these affirmations of Dulles with a certain measure of equivocation. First of all, there was a consensus, shared by Eisenhower, that Ho Chi Minh might have behind him the majority of the Vietnamese.[19] Therefore, it was not entirely true that acceding to the establishment of his government in North Vietnam was acting against the wishes of the population's majority. Second, the partition was not Ho Chi Minh's or China's idea. It was a political solution conceived more to satisfy the interests of the Free World than those of its opponents. Otherwise, it would not have been imposed by the joint effort of Britain and France upon the Vietnam Government of Bao Dai and Diem. Finally, those principles were promulgated by the United States and Britain above the joint signature of Dwight D. Eisenhower and Winston S. Churchill. Did Dulles want to imply that the full participation, consent and willingness of the British delegation to sign would mean that Churchill abandoned those principles or departed from them? If the straightforward British consent to the Geneva agreements was not surrender of those principles, why would United States consent be such? These are the reasons why the sceptical historian has difficulty in agreeing that the partial boycott of the conference and refusal to sign the General Declaration was performed because of those principles, and why he may look for the true cause in domestic political considerations.

Whatever the reason, the relationship of the United States to the Geneva *oeuvre* became sharply distinguished from that of the seven governments (Cambodia, North Vietnam, France, Laos, Communist China, Russia and Britain) who acceded without reservation to the joint text. As it was already pointed out, it differed from the other seven not by a qualification of "unilateral" stamped on it. In that respect there was no dissimilarity. The refusal of the United States to sign transformed the joint text, otherwise a conventional multilateral agreement, into seven unilateral statements with strictly identical text.† Neither Chou En-lai nor Molotov were willing to endow the agreements with their firm guaranty or interconnected obligation unless the United States also did so. Thus, as Eden reports, the American repudiation could not be made palatable to them otherwise than by injecting and spreading its dissociation into the entire accomplishment of the conference. "I do desire we may be better strangers," said Bedell Smith in essence.

One cannot have serious doubt that in July, 1954 in view of the threatening military catastrophy,†† Eisenhower and Dulles were elated that the war was over, that half of Viet-

---

† Au cours de la réunion du 21, rien n'est signé. Les textes préparés consistent en des 'déclarations unilatérales' et une 'déclaration finale', considérée comme un 'acte de la conférence', implicitement approuvée par les Neuf—ce qui permet d'épargner à la délégation américaine l'épreuve d'avoir à contre-signer un texte aux côtés de M. Chou En-lai. On a été adroit et ingénieux jusqu'aux dernières minutes. La conférence de Genève aura inventé une forme nouvelle de coexistence pacifique—celle qui résulte du consentement tacite des négociateurs, et une forme nouvelle d'obligation légale entre les Etats—le traité non-signé. (Lacouture-Devillers, *La fin d'une guerre*, pp. 273,274).

†† Infra Chapter 12.

nam was rescued and saved from Communist conquest, and that for Malaya, Burma, Thailand and the island chain of the Southeast Pacific a buffer state was coming into existence. Eisenhower in his press conference of July 21 stated his satisfaction. Therefore, in order to justify the separate and unilateral feature of the United States' relationship to the Geneva settlement Eisenhower retroactively downgraded United States participation in the Indochina war into the lower rank of "not a belligerent" (as if the entire military equipment and financial support had not been American) and he claimed that the United States—represented at the Conference by Bedell Smith and by a strongly staffed delegation—had not been a party to the conference decisions.[20]

The separate American declaration† takes note without reservations of the military arrangements separating the Vietnamese forces from the Vietminh and securing the evacuation of Laos and Cambodia. When the declaration reaches the joint seven-power document it "takes note" of the *first twelve paragraphs only* and ignores the existence of the thirteenth. This 13th paragraph is the one which obliges the members of the Conference to "consult one another . . . on such measures as may prove necessary to insure that the cessation of hostilities in Cambodia, Laos and Vietnam are respected."

Neither the United States delegation in Geneva, nor the State Department, have ever pointed out in any document the reason or the purpose of this peculiar feature of the United States declaration. As far as can be ascertained, no analysis or report exists that would explain why the American declaration scaled down United States interest in the Geneva settlement and limited the "note-taking" to the first twelve paragraphs. Dulles might not have wanted to consult or be consulted by any of the members of the Conference. It is probable, almost certain, however, that he did not want

---

† Text of the Final Declaration of the Geneva Conference and President Eisenhower's statement in regard to the Conference results are reprinted in Appendices II and III.

to expose the United States to the possibility that if Communist China might want to consult with it about anything he would be obliged by paragraph 13 to listen and be party to such contact. More specifically, he might not have wanted to admit the possibility of consultation of China by the United States in any event either.[†]

Whatever Dulles' reasons and purpose were in 1954, it might have been advantageous to have the diplomatic channel of paragraph 13 available for political contact during the past four years since the guerilla war in Vietnam started. If, in this respect also, United States policy was dictated not by rational considerations but by domestic politics, it is another instance of careful respect by the Eisenhower administration for domestic politics resulting in an inexpedient diplomatic situation.

[†] Answering the inquiry of the author about the background of ignoring paragraph 13 of the final Declaration of the Geneva Conference the Department of State in an informal answer confirmed almost literally the interpretation given by the text to that special feature of the American unilateral declaration.

12

I<small>N</small> J<small>ULY</small>, <small>WHEN THE</small> G<small>ENEVA</small> A<small>GREEMENTS WERE CONCLUDED</small>, nobody but the inner circle of the French military command, the heads of the French and British Governments, and, no doubt, Dulles, knew how tragic, desperate and irretrievable the military situation in Vietnam was. Mendès-France on December 21, 1954, forced by the hard attacks of parliamentary opposition to his Government, gave the Assemblée Nationale a heart-rending account of what had been the catastrophic military situation in Vietnam in July, during the final days of the Geneva Conference. General Ely, the French Commander-in-Chief in Indochina, had cabled him during the final phase of the Conference, that the casualties of the first six months of 1954 had reached the figure of 1,300 officers and 3,600 non-commissioned officers. In the Tonkinese Delta, held by the French Expeditionary Force, 77 French-Vietnam battalions—33 of them battle-fatigued— were surrounded and under attack by 124 Vietminh battalions. South Laos was considered lost. In Paris, all military advisers of the Government had agreed that unless three regular army divisions were to reach Vietnam speedily a debacle was unavoidable, and nobody was willing to say with any kind of certainty that the Expeditionary Force would be able to hold the line until their arrival. In view of this situation, the transfer of the northern part of Vietnam to the Communist rule of Ho Chi Minh was not only a wise policy but an unavoidable sacrifice. It was a desperate, last-minute operation to save something. No responsible statesman could possibly object. In essence, none did.

Thus legally, diplomatically, on paper the settlement made in Geneva was faultless. The Free World saved a substantial part of Indochina by sacrificing North Vietnam. But was South Vietnam really saved?

Prospects were dim for its survival. From the outset Diem's Government was challenged from many directions. He could not expect general international confidence in the stability and safety of his newly created country, an expedient truncation. He had to bear the political and psychological consequences of the defeat of anti-communist resistance and the collapse of Catholic and pro-Western forces in North Vietnam. To the north he faced a disciplined and confident army. Ho Chi Minh—supported by Peking and, though modestly, by Moscow—was riding a wave of popular sentiment in the wake of the victory at Dien Bien Phu. It was obvious that Ho would establish a Communist regime in North Vietnam—including the rich Hanoi-Haiphong area which until Geneva had been held by the French. It was equally obvious that international Communism would throw its bellicose shadow south across the seventeenth parallel.

The danger from the north was, however, only one of the many problems which confronted Diem at the time when the Geneva deal was completed. His authority was virtually nonexistent outside the capital—Saigon—and a few other large cities. For years the regimes which had preceded the Diem Government had exercised only nominal authority in the rural areas of the south and even that only with the aid of the French Expeditionary Force. Real control rested largely in the hands of the Vietminh Communists, and after their departure pursuant to the Geneva Agreement, in the hands of semi-autonomous sects, such as the Hoa Hao and the Cao Dai. These sects operated through a strange mixture of terrorism, protection, mysticism and subsidies from the Government in Saigon. Much the same chaotic situation existed in Saigon itself, the largest city in South Vietnam. The city was dominated by Binh Xuyen, whose principal revenues were derived from semi-official corruption, the narcotics trade, and other such activities. It also controlled the Saigon police.

There were other elements of weakness also in the situation in South Vietnam. It was anticipated that many residents of North Vietnam would avail themselves of the free choice opened to them by the Geneva Agreements to move into South Vietnam. Among those who would certainly go would be all Catholics living in the Tonkinese area, supporters of the previous French regime, alumni of French cultural institutions and those whose anti-Communist political orientation was known. Obviously, their re-settlement could be expected to over-tax the southern administration's ability to maintain tolerable order. In addition, conspiracy and subversion, rampant in anticipation of the "probable" debacle of the Diem regime, grew beyond control after the fall of Dien Bien Phu in May 1954. Majority opinion expected a coalition regime to be formed, with Communist participation—changing into concealed Communist control —working by all possible means towards unification with North Vietnam.

"Rarely, if ever, in history has a State come into being amid such inauspicious circumstances: arbitrarily split in two at the end of a bitter eight years war; suddenly given independence after a period of colonialism during which the colonial power made no effort at all to train civil servants or to prepare the people for self-government in other ways, with an influx of 800,000 refugees from the north; confronted with open rebellion on the part of pirates and bandits masquerading as religious

151

sects,† threatened by Communist infiltration and subversion and—with virtually no economic resources . . .
The most impressive thing about Vietnam is that it
exists."[1]

In 1954, the politics of South Vietnam were commonly
described as "anarchy," Diem as "inept," his Government as
ready "to fall of its own corrupt weight."[2] Senator Mike
Mansfield considered the outlook "grim and discouraging."[3]
French sources of information give, by and large, the same
picture.[4]

In comparison, North Vietnam already had at this time—
in spite of its many internal difficulties—at least two obvious
advantages. First, Ho Chi Minh had no reason to feel concerned about an armed attack from Diem,†† nor was there
expectation that any sizable opposition would assert itself
against the new Communist regime, especially if the Catholic and pro-French residents of the Tonkinese area moved
to the south.[5]

Accepting the truth of these descriptions of the political
situation it is obvious that Ho Chi Minh's North Vietnam
was in no great need of general guarantees by Britain and
France; nor did he need protection from his only possible
outside enemy, the Diem Government. South Vietnam, however, was in mortal danger of internal collapse and take-
over, in one form or other, by Ho Chi Minh. If this took
place—as of 1954—the otherwise reasonably safe Laos and
Cambodia would follow it behind the bamboo curtain.

Keeping this situation in mind, the Locarno-type system
of mutual guarantees devised and described by Eden in his
House of Commons speech of June 23, 1954 probably would
have been the most expedient and fitting instrument to assure South Vietnam's survival. But, as we have seen, at the

† Though this characterization of the religious sects is biased, even if
discounted, it still proves the point.
†† "Unlike Syngman Rhee in Korea, Diem's posture toward Communist
China was not a bellicose one. He apparently felt that new military conflict
would more likely lead to disaster than to national unification." (Doak
Barnett, *Communist China In Asia*, Vintage Book, New York, 1961, p. 239).

time the final documents of the Geneva Conference were written and the declarations, embodying the result, were made, Eden's scheme had already been vetoed by Washington. But for Eisenhower and Dulles, firm in their resolve to insure the survival and independence of South Vietnam, Laos, and Cambodia there would have been another approach available for the asking. Both Britain and France made repeated overtures prior to the final day in Geneva for the defensive protection of Indochina.

Prime Minister Churchill, on April 27th, answering a parliamentary inquiry, put it on record that should a settlement be reached at Geneva

> "the [British] Government will be ready to play their full part in supporting them."[6]

At about the same time, Eden, in a message sent to the Asian Commonwealth Prime Minister's meeting at Colombo, asked

> "if they were prepared to participate in a guaranty to assure the future of Indochina should the Geneva Conference arrive at an acceptable decision."[7]

In early May Eden, at one of his two meetings with Dulles, told him

> "that if a settlement were achieved at the Conference, the United Kingdom would be prepared to join in guaranteeing it."[8]

On May 17, Churchill, in a speech in the House of Commons, set forth that the British Government was resolved to

> "exercise their influence to ensure that any acceptable settlement should be backed by effective international guaranty."[9]

The French Delegation at Geneva made similar suggestions. In its opening proposal to the Conference on May 8 it expressed the readiness of France to guarantee—by itself— the results whatever they might be. On July 16, it published its draft of a final act for the Conference—to be signed by *all* Conference participants (including the United States) collectively and severally—which included a declaration of guarantee by all of them.

All these suggestions and offers of guaranty were ignored or snubbed by the United States. The second proposition of the French Delegation, just mentioned, was specifically killed by immediate American refusal.[10]

These refusals were coupled at the end of the Geneva Conference with a strong promise of United States action should the new political situation established in Indochina be disturbed. As has been pointed out earlier,† none of the seven participants who consented to the Geneva settlement undertook to defend it should any of them or an outsider, disturb it. They restricted their obligation towards each other to consultation and undertook even this obligation only if recommended by the International Control Commission.[11] The United States Delegation, however, made known in its separate Declaration, that it

> "would view any renewal of aggression in violation of the aforesaid agreement with grave concern and as seriously threatening international peace and security."[12] ††

In the idiom of diplomacy this is recognized as signifying the assumption of a liability. Thus, paradoxically, the sole Great Power participant at the Geneva Conference which dissented became by this pronouncement the only one to consent to an obligation to defend the settlement from violation by the consenting seven participants or anyone else.

By adopting this line of negative-positive policy the United States passed the first gate to the unenvied position it occupies today as the sole defender of South Vietnam's independence and territorial integrity.

This policy line was not nonsensical or irrational as hind-

---

† Supra, Chapter 11.

†† President Eisenhower in a statement on the results of the Geneva Conference, made July 21, 1954 (Documents on American Foreign Relations, 1954, p. 317) restricted the "grave concern" to Communist aggression only.

sight wisdom or sarcastic wit would make it appear. One must view the situation from the watchtower of a President and Secretary of State, who were leaders of the Republican Party, who were inspired by a crusading spirit against International Communism, and who sincerely believed that outside of Europe the international status of the United States was hurt by close association with Britain and France. These two countries were the foremost "colonialists" in the eyes of Asiatic and African people and it would have required unusual objectivity for the American leaders to act differently. Had they associated themselves with Russia and (even more) Communist China in a combination of joint guaranty, they would have had to face a revolt in Congress and by the majority of the Republican Party. Had they confined U.S. policy to association in joint guarantees with Britain and France only, it would have violated their anti-colonialist prejudices. Thus, logically they had to rebuff Russian and Chinese guarantees, they had to give the cold shoulder to the individual undertakings of Britain and France. Therefore, limited in their policy by their domestic political affiliations and by their conditioned mental reflexes to the cold war, Eisenhower and Dulles had no other choice but to put all their eggs in one basket, entrusting the protection of Southeast Asia to the defense treaty that was designed to bring into being the mixed European-Asiatic, militant, NATO-type, anti-communist alliance, later known as SEATO.

Thus, Dulles' diplomacy would have been along these lines anyway, but having obtained on June 25 Churchill's and Eden's acquiescence in the American plan to form the Southeast Asia defense pact with mixed participation of European and Asiatic countries, *immediately* after the Geneva Conference, and having obtained the seal of approval on this understanding from Australia and New Zealand on June 30,† it was not unreasonable of Dulles to anticipate that his project, the Southeast Asia defense pact, would well take

† See below p. 161.

care of the post-Geneva defense of Indochina and the entire area. At the end of the Geneva Conference, the then head of the United States Delegation, Bedell Smith, on taking leave of Mendès-France, put this American policy in unmistakable words: "We must get that pact."[13]

Had the Dulles plan been fully realized, had SEATO become a militant anti-Communist, NATO kind of alliance, with efficient deterrent power to protect Indochina as a viable part of the Free World, the diplomatic and political campaign so inauspiciously launched by Eisenhower and Dulles in the last days of March, 1954 would be hailed as a crowning success and consummate achievement. But, as SEATO did not meet these expectations, the diplomacy that restricted the international protection of Indochina to SEATO is now considered a fiasco. Its weakness, in view of the initial opposition of Britain, ought to have been anticipated. It was overly optimistic to expect that the general British policy, supported by Australia and New Zealand and giving weighty consideration to the views of India, Ceylon and Burma and to all the other features of the Eden plan, would not reappear in one form or other at the Manila conference table when the project would be negotiated in detail. In fact, that is exactly what happened. SEATO became a misformed compromise, halfway between the Eden project and the Dulles plan, a body lacking a proper bone-structure.

13

THE IDEA OF AN ANTI-COMMUNIST PACT FOR THE PROTEC-
tion of Southeast Asia and the Western Pacific was first
launched by Dulles as the all-embracing operational base in
his "crisis" speech of March 29, 1954. This would have been
in his "united action" plan the tool for action along two distinct but related lines. First, it would have become the basis
of an "ad hoc coalition, comprising the United States, Great
Britain, France, Australia, New Zealand, the Philippines,
Thailand and the three Associated States of Indochina
[issuing] *before** Geneva, a solemn declaration of their readiness to take concerted action under Article 51 of the United
Nations Charter," threatening naval and air action against
the Chinese coast and active intervention in Indochina itself.[1] Second, this *ad hoc* coalition would simultaneously set
about organizing the collective defense of Southeast Asia.
At this juncture only the second plan of action, aimed at the
future collective defense, will be dealt with; the first one
has already been extensively treated in previous chapters.

Eden records that the idea of a collective defense system
was welcome to him

"since this would contribute to the security of Malaya

and Hong Kong and would remove the anomaly of our exclusion from the ANZUS Pact."[2]

This plan must have become more palatable to Eden since Dulles, by the time of his trip to London on April 11, does not seem to have insisted on the first militant phase of the plan that was, as we know, firmly resisted by the British. On that occasion he put the entire weight of his power and persuasion behind the Pact and Organization for the future defense of Southeast Asia.

Dulles' plan was catapulted into existence by the anticipated threat to the Free World in consequence of the loss of Indochina. This consideration made the immediacy of its realization logical and necessary. Likewise, as the purpose of the coalition was the defense of Indochina against Communist conquest, it stood to reason that the participants should be only those countries which would be willing to adopt militancy, employ pressure and fight against expansion of Communist power should such measures become unavoidable. Thus, focusing the Southeast Asian situation the way that Eisenhower and Dulles did, their policy was far from ill-considered. It seemed to them to be unavoidably the only practical line of action. Neither was it emotional from their viewpoint to oppose the membership of India and likeminded Asians. This opposition stemmed from the certainty that, if members, they would never agree to a militant anti-Communist policy.

> "To the Indians Ho Chi Minh was and is first and foremost, an Indochinese nationalist, a leader in the struggle for Vietnamese independence, and the fight in Indochina was almost completely a colonial struggle. The fact that Ho was and is an old-line Communist, if admitted at all, is regarded as inconsequential."[3]

Eden was in agreement with a Southeast Asia Defense Treaty but subject to strong qualifications. At the first meeting when the Dulles plan was discussed between them in London on April 11 he set forth that it

158

"would require the most careful thought and study, particularly on the question of membership . . . [because] on no account shall India and the other Asian Commonwealth countries be deliberately excluded."[4]

This qualification had behind it the conviction of the Churchill Government and both Parties of the British Parliament that although India and the others might want to remain outside of such a Pact, they should nevertheless be given every opportunity to participate or, as a second best result, should bear good will towards it.

For Eden Indochina was to be taken care of by settlement and special individual and interconnected guarantees. Entirely separate from this, Eden wished to create a safeguard with little or no relevance to current, 1954, events, a safeguard which would *not* be primarily anti-Communist in its character but would deter and curb local Asian conflicts by its existence and, if they erupted, keep them localized and arrange their settlement rather than allowing them to become part of the global controversy. The organization could thus unite all non-Communist states of the area in a union of defense. As Eden pointed out in his speech in the House of Commons on June 23, his plan "has been canvassed for years" and though ultimately, as a secondary result it might eventually be effective to protect the settlement in Indochina, its primary purpose ought to be "to assure security" of the entire Southeast Asia area.[5] The Eden project had the approval of Canada, Australia, New Zealand and, last but not least, of his Parliamentary Opposition.[6] Robert Menzies, the Australian Prime Minister in the House of Representatives in Canberra, said:

"We in Australia, attach great importance to rallying the opinion and influence of the great new democracies in South and Southeast Asia."[7]

The contrast between Eden's and Dulles' position was made by Eden as clear as language permitted, in his House of Commons speech on June 23. He regarded with pride and self-satisfaction his refusal to agree to the "precipitate action" demanded by Dulles, for by this refusal he felt he had advanced the cause of two systems of guarantee: one to take care of the Geneva settlement immediately and the other, a NATO kind of guarantee, to provide exclusively for defense of all countries of the area. He gave much weight to his opinion that

> "there never will be any real security in Southeast Asia without the goodwill of the free Asian countries. If peace will be restored in Indochina, these countries will be willing to take part in supervising and guaranteeing the settlement to last. . . . The Southeast Asia defense organization will not be fully effective without their support."[8]

The composition of the defense organization was the subject of a running fight between Eden and Dulles until June 23 when, as seen already, Churchill and Eden, for the sake of mending the ailing alliance, surrendered, letting Dulles have his way. They agreed, though obviously with much reluctance, that the Southeast Asia pact should

> "be limited to those powers willing to undertake specific commitments for military action in the event of renewed Communist aggression [and] the United Kingdom was willing to examine the possibilities of this . . . arrangement *at once*."[9]

This capitulation required from the British statesmen much elasticity and self-possession. They had committed themselves publicly and firmly to their own plan and laid emphasis on it by contrasting it to the main features of the Dulles scheme which, they said, was unacceptable to them because it defeated the desirable aims of such an alliance.

Eden no longer mentioned, after June 25, the controversy that had been so clearly and sharply underlined in his speech before his trip to Washington on June 24. Upon his return he carefully avoided the task of reporting to the House of Commons the result of the Washington Conference. Instead, it was Churchill who—not as deeply committed in this respect—gave an account of the agreements made in Washington. He succeeded, in his speech of July 13, in getting around the concession to Dulles by using the formula of the "study group" which was prefabricated for this purpose. Not the two governments, but a study group only, would prepare the *immediate* formulation of the defense pact and the possibility of having Asian members join it.[10] Eisenhower records the elimination of the controversy with polite understatement: "I was delighted with this particular reaction [of Churchill] to our *earlier* suggestion."[11] Dulles' victory, of course, is contained in the word "earlier."

Dulles, however, wanted to have the British agreement on the timing and membership of the organization nailed down and sealed. Therefore, he convoked for June 30, Australia and New Zealand to an ANZUS meeting in Washington for the discussion of the Southeast Asian situation in the light of the talks just concluded in Washington between Britain and the United States.

"The Australian and New Zealand representatives expressed satisfaction with the statement by President Eisenhower and Sir Winston Churchill that plans for collective defense in Southeast Asia *should be pressed**** forward."

The representatives of the United States, Australia and New Zealand all "agreed on the need for *immediate***action" to bring about the early establishment of collective defense.[12] Dulles' victory thus precluded SEATO from playing the role that it would have, had Eden's plan been realized.

The Geneva Conference ended on July 21. In the absence of any specific guarantee of the Conference participants that had been eliminated by United States policy, the need for an urgent and immediate defense pact as the only shelter protecting South Vietnam, Laos and Cambodia led, only 43 days later, on September 6, to a meeting in Manila of the representatives of three countries from Asia—Pakistan, Thailand and the Philippines—and those of Australia, New Zea-

161

land, France, Great Britain, and the United States. Only two days later the Southeast Asia Collective Defense Treaty, the Protocol to it and the so-called Pacific Charter, embodying a few bombastic pronouncements, were already approved.[13] This timetable demonstrates the urgency dictated and imposed by Dulles' policy to realize the solution he advocated. Dulles got his pact.

The participants of the Manila Conference could have no illusions about the military strength of an alliance backed in Asia by such lightweights as Thailand, the Philippines, and Pakistan if opposed to China or even Ho Chi Minh, unless the full striking power of the United States were to be in the first line of defense. Dulles promised, in fact, to provide this backing:

> "The Treaty will, to the extent that is practicable, throw a mantle of protection over Cambodia, Laos and the free territory of Vietnam,"

he said in a broadcast on September 15, 1954.

> "The Manila Pact," he continued, "will, in fact, make a substantial contribution to preserve free governments in Southeast Asia and to prevent Communism from rushing on into the Pacific area where it would threaten the defense of the United States."[14]

Thus, this pilgrimage to Canossa, represented by Manila was not a mere gesture of one ally towards another for the sake of showing cooperative spirit. In the absence of any other guaranty it became for Britain and France, too, *conditio sine qua non* for the protection of the three associated States. But France's and Britain's participation at Manila was also a helping hand to alleviate United States' terror of appearing as an imperialist meddler; and, at that stage of the Indochina crisis, it was an attempt to make the solitary United States guarantee of the Geneva settlement palatable to the uncommitted countries of Asia. In the absence of a reciprocal international guaranty it was vital—said Turton, Joint Under-Secretary of Foreign Affairs in the House of

Commons on November 8th, 1954—"that there should be a final declaration and some collective safeguard; otherwise there would have been a dangerous gap."[15]

Nevertheless, the British and French put up strong resistance to American insistence on admitting Cambodia, Laos and South Vietnam to the Treaty. Jean Chauvel, the chief strategist of the French Delegation both at Geneva and at Manila, fought valiantly against this. The United States thesis was that these three States could be participants because the Geneva document prohibited only alliances which violated the United Nations Charter, i.e., were openly of aggressive intent. Chauvel insisted that if not the letter, at least the spirit of the Geneva settlement would be violated by an alliance of the three Associated States with the Manila powers and, besides, it would not add strength to the Treaty.[16] A compromise solved the disagreement. By unanimous agreement, but by designation in the Protocol only and, without making them Treaty Participants, Cambodia, Laos and South Vietnam were added to the area protected by the Treaty. By choosing such a middle course the hostile response of the Communist world did not go beyond verbal protest. Ho Chi Minh and the Chinese did not take action beyond issuing a communiqué in July 1955, in which they accused the United States of violating the Geneva accord by putting Laos, Cambodia and South Vietnam in the designated area guarded by the Southeast Asia Defense Treaty.[17]

The debate on the Manila Treaty[18] preceding its ratification began in the House of Commons on November 8. On that occasion Eden could not avoid the grilling. It was well known to the British that the Manila Treaty was Dulles' answer to the guarantee requirement of the Geneva settlement. But Eden's plan—the general guarantee arrangement for Southeast Asia—had appeal in opening vistas of a peaceful future not only because as a reciprocal guarantee it would have taken care of the Indochina settlement proper but because the participation of India and other non-com-

mitted Asian countries might have calmed the Asian rever-
berations of the cold war and created a neutral belt there.
It was, therefore, to be expected that the Labor Party would
take for its line of attack that Eden had yielded to American
pressure by discarding his own plan for the sake of mending
the cracks in the alliance. Eden, on the other hand, felt it in-
cumbent upon him to maneuver in the House of Commons
so that the concession made for the sake of allied unity
would not be made the subject of public censure. Such a result would have defeated his and Churchill's gambit.

The leading speaker of the Labor Party, former Minister
of State in the Attlee Cabinet Kenneth Younger, opened
the debate with the question:

> "What proposal has the Foreign Secretary made to the
> participating countries of the Geneva Conference for
> a reciprocal guaranty?"

Here is Eden's explanation:

> "Unfortunately, it proved impossible to obtain the kind
> of reciprocal guaranty which we had in mind. This was
> due to the insistence at Geneva of the Soviet, China
> and Vietminh delegations that any guaranty must be
> collective. In other words this introduced the principle
> of veto once again and this was completely un-accept-
> able to us. That is why that form of guaranty lapsed."

As it was obvious that Eden evaded the essence of the question, the Labor Party speaker repeated the question:

> "Would the Foreign Secretary say whether any attempt
> has been made since Geneva to pursue the idea of re-
> ciprocal guaranty?"

Eden's answer was in the negative.

The Parliamentary Opposition now turned to two features
of the Manila Conference—the urgency that had attended
the creation of the Treaty and the elimination of India and
the other Commonwealth powers from participation. Kenneth Younger referred to Eden's speech of June 23 in which
he said, with the approval of the whole Parliament, that

without general Asian support a treaty of this kind would be of little value at best and it might even be harmful. The changes in the Asian political situation since Geneva, Younger said, had lowered political tension and should have strengthened the case against moving rapidly.

> "Why is it that the Government acted so rapidly, especially in view of the fact that the Commonwealth was split? It would be irresponsible—and this is a fault into which the Foreign Secretary did not fall—to assume that [the Manila Pact] had achieved anything important [in view of] the crippling gaps in Asian membership and [that] Siam is the only area really covered by the Treaty, outside of Indochina's odd inclusion. . . . The Treaty is unimpressive militarily, open to certain abuses; . . . it is a paper treaty."

Nehru said the same:

> "The Manila Pact does not help peace-making in the area and it is a positive hindrance to peace-making policies."[19]

The Manila Treaty differed from Dulles' project not only in regard to the membership of Cambodia, Laos and South Vietnam. The main deviation was the absence of a direct and clear anti-Communist line. The original text of the Pact drafted and sent to all participants by Dulles before the Conference, specifically referred, as Eden in his House of Commons speech set forth, to "Communist aggression." The word "Communist" had been eliminated when Eden objected. On the other hand Dulles was interested in one kind of pact only, in an anti-Communist one. He "had always wanted primarily to direct the treaty against Communist aggression."[20] Consequently the Treaty had been signed by Dulles with the reservation that, as far as the United States was concerned, its application would be restricted to Communist aggression. In view of the fact that a military backbone of the Treaty was, for all practical purposes, lacking without the United States, SEATO became, on account of the American reservation, an anti-Communist tool to be used or not used by the United States as it pleased.

There is no doubt that the expectations which Eisenhower and Dulles had for SEATO, the hopes they had set on it, have been unrealized. Its members do not allocate part of their armed forces to the Organization. Peking's denunciation, dubbing it a symbol of American militarism and imperialism, is widely accepted in Asia. The only Southeast Asian *area* members in SEATO, the Philippines and Thailand, are not generally considered representative of Asian solidarity. Pakistan's membership is a major factor in the malice borne towards it by India. Whatever weight the Organization carries derives from the non-Asian members, and so in Southeast Asia SEATO is an easy target for the anti-colonialists. According to Nehru, for instance, it smelled of colonialism. Thus, on the political balance sheet SEATO is not an asset, it is a fiction. But even militarily as an international instrument, SEATO is not a plus factor. It lacks "definiteness, cohesiveness, organization and committed power."[20a]

The weakness of SEATO had to be admitted even by its principal architect and sponsor, Dulles. In his New Year address for 1955,[21] in which he reviewed United States foreign policy in 1954, he forecast SEATO's development into a

"deterrent to Communist designs on Southeast Asia . . . a combined allied security unit for policing the area. The possibility of creating such a task force will be explored" [at the next meeting of SEATO].

The Secretary regarded SEATO as a

"defense weapon of great potential power, capable of mounting a mobile striking force against attack or aggression in Southeast Asia."

Dulles' statement was immediately challenged, and rejected by the British Government. What had been surrendered by Britain in June, 1954 in Washington, was reinstated and revalidated by the wording and interpretation of the Manila Pact.†

> "Surprise was expressed in diplomatic quarters tonight at reports of Dulles' press conference statements about the defense of Southeast Asia,"

especially on the creation of joint defense forces or mobile striking forces to deter aggression.

> "Britain's objectives in the Southeast Asia organization have always been predominantly to create *political and economic solidarity* by creating an organization in which India, Burma and Ceylon and other currently neutralist powers in the area might join or cooperate."[22]

Therefore, the view of Eisenhower and Dulles that SEATO would become an *international* structure, in which America would not carry the entire political and military weight and would give a strong guarantee of the defense of Southeast Asia has certainly not been vindicated. Even in the second Vietnamese War SEATO has not made, and until recently was not expected to make, any contribution to the protection of the Geneva settlement and South Vietnam. At the time of the 1962 Laos crisis, the United States made no use of the SEATO machinery. Neither was the slightest attempt made in 1960 to turn to SEATO and obtain support from it in Vietnam for the American military action there. More recently, however—the first such move since 1954—the Kennedy-Johnson administration began a campaign to bring other nations who are members of SEATO into Indochina with contributions to hold the defensive line jointly with America.[23]

From time to time in the past some tentative moves were made to clothe SEATO with the appointments symbolic of genuine existence. Successive SEATO Council meetings appointed a Secretary General, military advisers, and estab-

---

† "[It is] characteristic British practice of affording temporary appeasements in fact while holding ground stubbornly in principle" and "yielding the substance while not giving up the principle." (Samuel Flagg Bemis, *John Quincy Adams*, Knopf, New York, 1956, pp. 66 and 138).

lished a secretariat, a public relations office and a military planning staff. Yet SEATO was not transformed into an international body of efficient military striking strength. Actually, the bilateral military programs strengthening SEATO's members individually could be maintained with or without its existence.

> "A Congressional Committee found that [SEATO] offers no security to the nations of the area . . . SEATO is not a going concern but a sham. We are more inconvenienced than convenienced by its rather loose treaty ties."[24]

According to Hamilton Fish Armstrong, SEATO has aggravated nationalist rivalries. It is partly responsible for anti-American feelings in Cambodia, and retarded the settlement of some local conflicts and stimulated new ones. He also believed it doubtful the United States needed any of the States that joined us in SEATO as military allies.[25] It most certainly did not become a good substitute for the broad cooperative defense structure that Eden's policy might have built. It was called by a keen observer of the international scene, in May 1962, "the alliance that really never was, never truly existed."[26]

In appraising our tool, SEATO, which countries can be said to guarantee the Geneva Settlement, or more particularly, which countries guarantee the three Associated States, Cambodia, Laos and South Vientam? China and Russia certainly do not. Nor do Laos, Cambodia and South Vietnam recognize any such mutual obligation towards each other. Outside of SEATO no such guarantee was undertaken by anyone. Within SEATO the three Asian member states— the Philippines on the east, Thailand in the center, and Pakistan far to the west—cannot and would not contribute military support, perhaps not even token forces. In any realistic sense, in case of a hot war, only insubstantial help could be expected from France, Britain and even from Australia and New Zealand. And in the developing hot war in South Vietnam, not even token assistance has until recently appeared. Thus, in sum, Dulles' Manila Treaty has become the second gate through which the United States passed to its solitary, unenvied military task in South Vietnam.

There was, however, a third gate which the United States chose to open that led, as we shall see, to a wasteland where we find ourselves almost completely isolated from our allies and associates, and where again we have to shift for ourselves.

14

THE GENEVA AND MANILA CONFERENCES TERMINATED THE 1954 Indochina crisis. They developed a settlement with four new entities—Cambodia, Laos, North Vietnam and South Vietnam. All four were in a sense independent, but with deficiencies which affected their foundations and structures in different ways. Whether they would develop into healthy, self-sustaining states, depended only partly on their own statesmen, population, and domestic politics. The final outcome was to be more or less determined by the policies of the five major powers which were the leading actors at Geneva and Manila.

Subject to these reservations, it can be said that Cambodia, as it was brought into existence in Geneva, was considered in 1954 an independent country with an anti-Communist political foundation. These two political characteristics could be threatened only from abroad by external political powers. Laos, too, had independence but the regime set up by the Geneva Agreements was a peculiar form of peace-front, a coalition of left and right. The Royal Government with its seat in Vientiane had no Communist participation. But the term "coalition administration" is justified on account of the allocation of two provinces to a Communist political group, called Pathet Lao, which then claimed the right of participation in the central government controlling ten provinces.[1] Both Cambodia and Laos, because of their modest size and moderate economic resources, could not and, in fact, did not play a decisive role in the immediate post-1954 history of Indochina. The crux of the political developments and the center of interest lay unquestionably in North and South Vietnam and, therefore, only development in Vietnam will be the subject of the chapters which follow.

This chronicle and analysis of the political history of Vietnam, mainly South Vietnam, will cover only the period from September, 1954 to July, 1956. In these two years can be found the roots of the critical political and military situation as it has existed in Vietnam since 1960. In 1954 and 1955 the United States could still have charted a different course. But once it chose the direction it did in 1954 and proceeded in that direction through 1956, it became a captive of its policy and committed to its continuation. In 1965 it is still committed to it.

At the time of the cease-fire (on the closing day of the Geneva Conference, July 21, 1954) the agreement for military withdrawal gave to the French Expeditionary Force, including its Vietnamese elements, control and mastery of the political situation. This, then, must be the starting point of our narrative, for the French Government could, at this time, have freely chosen which way to chart as a course for Indochina's future.

It must be remembered that after the fall of Dien Bien Phu, at the time when the success of the Geneva Conference could not yet safely be anticipated, the Laniel-Bidault Government realized that Indochina was the most critical problem for France and that the difficulties of communication did not make it possible to have all important decisions reserved to Paris. This being so, the Government decided to create in Indochina a special command position and to give overall political and military power to one person who would have decision-making authority without consultation with Paris.

The Chief of Staff of the French armed forces, General Paul Ely, one of the highest ranking military figures of France, with long experience in diplomacy and several years of previous service in Washington and at inter-allied organizations, was chosen for this extraordinary position. He had already previously, after the fall of Dien Bien Phu, sized up the Indochina situation during a special investigative trip. His military rank and previous command position lent him a special aura that would command respect and ready compliance from any military or civilian official and from the French settlers' community. Thus, French post-Geneva policy was largely devised by him and, insofar as he acted on the basis of decisions made in Paris, he was the commanding officer and political emissary who directed its execution. Fortunately for historians, he published in his memoires a detailed account of his stewardship.[2]

Following the cease-fire and withdrawal agreement in Geneva no power existed in Indochina that could have forced General Ely to do anything that was not his own chosen policy for South Vietnam. The Vietminh Communist guerillas, assembled at the points designated for their exit operation, were in the process of leaving South Vietnam following a timetable set by Geneva. Insofar as a Vietnam army existed, it was mostly merged with French units and thus was necessarily in operational harmony with the French policy. The armed forces of the so-called "sects"—organized partisan and religious political groups—had fought for many years in association with the French Expeditionary Force against the Communists and were politically committed to the anti-Communist policy line of Ely's command. American military presence was insignificant and the United States training units also were subordinated to General Ely. General John W. (Iron Mike) O'Daniel, Head of the American Military Advisory and Assistance Group (MAAG), recognized General Paul Ely as his superior; General Gazounaud who was in operational charge of the training of the Vietnamese was himself, of course, subordinate to Ely.

In addition to the chaotic situation already described, all available sources of information agree that in the fall of 1954 the Vietnam political administration, presided over by Prime Minister Ngo Dinh Diem, was powerless. According to a report on Vietnam by Senator Mike Mansfield, Diem's authority in 1954 was virtually nonexistent outside Saigon-Cholon and a few other large cities.[3] For years, the regimes which had preceded the Diem Government—installed in June 1954—had exercised only nominal authority in the rural areas of the South and even that only with the aid of the French Expeditionary Force.

> "Real control rested largely in the hands of . . . semi-autonomous sects. . . . Much the same situation existed in Saigon-Cholon, the largest city, and the administrative core of South Vietnam. . . . [There] the head of the organization [Binh Xuyen] controlled the police through his relationship with Bao Dai, the Chief of State. . . . Not only the Binh Xuyen but the Vietnamese army command and certain sect leaders were conducting themselves in open contempt of [Diem] the President. An orgy of conspiracy and subversion was the order of the day. The tea-cup speculation centered on predicting the day, the hour when the Diem Government would be ousted."[4]

William Henderson, Director of Meetings, Council on Foreign Relations, though greatly impressed by Diem and his political achievements, admitted in a *Foreign Affairs* article that in 1954 and 1955

> "there was nothing and no one on whom he [Diem] could rely, neither the army, nor the police, neither the government nor any significant segment of popular opinion."[5]

Thus, Diem could never have survived without French support. He survived because he did receive it. Ely kept the opposition of the three powerful Vietnam sect-organizations to Diem within limits and he restrained the anti-Diem activities of the Vietnam officer-corps and the French subaltern commanders by disciplinary measures and similar activities of the French settlers' community by persuasion.

It is, therefore, a completely erroneous belief, though unanimously voiced in contemporaneous American newspaper reports that Diem, during the year following the Geneva Conference, drove the French out of Vietnam. Had the French wanted to maintain a direct or concealed political control, it would have taken no time to get Diem's acquiescence. As late as March 27, 1955, when Diem's attack against Binh Xuyen was about to begin—signalling the start of his civil war against all oppositional elements of the population—General Ely, in his role of decision-maker, enjoyed the full confidence of the French army, the sect leaders (with the exception of one whom Diem had bribed into conspiracy with him), the American Ambassador (General I. Laxton Collins) and the regular Vietnam army units which abided by their sworn loyalty to the head of the State, Bao Dai. Indeed, on that very day, March 27, the Chief of Staff of the Vietnam army called on General Ely, begging him to intervene and prevent the attack against Binh Xuyen by Diem and assuring him that the regular Vietnamese army would loyally follow and execute any command which he, Ely, might give.[6]

American sources at this time, however, almost uniformly professed that it was Diem's statesmanship, energy and political drive that had built up his dictatorial position and that with an iron hand he had thus been able to make over Vietnam into an anti-Communist, pro-American power. He had achieved this against bitter opposition from the French and French intrigue with the sects, wrote Henderson in *Foreign Affairs*.[7]

The heart of the matter is that the French had no need to oppose or intrigue; they had their own military power and the support of the Vietnam army, and a large segment of the organized elements of the social structure—the powerful sects. They could have driven the unpopular Diem out of Vietnam by a wave of the hand. Thus, the true story of French policy and withdrawal from Vietnam was entirely different from the one put out by American sources.

The first problem facing France in Vietnam was to choose between full-fledged support of South Vietnam, on the one hand, and a policy of balanced neutrality between the two Vietnams, prompted by substantial French cultural and business interests in the North, on the other. It was only natural that concern for the investments in the northern Hanoi area—which until the armistice was safely held by the French, but according to the Geneva Agreements was to be surrendered to the Ho Chi Minh regime—weighed heavily in the scale of policy decisions. This consideration was so acute that despite the fact that General Ely was not yet established in Saigon and was engaged in the military problems created by the cease-fire and withdrawal, the Government in Paris took a definite step towards establishing a semi-diplomatic relationship with the new North Vietnam regime. It appointed Jean Sainteny, a French Indochina expert who was on friendly personal terms with Ho Chi Minh, as "délégué général" in North Vietnam.† The appointment was based on the assumption that the French should establish a policy of symmetry towards the two Vietnams. But this step was in conflict with what Ely planned to make the policy towards Vietnam and therefore, upon receipt of the news of Sainteny's designation, he immediately left for Paris. There he appealed directly to Prime Minister Mendès-France against the Sainteny appointment. This issue was de-

---

† Immediately after the Japanese evacuation Ho, supported by United States military aid, negotiated with the commanders of the French army re-occupying Indochina and with Sainteny, the political delegate of France, a peaceful settlement which would have made Ho, by consent of France, head of a new, all Indochina regime, maintaining some political and financial ties with France through a Commonwealth-type arrangement, called the "French Union."

cided as he had wanted it: no symmetry, no hesitation or equivocation. South Vietnam was to receive full diplomatic support, economic aid and, also, all possible tolerance during the difficulties of the building-up period of independence. The Prime Minister decided that it should be made clear publicly to both Vietnams and to Sainteny himself that he would have no political mission, that his delegation would be restricted to the defense—within the terms of the Geneva Agreements—of French cultural and economic interests. Mendès-France authorized Ely to make a public declaration defining in detail French policy towards Vietnam, expressing recognition of complete and unrestricted independence and full support. This declaration would be a natural sequel of the Prime Minister's statement made on July 25, two days after the end of the Geneva Conference, that the mission of France in Indochina had not come to an end, that France would stay in North Vietnam through her cultural and economic institutions and in South Vietnam by assisting the building of a national, independent, and high-principled progressive regime that would eclipse North Vietnam both morally and politically.

The policy declaration was made by Ely in the form of an interview given to France-Presse on August 31, 1954. Thus, it is not rationalization after the fact. In the declaration Ely repeated the total recognition of independence and the unrestricted backing that France would give to Vietnam for its national development and progress, in all the spheres of political and social life where this would be requested by the Vietnam Government. He declared that the French Expeditionary Force would not stay in Vietnam a day beyond Vietnam's wish for it and its reduction to the required size would begin immediately. Ely put it in unmistakable terms that France would pursue a policy in harmony with that of America, bearing in mind that conflict with it would endanger the Western position generally, and might defeat it in Indochina. Ely was asked what was France's interest in aiding an *independent* Vietnam without a local power-position for itself? France, he answered, wanted to be and remain a great power *in Europe*. But, as a necessary element of that position, France intended to maintain an interest in the political development of such other independent countries outside of Europe which needed aid and support from more advanced nations and an alliance with them. This, he said, was especially true in regard to Southeast Asia where French investments and cultural institutions were important parts of the social and political life.[8]

General Ely set about making his general declaration of policy a political reality. One by one, without any hesitation or delay, French participation in the management of Saigon harbor, of civil aviation, in the judicial, as well as all other fields of civil administration was immediately terminated without fanfare. The French managers of all public utilities including the institutes for fiscal and monetary management resigned and withdrew on Ely's instruction. All this was coupled with genuine cooperation with the Vietnamese successors in solving the difficulties of transition.[9]

Nor did Ely neglect the symbolic aspects of independence. He attached special importance to them because the unavoidable continued presence of the reduced French Expeditionary Force—even if only temporary and inconspicuous—might have weakened the significance of all these steps and might have appeared to reinvest all final authority in the hands of the French Commanding General. Therefore, Ely moved out of the traditional residence of the French Governors, the Norodom Palace, which had always been the symbol of supreme command position, and Diem moved in, taking over the Palace as his office and residence. Ely then occupied the former office of Diem and took a modest villa as his personal home.

Ely's policy, offending at almost every step vested interests, institutions and personal sensitivities, could naturally not be put into effect without resistance from the high-ranking officers of the Vietnam army as well as from French settlers, subordinate commanders of the French Expeditionary

Force, and those Vietnamese who had shared colonialist privileges before the change-over. This last group included almost the entire intelligentsia of Vietnam who resented Diem's dictatorial, uncompromising, inimical and often brutal response to those who dared to disagree.

To counteract resistance among the military, Ely found it necessary to take disciplinary action. Thus, one of his first steps was the retirement of General Salan from the second-in-command position, the removal of French extremists from sensitive posts, and, finally, orders for vigorous breakdown of open or latent resistance. Even the transfer of the Norodom Palace to Diem had not taken place without friction, though it affected primarily only Ely's private life.

Only in one respect did General Ely go outside of complete non-interference with Diem's independent administration. He insisted that Diem should include in his Government at all levels all available anti-communist elements, especially the local intelligentsia, that their amalgamation into the political life of the country should be especially sought, and that their cooperation, if offered, should be accepted. This policy was based on an agreement worked out in Washington between a French delegation consisting of two Cabinet members and Ely himself, on the one hand, and Under-Secretary of State Bedell Smith, on the other, between September 25 and 27, 1954.[10] It had been agreed upon to support Emperor Bao Dai as impartial head of State coupled with assistance and support of Diem as head of the administration, subject to the peaceful settlement of partisan controversies.

This general policy of Ely, conceived in the fall of 1954, had the support of the American envoys in Vietnam. Ambassador Donald Heath was in complete agreement. In November 1954, when he was replaced by General Collins, the personal envoy of President Eisenhower, the President's intervention was at first believed to signify an anti-French shift in policy. Ely himself, in fact, interpreted the recall of Heath as disapproval in Washington of Heath's support of

179

Ely's policy.[11] Whatever anxieties Ely felt in regard to Collins' appointment, they were soon dispelled however, for it took but a little time for Collins to form a view about the Vietnam situation identical to that of Ely. He soon joined hands with Ely in the attempt to prevent Diem from abandoning the all-important task of bringing about political stability to gain the support of the politically conscious Vietnamese and to undertake instead full scale offensive activities against all organized religious and civil groups opposing him.[12] The report of William Henderson—who was at that time on a study trip in Indochina—confirmed the veracity of General Ely's report.†

There is little doubt that had the Geneva conference failed and the fight against Ho Chi Minh been carried on, Ngo Dinh Diem would probably have been an admirable war-time leader—incorruptible, bold, ascetic, an intransigent nationalist, a fanatical anti-communist and finally, the recognized leader of the Catholic North Vietnamese. But, after Geneva, the creation of a unified, cohesive new state needed other qualities which Diem did not possess, among them, flexibility, tolerance, willingness to make conciliatory compromises and skill at political manipulation. Many observers of the Vietnam situation, French and American alike, were convinced that Diem was by his nature unable to adapt himself to this mission. French Prime Minister Edgar Faure, in spite of the restraint that his official position demanded did not refrain from expressing publicly his opinion that Diem was "not equal to his task," that he had little if any popular support.[13] The United States by the manipulation of foreign aid might have attempted to influence or even bring direct pressure to bear upon Diem to build a broad popular base for his government and to pursue a policy of conciliation.

† "We played a less distinguished role at the time of the showdown with the Binh Xuyen. General I. Lawton Collins, President Eisenhower's special ambassador in Saigon at the time, is known to have wavered in his evaluation of Diem's prospects during that moment of supreme danger." (*Foreign Affairs,* January 1957, p. 286) Collins's policy line, supporting Ely against the dictatorial policies of Diem is confirmed by Wise and Ross, *The Invisible Government,* Random House, 1964, p. 157.

General Ely, Mendès-France, Edgar Faure, Cabinet members of their government, and French statesmen with long previous experience in Indochina, fought hard to gain the approval of Dulles and the State Deartment for such a policy line. Their efforts were to no avail.

President Eisenhower, on February 19th, sent a special message to Bao Dai, Chief of State of Vietnam, assuring him that "it is encouraging to me to know that Prime Minister Diem is making substantial progress. The United States Government intends to continue its support of his Government."[14] Senator Walter F. George, Chairman of the Senate Foreign Relations Committee, while he was a member of the American Delegation at the NATO conference in May, 1955, published a strongly worded statement supporting Premier Diem in his fight to "clean up some of the lawlessness (opposition would have been the right word) out there." He attributed—no doubt, erroneously—French opposition to Diem's dictatorial rule to their wish "to protect their commercial interests."[15] These policy statements were preceded and based upon a report of Senator Mike Mansfield made in October 1954 in which he recommended that

> "In the event that the Diem government falls . . . the United States should consider an immediate suspension of all aid to Vietnam and the French Union forces there."[16]

With this unanimous domestic political opinion behind him neither American critics of Diem, among them General Collins, and the local political agent of the Central Intelligence Agency, Col. E. Landsdale, nor the French could persuade Dulles to withdraw the unconditional support from Diem and exercise both direct and indirect influence on the internal politics to affect the social and financial development of South Vietnam. Dulles and the Department of State did not budge. To them, the only feasible Indochinese policy remained the complete dependence on Diem.[17] On April 5, 1955 Collins was informed that his recommendations were not acceptable, that he must back up and work for Diem in every respect, including the use of available armed forces against the opposition, the so-called sects.[18] The French effort reached its climax on May 7, 1955 in the course of a five-hour long conference on Indochina between Dulles and Prime Minister Faure. The result was published in a semi-official communiqué announcing that the two statesmen could not as yet foresee any solution of French-United States differences although both sides had made great efforts to reach an accord.[19]

There cannot be much doubt that the first positive push towards the elimination of French influence showing the means of its realization came from President Eisenhower. His narration of the Indochina crisis in his *Mandate for Change* ends with a short, one-sentence paragraph:

> "On August 17" (twenty-six days after the signing of the Geneva Agreements), "I directed that aid to Indochina henceforth be given directly to the Associated States rather than through France."[20]

For the realization of the full significance of this personal directive it must be remembered that until then all American aid had been given to Indochina through France. The United States had paid all or a large part of the war budget of France, including military equipment shipped from American bases. It reached over one and one quarter billion dollars. These United States funds made it possible for France to aid the Indochina economy. Thus, to give American financial support directly to the three Indochinese states must have been meant as a wedge to introduce and establish American presence. It certainly served that purpose.

The background struggle between those favoring a policy keeping France, and perhaps Britain, as associates in Indochina, and the anti-alliance, go-it-alone internationalists, must have been going on between August 17 and October 27. In September the French Government had not yet given up hope that French-American cooperation might be worked out, and that the funds, no longer needed for a war budget, could be used by France for the support of a vigorous economic policy and maintenance of vigilance against communist infiltration. French authorities offered ten divisions as the backbone for the defense of Southeast Asia, serving the protection of the entire Free World. A *New York Times* editorial, written after Manila, expressed the view that free Indo-China

"cannot remain free without defense by French troops there. . . . There has been consummated the multilateral defense accord upon which we were insistent, so we cannot weaken it by quibbling over helping France because we are not satisfied with her over E.D.C."[21]

The agreement September 25-27 (Supra p. 179) signaled a temporary victory for the "united action" group. It split the budgeted 700 million dollars of United States aid in two equal parts, one-half to be given to the French Expeditionary Force, the other 350 million dollars to be given directly to the three Indochina states. But a decisive turn in the opposite direction was revealed on October 27 when Prime Minister Diem received a letter from Eisenhower which, after suggesting domestic reforms, assured Diem of the unconditional suport of the United States. Officials of the State Department leaked to the press that the reference to domestic reform was

"not the main point. The President wanted to make the support of Diem evident."[22]

The *New York Times* commented two days later that

"the delivery of that letter drafted already early in September prevented France from influencing policies."[23]

The interval between the drafting and the delivery date indicates that Eisenhower was hesitant about embarking on the policy which the letter forecast.

On November 18-20, 1954 Mendès-France was on an official visit to Washington and made an attempt to bring back to life the Ely-Bedell Smith agreement, the common United States-French front towards Diem and joint handling and control of the Vietnam situation. By that time, however, policy in Vietnam was no longer determined in the State Department. It followed the direction of Congress, more particularly that of Senator Mike Mansfield, head of a special subcommittee on Indochina who associated the unconditional support of Diem with resolute policy to eliminate "colonialist" France. Congressman James P. Richard, soon to become Chairman of the Foreign Affair's Committee of the House of Representatives, in a statement made public insisted that in Vietnam "the task of building up an anticommunist force be assumed by the United States."[24]

The instrument for the execution of this policy was available in the manipulation of United States military and financial foreign aid. French assistance in the build-up of a strong Vietnam could have been easily obtained by channelling part of the aid to Vietnam through France. At that time in 1954, the many millions of dollars passing through French foreign exchange institutions would have been a strong inducement for France to continue the presence of her army, as well as her own contribution to the Vietnam economy, despite the great sacrifices and losses suffered in the war years. But as it has been pointed out, an opposite policy line was adopted. The French were forced out by the United States withdrawing its aid from all French activities in Vietnam.

Eden and Mendès-France, however, made one more energetic attempt to turn back the clock and re-establish the partnership in Indochina. On December 18-19, 1954 on the occasion of a NATO meeting, they brought to Paris General Ely and Sir Hubert Graves, British Ambassador to Vietnam and arranged a conference with Dulles with their assistance.[25] The result was defeat. At that meeting Dulles made it clear that the United States was not prepared to give financial aid to France for the maintenance in Vietnam of the French Expeditionary Force and if the Force would quit Vietnam, the move would not be unwelcome to the United States. Dulles stated further that the training and build-up of the Vietnam army would be done by the United States, thus making Vietnam sufficiently strong through the support of SEATO and the striking power of America. This United States policy was publicly announced by Dulles on December 20 when he stated that United States and French thinking had been brought in line in regard to Indochina through the acquiescence of Mendès-France to the principle that the defense of Vietnam, Laos and Cambodia would rest on the Manila Treaty—the strength of which, as we know, consisted of American military striking power. This implied the withdrawal of French forces more rapidly than had been contemplated, reducing them by the end of 1955 to 30,000 instead of 100,000 which Mendès-France considered a proper minimum. Consequently, American financial aid to the Force was cut from the promised 300 million dollars to 100 million, a fact made public by Mendès-France in the Assemblée Nationale on December 18, 1954. All this was made official by the Department of State in a press release of December 31, 1954, which announced that

> "arrangements have been completed so that on January 1, 1955, United States begins supplying financial aid directly to Vietnam, Cambodia, and Laos for the purpose of strengthening their defense."[26]

In execution of this policy decision, on February 9, 1955, General John W. (Iron Mike) O'Daniel assumed charge of the United States Military Support Mission and carried a special contribution of 200 million dollars to South Vietnam as military aid to make sure that no French military presence would be needed.

For a short while a secondary role was conceded to the French in the military training program, by appointing General Gazounod second-in-command and retaining a number of French officers and other military personnel as instructors. Also, General O'Daniel himself was placed formally under the authority of General Ely who by that time was back in France as Commanding General. Soon, however,

SOUTHEAST ASIA

Canfield in The Newark Evening News

"When I started, he was just about so big."

this facade was dismantled. By April 1956, the French command in Indochina had been dissolved and the French Expeditionary Force, no longer supported by United States aid, had departed.[27]

Summing up the essence of these developments, it is obvious that the hands of France were not tied, and her policy choice could have been made in any direction. Certainly Diem was not in the position to direct, or decisively influence it. Indeed, the French Government might have resisted Washington's chosen policy—to support Diem and eliminate French influence—in spite of the big stick of foreign aid which could be arbitrarily manipulated by the American Administration or by Congress. Even in 1954, after the Geneva Conference, France faced a United States policy fearful of losing all Indochina—which was protected only by the French Expeditionary Force's armed might—and could have insisted that the continuation of its army's presence be subject to conditions not to the liking of the State Department. Dulles himself admitted this feature of the post-Geneva political situation.

> "The French have a substantial military force in South
> Vietnam. . . . The Geneva accord bars the importation
> in Indochina of new military aid. The United States
> cannot increase the number of its military advisers. That
> places a strong dependence on France."[28]

A "General DeGaulle" might have indeed done it. Mendès-France and General Ely, however, were inspired by another conception of alliance policy. As Ely set forth and emphasized in his general Indochina statement, quoted in the preceding chapter, respect and consideration of United States policy and the weight attributed to the Atlantic alliance, to the protection of Europe and to France's future as a European Great Power made them forego a defiant "DeGaulle-ist" policy line. Instead of defiance, Paris chose to cede the helm to Washington. General Ely was instructed to coordinate his command with the intransigent American policy, to give Diem complete and unconditional support. This was,

"Alliance, Any One?"

however, in conflict with all tenets of Ely's appraisal about the interest of France, the Free World and the future of Vietnam. He knew that both successive American ambassadors shared his view. Under such conditions he took the only honest step open to him. He resigned and soon afterwards returned to France.[29] American political and military organizations moved in and successively took over all functions which might have been the joint responsibility of the United States and France.† Thus, when Assistant Secretary of State, Walter S. Robertson, on June 11, 1956, described United States policy and its achievements in Vietnam, he did not mention the French presence there.[30]

Simultaneously with the elimination of the French presence, Britain too was gently elbowed out of Indochina. For a few months after Geneva at conferences on the Foreign Minister level, Britain still participated as an interested party. In December 1954, Eden still tried to influence the Vietnam situation. The joint communiqué of France, Great Britain, and the United States issued on December 19, 1954 after a meeting of the foreign secretaries held in Paris, calls the agreement of November on Indochina an "accord between France and the United States," without reference to Britain.[31] The joint pronouncement about the defense of Indochina issued at the Bandung Conference in March, 1955, still carried Eden's signature. But Eden in his broadcast of March 3, 1955, from Kuala Lumpur, Malaya, discussing the Conference, omitted any reference to Indochina.[32] Soon afterwards, however, reports reached the British press that the British Government objected to being left out of French-American talks regarding Indochina, since it was felt that

"her vital role in Geneva, her prominent position in

---

† "When Ngo Dinh Diem became President in 1955, the United States assumed the preponderant burden of outside support for the new Republic in South Vietnam. . . . [In] matters of defense, internal stability, and economic support, the Vietnamese Government has come to depend almost wholly on the United States for outside assistance." (Report of Senator Mike Mansfield, *Vietnam and Southeast Asia*, 1963, p. 3).

SEATO and her concern for the future of Southeast Asia entitled her to play a part."[33]

Despite this insistence, in May, when a temporary arrangement was worked out between France's Prime Minister Faure and Dulles regarding Vietnam, the United States opposed British participation and presence.[34]

"The French long sought to bring Britain into the discussion while the United States resisted, preferring a French-United States accord."[35]

In these conferences held in May 1955, regarding Vietnam, Foreign Secretary Harold MacMillan, though he was present in Paris on the occasion of a meeting of the Atlantic alliance, "joined in the latter part of the discussion only."[36] Since 1955, in no phase of the Vietnam situation can the influence of Britain be traced.

Thus, as of 1956, by giving honorary discharge to France and Britain as fellow associates in Indochina, the United States passed the third gate and achieved thereby American monopoly and solitary responsibility for the survival of Vietnam as an independent, non-Communist state. The United States was at last, all by itself, in the China shop. It has taken eight years of laborious struggle and a change of Administration to induce our foreign policy-makers to invite our allies to join the fold again.[37]†

---

† According to the *New York Times*, on August 14, 1964, a report from Saigon stated that "President Johnson's effort to bring more flags to South Vietnam, to induce aid from many nations in the country's counter-insurgency effort, is well under way. . . . Complicated negotiations between the South Vietnamese Government and 35 foreign governments are now in process with the United States taking an assisting role in Saigon and in foreign capitals. To date commitments have been made by twelve nations (Australia, New Zealand, Japan, South Korea, the Philippines, Thailand, China (Taiwan), West Germany, Italy, Iran, Britain and Canada).

15

T HE ACCOUNT OF THE EVENTS WHICH LANDED THE UNITED
States in its present involvement in Vietnam raises three
puzzling questions whose consideration does not change the
history, but may add to its meaningfulness.

One question—the *first*—will be: was the United States, in
connection with the critical difficulties in which its close
European ally and friend, France, became increasingly, and
in the nineteen-fifties, fatally entangled, a helpful friend, a
cooperating ally? As the subject of this writing is the description and analysis of United States diplomacy generally,
especially during the Eisenhower-Dulles era, its main features regarding relations with Britain were extensively
dealt with, and it may be enlightening to look at it from
another angle, focusing it on the French aspect.

The *second* question would be: in view of President Eisenhower's and his Administration's strongly held conviction
that the conquest of Indochina by Ho Chi Minh," an agent of
"International Communism", must not come to pass, and
their assumption that the Geneva Conference could not possibly produce an acceptable solution, why did the President
not follow up his "serious and far reaching decisions" to

undertake direct military intervention in the first war in Vietnam? Why did the United States foresake the policy of intervention and fail to back up its bold words with action?

The *third* question is: why did the United States, after the Geneva settlement, suddenly abandon the coalition policy—which had been so strong in Eisenhower's thinking before Geneva that "no Western Power can go to Asia militarily except as one of a concert of powers which must include local Asiatic people"[1]—and, by freezing out Britain and France, assume alone the defense of South Vietnam?

Having put the queries, the answers shall be postponed to the following chapter because the roots of all three answers are in the very same political problem, which appears variously under the names of "colonialism", "anti-colonialism" and "imperialism."

It was Eisenhower's and Dulles' contention that:

A) the United States "was the first colony in modern times to have won independence, and it *therefore* had a natural sympathy with those everywhere who would follow our example."[2] "We have not forgotten" said Dulles on another occasion, "that we were the first colony to win independence."[3] According to Eisenhower, American anticolonialism "was born in the circumstance of our national birth in 1776."[4]†

B) That the United States had a long anti-colonialist tradition, and that it had been a prevalent feature of American foreign policy since the United States had attained its independence.

> "The standing of the United States as the most powerful of the anti-colonial powers is an asset of incalculable value to the Free World."[5]

C) That the United States can, and in fact, did avoid a

---

† The same verbatim statement appears in many foreign policy pronouncements of Dulles. See, for instance, Press Release, Department of State, April 7, 1954 p. 5; Dulles' nation-wide broadcast, May 7, 1954. *Department of State Bulletin* May 17, 1954, I. p. 740; Hearings, Senate Foreign Relations Committee, June 4, 1954, p. 19.

policy of imperialism except "for a time in the nineteenth and early twentieth centuries" when this policy-line was "violated—almost accidentally."[5]

D) That this anti-colonialist, anti-imperialist policy "means that our counsel is sometimes trusted where that of others may not be," and that it is essential to our leadership and gives a "moral position" to America.

These four propositions will be taken up in this chapter to enable us to deal in the following chapter with the three paramount questions previously posed.

First, neither the United States, nor the thirteen states which formed it and which had won independence and political separation from Britain had ever been colonies in the sense in which political literature or the language of international diplomacy now use that concept. The British immigrants who crossed the Atlantic Ocean and settled in another continent spoke of "colony" because, as the Oxford Dictionary states, following Roman use, "colonia" meant a settlement of Roman citizens in a hostile or newly conquered country. At the time of their emigration to America, "colony" meant a body of settlers in the new country forming a community politically connected with their parent state, which political connection, in view of hostile, desperate resistance by Indians, French and other groups of settlers—was very much in the colonists' interest. The immigrant British settlers annihilated or expelled the native inhabitants. *They* colonized the land as an integral part of Britain and enjoyed there more liberties than their British brothers back home. In other words, these Anglo-Americans were not oppressed natives, they were proud conquerors.

If the Eisenhower-Dulles use of the word "colony" were correct, it would imply that the immigrant Britishers voluntarily degraded themselves to the status in which the native inhabitants were found in Africa, in the Pacific islands, in Zanzibar or Polynesia and were willing themselves to agree that their body politic should be of the most inferior sort. It would be equally improbable to assume that the government of England expected that the colonies to be created in America would be constitutionally or administratively at the level of Togoland, Okinawa, or Vietnam.

Colonial relationship requires political domination not over the colonizing settlers but over the people in whose land the expanding imperial power penetrates, whose country it conquers. The revolution of 1776 was an act of separation, not a revolt of oppressed natives. The British who were to become Americans crossed the ocean as conquerors. They severed their political ties with their motherland because of disagreements over their constitutional rights, their religious and political self-assertion. As a leading authority of political history set this forth:

> "This struggle should be compared, not to the movement for Algerian independence, but rather to a hypothetical attempt on the part of the French settlers there to establish their independence from the French Motherland in order to exploit Algeria to their own advantage."[6]

Separations do not make over retroactively the preceding political connection into a colonial relationship in the sense in which this concept is used in the twentieth century, even if the seceding units which colonized the foreign lands called themselves "colonies" because of *their* relationship to the newly acquired world. Had the Southerners seceded in 1861-65 as a result of the Civil War, could they call their independence from Washington "decolonization"? If the French Canadian provinces were now to secede, would that make the French Canadian provinces colonies that had won independence? There is no reason why the Americans should not sympathize with those who want to become independent, but these sentiments have emotional sources which exist in many other countries whose history does not include a war of independence. In fact, these feelings appeared in Britain just as often, and have been just as widespread as in the United States. It is rather an Anglo-Saxon phenomenon than an exclusively American one.

194

Although historical comparisons are always faulty there is at least one international relationship which may be used to demonstrate the historical and political error underlying the Dulles thesis. A parallel to the separation of the American "colonies" appears in the connection between Denmark and Norway. Denmark in the last part of the 16th century was one of the great powers of Europe. Its monarch, Frederik II, dominated at that period all the seas surrounding the northern part of Europe and was able to force all foreign ships to strike their topsails to a Danish man-of-war as a token of Danish rule. Denmark and its kings at the same time, reigned over Norway and Sweden. For the purpose of comparison only the dominion over Norway will be used because, after the Black Death had wiped out almost the entire Norwegian population, Norway was re-populated by Danish immigrants. These Danes soon abandoned their loyalty to their old homeland, mainly to free themselves from the burden of Danish taxation and other kinds of commercial exploitation, such as a law that prohibited importation of grain from anywhere except Denmark.

In 1814 the Treaty of Kiel separated Norway, after a union of nearly 400 years, from Denmark. A new union was established with Sweden by a treaty which declared Norway "a free, independent and indivisible kingdom, united with Sweden under one King." Ultimately, in 1905, after a long series of disagreements, this union also was dissolved.

For the purpose of the historical parallel it is sufficient to point out that no Danish or Norwegian historian or political writer has ever characterized Norway's political position as a former Danish colony or its independence as emergence from colonial status. Neither would a Norwegian Government, if sympathies in Norway existed for struggles of independence in other parts of the world, equate it to the achievement of Norway's independence from Denmark.

Turning now to the second thesis of Eisenhower and Dulles, it must be recalled that anti-colonialism is not determined by the possession, or non-possession, of colonies.

Sweden, Norway, Austria, Canada and Finland, for instance, have no colonies, yet they are not anti-colonialists. Thus, the fact that the United States terminated its policy of imperialist expansion in the Philippines, Puerto Rico, Guam, the Hawaiian Islands, Tutuila, Cuba, Panama, Haiti, the Dominican Republic and Nicaragua should not be confused with anti-colonialism. Nor did the United States in the nineteenth century, opposed as it was to *new* colonies of European powers in the Western Hemisphere, demonstrate through its use of the Monroe Doctrine and other political moves, any but an imperialist foreign policy. Anti-colonialism signifies active criticism, antagonism, or even hostility towards powers which are superior to the "anti-colonialists" culturally, economically and financially, but especially politically and socially. The anti-colonialist governments nurture such feelings and follow such policies, regardless of whether they do or do not have direct or local interest in the situation. The Africa-Asia group of states do use in their foreign policy an anti-colonialist approach to nearly every problem. They are the proletarians of international life to whom antagonism against West Europe, North America, white skin and wealth is the dominant source of political emotions and actions. The present day leading rivals of the United States, Soviet Russia and China, exploit the anti-colonialism of these Asian and African nations for their aggressive imperialism. In applauding this emotional animosity Eisenhower and Dulles were giving aid and support to the hostile policies of Russia and China.

The United States was not anti-colonialist under either the Democratic Administration of President Wilson and President Franklin D. Roosevelt or under those of the Republican Presidents, Harding and Hoover. Woodrow Wilson in his celebrated Fourteen Points address on January 8, 1918, did not condemn colonialism as such, but only its abuses. In an address to the Council of Ten on January 27, 1919 in which he explained his theory about colonies, there was not the slightest hint that the colonies of Britain, France or any other country should be given self-government or independence. The mandate system, he proposed, was to be applied only to former German colonies. Anti-colonialism was not so much as mentioned or even contemplated. Self-determination—one of the general principles of his Fourteen Points—had application only to European peoples of high culture who were recognized members of European upper civilization, but neither Wilson nor anybody else in his Administration thought it applicable to under-developed dependencies or to colonies of European powers. (What an irony of our era, that today self-determination and independence is the birthright of every nation, group, or tribe of the globe with the exception of exactly those European nations which in Wilson's thoughts, were the intended beneficiaries!)

Anti-colonialism first appeared in American official pronouncements as a principle of American policy during and after World War II. Secretary of State Cordell Hull produced in 1943 the draft of a document called "Declaration by the United Nations on National Self-Government" which comes close to being "anti-colonialist." But, under pressure from the United States Defense Department, its application definitely excluded the former Japanese-mandated islands which became strategic outposts of the United States,[7] and the whole document has never been accepted by Presidents, Congress or any other American policy making body as a basic pronouncement. The Charter of the United Nations addressed itself only to "respect for the principle of equal rights and self-determination of peoples," not to independence.[8] In terms of United States policy, the Charter was thus a retreat from the attempt of the anti-colonialist pronouncement of the Hull Declaration, and it was President Roosevelt who was the prime mover toward this conservative position. Before the Eisenhower-Dulles regime, there existed no tradition or set attitude of American policy that would have demonstrated opposition or hostility to acts of an alleged "colonialist" nature, whether these acts were our own—supporting a European ally—or those of our allies whenever they might be influenced by considerations of power politics. It was the Eisenhower-Dulles team that introduced an anti-colonialist moralism into the theory of United States Government and fancied that it had been the tradition of American policy before them. Anti-colonialism did appear once in a while as a verbal catch-phrase of political rhetoric but before the Eisenhower-Dulles era it had never influenced or determined actual policy.[9]

Third, foreign policy for the attainment of concrete, definable goals, regardless of whether it is directed at the acquisition of territory or at some other kind of changes in international life has never been regarded as "imperialism" by political observers, historians, or statesmen who were not already strongly prejudiced anti-colonialist partisans. Armed aggression or political pressure for acquisition of a given area held by another state is not imperialistic if it is the result of a locally delimited purpose, justifiable by identity of language, by need to protect a country's own nationals or its co-relegionists, or by other similar motivating factors. Such actions may be violations of international law or agreements and they may be condemned as aggression, but this does not make them acts of imperialism. "Rationally limited objectives which in themselves are compatible with the maintainance of the status quo" in the power-relationship of opponents and rivals are not imperialistic and therefore may "be disposed of either on their intrinsic merits or by compromise."[9a] For example, the extension of India's territory in Goa; the war to incorporate Katanga in the Congo; the incorporation into Austria of the Hungarian Burgenland, inhabited by people of German mother tongue; the acquisition of Louisiana and Florida by enforced purchase; and the unification of Italy by Piedmont are all instances of a policy serving a special local purpose which, once realized, would result in no further expansion. It is understood, of course, that the local interest cannot, like the occupation of Sudetenland by Hitler's Germany, be merely a cover-up for general expansion planned to follow it. Successive demands which are "links of a chain at the end of which stands the overthrow of the status quo" of power relationship are the main characteristics of imperialism.[9b] The maxim, *c'est le ton qui fait la musique*,† plays an important role here. Turning to other kinds of illustrations, if water-deficient states attempted to satisfy their vital water requirements or if countries in need of food reached out for larger fishing areas, their acts would not be called imperialist. Thus, imperalism would not be involved when a state pursued, no matter how vigorously, concrete *limited* interests and could be expected to abandon its aggressive attitude as soon as it had attained its ends.

Imperialism implies an aggressiveness for the sake of expansion, for an increase in prestige. And it even implies aggression for the purpose of protecting existing hegemony and global influence.††

Applying these principles, Russia and China are today the foremost imperialists. Russia has no substantial interest in Eastern Europe and none in Africa. China has little or none in South and Southeast Asia or in Central Africa. Minor local advantage may accrue to them through their imperialism but their expansionist, aggressive policies do not aim at such local advantages. Egypt, under Nasser, is another imperialist country, seeking extension of Egypt's power over all Arab countries and beyond that, over a large part of Africa. Indonesia, too, pursues an imperialist policy in

_____

† Rhythm and harmony make the melody into music.

†† This interpretation of imperialism is mainly based on and follows closely the recognized classic of literature on imperialism. The *Sociology of Imperialism*, by Joseph Schumpeter, World Publishing Company, New York 1955 first published in *Archiv für Socialwissenschaft und Socialpolitik*, Vol. 46, 1919. "This essay on imperialism is indeed a classic work and it is rightly accorded a prominent place in contemporary discussion on the subject." (Leon D. Epstein, *British Politics in the Suez Crisis*, University of Illinois, Urbana, 1964, p. 8, n. 3; Klaus Knorr, "Theories on Imperialism," *World Politics*, Vol. 4, pp. 402-431, April 1952). See also for diagnosis that is in essence identical: Hans J. Morgenthau, *Politics Among Nations*, pp. 44-71, stressing for identification of imperialism the overthrow of political equilibrium and status quo rather than limited intention.

Southeast Asia as manifested in its hostility towards Malaysia and its expansionist claims in New Guinea. Any listing of countries engaged in *aggressive* expansion would perforce, include the United States at the last part of the 19th century and the beginning of this century, when it extended its power to the islands and countries of the Caribbean and Pacific. (supra. p. 196). But it is certainly erroneous to believe that Theodore Roosevelt's expansionist, aggressive foreign policy and the acquisition by him of foreign lands was done "almost accidentally," as Eisenhower described it. In fact, debate, strong disagreements, and political opposition accompanied it. But majority public opinion was in its favor.

The United States, however, is still imperialist in another sense within Schumpeter's definition. By its interest in protecting its existing power position in the Western hemisphere, in Asia, indeed, all over the globe, the United States pursues an imperialist policy and cannot avoid it even if it is in essence defensive.[10] The several dozen regional treaties serve this defensive imperialism as a "legal, moral and practical basis for helping our friends,"[11a] those who support America's power position against the aggressive imperialists who would encroach upon them.

> "Looked at from the standpoint of the sum total of its history . . . the United States becomes by its very essence an expanding imperial power."[11b]

The limited wars in Korea, Vietnam, Guatemala, Lebanon and the Congo are testimony to this policy of defensive imperialism. Was not Rome, under the Empire, not only expanding but defending around the perimeter of the Empire against the encroachments of migrant Germanic, Slavic, Gallic, and Gothic peoples—the prototype of imperialism? The argument of Eisenhower that we fought a war in Korea in which "we as a nation never had any of our political or economic interests involved"[12] is not only error, since strong political American interests were involved but, surprisingly, denies American interest in Korea. This statement comes very close to the much criticized Acheson reference to Korea as being outside the American defense perimeter. In addition, this Eisenhower statement defeats its own thesis. Absence of local interest makes the American war in Korea essentially imperialistic.

Using as a tool of analysis Professor Morgenthau's definition which restricts the concept of imperialism to policy aimed at overthrowing the previous equilibrium, we reach the same result. The entrance of the United States by diplomacy, economic devices and force into Southeast Asia— an area controlled in the main and for long periods by China —upset the status quo. If China had not become communist, the United States would not have interfered. In fact, it would have supported it. This alone proves that the United States' entrance alone comes close to overthrowing the previous status.

Fourth—and last—even if the United States had an anti-colonialist tradition, even if it had not pursued a defensive imperialist policy in Indochina, Eisenhower's claim that this policy was inspired by moral and ethical considerations could be seriously questioned. The United States demanded from France its abdication of all the cultural, economic and emotional ties which had been created in Indochina by the presence of French settlers, by French schools and by historical memories. American policy in this regard was dictated by the fear of appearances, by fear that the continuation of French influence in Indochina would impart to American support of France an aura of colonialism. Also, the United States' drive for a coalition was not motivated by the existence of British or French colonialism. Britain did not want to bite a little colony out of Indochina and France was eager to liquidate its political involvement. America was driven by terror of a phantom, *the specter of American imperialism or colonialism*. Eisenhower himself declares that United States military intervention "would lay ourselves open to the charge of imperialism and colonialism or—at the very least—of objectionable paternalism."

Therefore, so this argument runs in a letter written to General Gruenther,

"no Western power can go to Asia militarily, except as one of a concert of powers, which concert must include local Asiatic peoples."[13]

Knowing that the "concert of powers," the much desired coalition, would have been a token one for show purposes only, it becomes obvious that such American intervention would have been, again, in essence, a move in power politics for the protection of legitimate global interests of the United States and the Free World.

In theory, if no aggressive imperialist power existed, the United States could withdraw into a neutralist, non-imperialist position. But facing Russia and China, eager to dominate our world, the United States cannot retire in peaceful solitude, undisturbed by un-American activities. We cannot be disinterested onlookers at local domestic conflicts in Vietnam, Laos, Lebanon, Cyprus, Guatemala or the Congo, as it is suggested by Lord Russell, Norman Thomas, Senator Wayne Morse and—until the Chinese attack in 1962-63—by Nehru. Being engaged in a global conflict, every seemingly local, though distant thunder clap carries dangerous sparks of fire that might develop into a conflagration that would destroy our house. Our interest and intervention need not be, and in fact, ought not to be military. Other means of diplomacy, persuasion, economic or financial intervention may produce the desired result. Thus, America's image cannot be that of a disinterested warrior of international morality, unselfish and impartial, whose "counsel is sometimes trusted where that of others may not be."[14] Unfortunately, we evoke the same reactions to power and fortune as all other nations.

"We [the United States] have become the principal

object of anti-colonial agitation because 'colonialism' does not end with the grant of political independence."[15]

We experience in Europe, in Asia, in South America, indeed all over the world, from friend and foe, suspicion of our policies and resistance to our economic and financial influence. America is not a favored impartial observer. It has not, for instance, participated in United Nations peace-keeping bodies. Indeed whenever impartiality is required, even we do not suggest our participation.

On the other hand, imperialism or colonialism is not an incurable disease of Britain and France. Already France is becoming a trusted friend who, in Latin America and even in Southeast Asia, is not suspected any longer of being colonialist. And Britain is in the process of acquiring this kind of standing in Africa.

Appraising the power situation of the United States in the world now, we learn that it is not possible to avoid between the powerful and the weak that relationship which was put by LaFontaine in the mouth of the donkey, facetiously, yet with gravity behind the jest:

"Que m'importe donc, dit l'Âne, à qui je sois
Sauvez-vous et laissez-moi paître
Notre ennemi c'est notre maître
Je vous le dis en bon francois."
(Le Vieillard et l'Âne)

No token coalition or any kind of fiction can mislead the donkey, still less the impartial or hostile observers of the international political scene. Coalitions as fronts cannot give the United States the position of an anti-colonialist power. Anti-colonialism has nothing to do with morals; it is a policy line serving the interest of its partisans. They call evil what they fear to suffer or have not the power to do themselves. But, be that as it may, such coalition most certainly could not have given us *moral* position. Ethics and morals inhabit the essence, the innermost nature of human acts; morality is in truth, not in appearance.

16

THE FOREGOING EXAMINATION OF IMPERIALISM, COLONIAL-ISM, and anti-colonialist tradition in United States foreign policy, provides the required background for understanding United States policy in regard to the 1954 Indochina crisis. It is relevant, in particular, to answering the three questions concerning United States involvement in Vietnam that were posed in the previous chapter.

The First Question. United States policy in the years 1941-1949—when no more than an outsider's indirect notice of Indochina was taken—was premised on the "strongly held" opinion developed in 1940 and 1941 by President Roosevelt, that France had misruled Indochina, that the native Indochinese had been so flagrantly oppressed that they would consider anything better than continuing to live under French colonial rule;[1] and that the French had no right to walk back into Indochina and repossess that rich land for no reason other than that it had been their colony. President Roosevelt's view that the French administration exploited and milked the Indochinese outrageously was hardly in keeping with the history of French colonial administration there. Yet he expressed many times his opinion that

205

France must not be permitted to reestablish her rule there. This opinion actually prompted Roosevelt to offer Indochina as an outright "gift" to Chiang Kai-Shek, who, incidentally turned this proposal down flatly, pointing out that the Vietnamese were for the most part hostile to the Chinese and had fought against Chinese domination intermittently for more than a thousand years whenever Chinese power was not overwhelmingly stronger. Roosevelt, however, took a firm stand that Indochina's future must not even be made the subject of negotiation with the Free French in order that it not again become the victim of French misrule and abuse.[2] Thus, at the Teheran and Potsdam Conferences, in 1943 and 1945 respectively, it was decided on United States suggestion—overruling Churchill's objections—that Indochina should be occupied north of the sixteenth parallel by the Chinese and south of that line by the Indians and the British, and that it should be placed under trusteeship without participation of France in its administration.[3] Even in the post-war period, as an extension of this approach to the Indochina situation during the first phase of the conflict between the French and Ho Chi Minh, American sympathy was definitely not on the French side. In fact, the United States policy decidedly favored Ho Chi Minh. This showed itself in a number of ways, but one example may suffice. Until 1950 the American Administration insisted that American-produced propellers be removed from British aircraft given by Britain to the French troops fighting against Ho.[4] "In the international field," wrote a British commentator, "the Americans show a tendency to kick into their own goal."[5]

In 1950, the year of Communist China's complete victory on the Chinese mainland, a radically new American policy towards France and Indochina was initiated, based on two eye-opening events of late 1949 and early 1950.[6] In December 1949, when Mao-Tse-Tung, after the conquest of Peking, Nanking and Shanghai, reached the Indochina frontier the Nationalist Chinese troops in Indochina deserted to the Communist regime. And, in January 1950, Mao's China and

Ho Chi Minh's Vietnam recognized each other as the only Chinese and Vietnamese Governments.

> "With the Communist victory on the Chinese mainland in 1949," writes Eisenhower, "the situation changed rapidly. . . . The struggle became more intense and began gradually, with Chinese intervention, to assume its true complexion of a struggle between Communism and non-Communist forces rather than one between a colonial power and colonists who were intent on attaining independence."[7]

On December 17, 1952 the NATO Council called for continued support for the French forces fighting in Indochina. Although United States aid funds to France took into consideration the costs of the war in Indochina, until the end of 1952 no funds were earmarked specifically for the war. But on December 18, 1952, the Mutual Security Administration, with President Truman's approval, announced a special defense-support program for Indochina with an initial contribution of 30.5 million dollars. In 1953, the specific aid for supporting the French war grew into hundreds of millions.[8] In May 1953, Eisenhower sent a message to Congress pointing out the need "in our own interest" to give to France full help, and Under-Secretary of State Bedell Smith made a statement in which he called the Indochina affair a global problem and the help to the French "a necessity for our nation."[9]

This progression of events answers the first question, how far, if at all our foreign policy is influenced by our alliances when our allies' interests and policies happen to differ from our own. Put another way, did we take upon ourselves a burden in Indochina for the sake of helping a friend in need? So long as the flag of Mao's Communist China was not openly unfurled on the battlefield of Indochina our policy was not neutral, but rather on the unfriendly side. In fact, even in January 1950 after Ho Chi Minh had taken off the freedom-fighter mask, our neutralism was not completely abandoned despite the fact that

> "NATO defense [in Europe] needed greater French participation [which] was largely denied [by France] because of her losses and costs in the Indochina war."[10]

Certainly after 1951, as we learn from Eisenhower's memoires, NATO's interests would have been better served had some part of the load of defending Indochina been taken over by the United States.[11] But not until 1953 did the United States do what the interests of NATO and the Free World required. Not until then, when Eisenhower fancied to have on his side the "support of world opinion," did the United States act. We began to support France, but not as a "friend in need." We aided her "fight to save Indochina" from Communist conquest because that eventually was dreaded by Washington for its possible external effects and domestic political repercussions.[12] One must always remember that the loss of China by the Free World figured heavily on the debit side of the Democratic Administration. To accept the disappearance of Indochina as well—and perhaps thereby the whole of Southeast Asia with 200 million Asians —must have appeared in 1953 an ominous prospect in the Republican imagination. The Republican Party was out of office throughout the cold war, but the loss of China and then the Korean conflict became the rallying points of those who were dissatisfied with American foreign policy and who, in 1952, gave to the party a "mandate for change." What would have become of this mandate had Indochina also promptly disappeared in the red maw? There cannot be any doubt that the interventionist policy developed in 1953-54 was not a "helping hand." It was part of the global crusade against International Communism and the defense of the United States. But, with Communist China at the gates, our foreign policy promoted the colonialist operation into a holy war, a crusade of the Free World.

The Second Question. In 1953-54, Eisenhower and Dulles made the defense of Indochina and its preservation within the Free World the basis of their Southeast Asian policy. They had no confidence that an acceptable compromise on

208

Indochina could be worked out, nor did they believe that an all-out military engagement or even a major war would be too excessive a price for the achievement of that goal. One must then ask why Eisenhower and Dulles did not act? Why did they yield to British opposition instead of putting their policy into action? Presently, we shall see that they did not shrink back because the loss of Indochina was not, after all, basically important. They did not recoil because the horror of war was too strong. They did not flinch because they were less pessimistic than they seemed to be about the chances of a good settlement. They did not sound retreat because United States' bellicosity was a front behind which they hoped to build negotiating strength for Eden, Bidault and Mendès-France. No, their stated convictions were genuine. They believed in them, and held them to be true and basic.

Yet the United States did not take the reins which guided the protection of the Free World from Eden's hands. It did not intervene. Although there were a number of occasions during 1953 and 1954, on which Eisenhower or Dulles sounded a note for military action, on no such occasion did military action take place.[13] There must have been considerations to which they attributed more importance than the losses which—in the absence of action—we might suffer. Discussion of these circumstances appears and reappears in information sources, in newspaper reports, and in the official statements of President Eisenhower, Secretary Dulles and other spokesmen of their Administration. It is not, therefore, impossible to list them even though some are discoverable by inference only.

It is half truth only that United States intervention was contingent on Communist Chinese forces joining or not joining Ho Chi Minh's troops *overtly* and *directly*. Dulles, in his speech of March 29, 1954, discarded this distinction entirely by threatening intervention against expansion of communism achieved by *"whatever means."* Yet, following this new policy move he reverted again to the subtle line of difference, threatening armed action only in case the Chinese pursued the path of direct and overt military agression.[14] Eisenhower himself restricted his own threats, on each occasion, to committing American troops "in the event of Chinese intervention."[15] The edge of this distinction was dulled by varying the diagnosis of the facts in keeping with the vacillating policy lines. Whenever Dulles needed an argument for his militancy, he went very far to assert that for all practical purposes the Chinese were already *directly* engaged in the battlefield operations. He asserted that Ho Chi Minh's forces were trained, equipped and provided with artillery by the Chinese, and that at division level the Chinese were in charge of operations and took care of signal, engineering, and transportation behind the first battleline. On the other hand, whenever he sounded retreat, he rediscovered the caesura between the size of Chinese presence and the line of direct intervention. In his address on May 17, 1954, after the fall of Dien Bien Phu, Dulles went so far as to attribute to his warnings against Chinese intervention the fact that China did not participate openly and directly in the battle of Dien Bien Phu. A few weeks earlier, on April 5 (supra, p. 54), he found Chinese participation at Dien Bien Phu already in operation. Thus, whether or not Communist Chinese forces were actually among the combatants, it was merely a peg on which he could hang direct intervention.

Eisenhower himself accorded the main reason for his decision for non-intervention to "anti-colonialism" and "the importance of America's moral position."[16]

> "The strongest reason of all for United States refusal to respond by itself to French pleas was our tradition of anti-colonialism. . . . The standing of the United States as the most powerful of the anti-colonial powers is an asset of incalculable value to the Free World . . . It is essential to our position of leadership in a world wherein the majority of the nations have at some time or another felt the yoke of colonialism. Never, throughout the long and sometimes frustrating search for an effective means of defeating the Communist struggle for power in Indo-

china, did we lose sight of the importance of *America's moral position**."

The President was strongly supported by the Secretary of Defense, Charles Wilson, in the optimistic belief that if the United States were only to disassociate itself from the colonialism of the allies, all people who had recently won independence would support America in its struggle against Communism.[17] In a nationwide radio and television address made on June 1, 1953, Dulles declared it was high time that more attention be given to the Near East and South Asia. He asserted that the peoples of those areas were suspicious not only of the colonial powers but of the United States as well. They were convinced that membership in NATO required America to preserve and restore the old colonial interests of its allies. Dulles' conclusion was that American policy had become "unnecessarily ambiguous" in this regard. The strength of this anti-colonialist myth in Eisenhower's inner sanctum is attested to by many sources of information, which do not need listing because he himself points to them more than once in his memoires. Sherman Adams, speaking of the result of Eden's visit to Washington —his first as Prime Minister—reports that the visit

"did not resolve one serious difference between the American and British positions on the Middle East question; our firm opposition to colonialism. . ."[18]

Even though this report concerns a later period, 1956, and a different subject, not Indochina, it is significant evidence of the paramount importance that Eisenhower and his entourage, most particularly Dulles, attributed to their anti-colonialist creed.

In the Indochina crisis anti-colonialism could not play a role outside of the relationship to France. During the crisis period prior to the Geneva settlement, not even the most rabid anti-colonialists accused the United States and Britain of colonialism. All the greater was the attention paid by President Eisenhower himself to the aspect of colonialism in relation to France. However, this was a situation that required subtlety. The French Expeditionary Force, he felt, had to be kept in Indochina so as to avoid the use of American forces. But actual fighting alongside the French would have projected to world opinion an America saving a colony for France. Thus, the United States had to bleach the tinge of colonialism from the French combattants and give them the colors of champions of freedom. For Eisenhower, aversion to association with France in Indochina was not a new tenet. As allied Commander of NATO, because of the insufficient contribution by France to NATO forces due to their losses in the Indochina war, he had already planned participation by the allies in that way but only if France would commit herself to granting complete independence to the three Associated States as soon as military victory were attained. This would have created

> "a clear appreciation throughout the Free World that war was in no sense an effort to sustain former French domination but was a clear case of freedom defending itself from Communist aggression."

To bring about such appreciation, there would have to be a "simple, sincere and selfless pronouncement."[19] After his election as President, Eisenhower continued this same approach to the Indochina problem. He felt it basic to persuade the French to take measures to convince the Vietnamese— "every man and woman" *and the world*—of their sincerity in intending to grant complete independence in the shortest possible time.[20]

Successive French Governments, one after the other, issued declarations to this effect. On September 17, 1953, Dulles said in a speech before the United Nations General Assembly that

> "the French Government by its declaration of July 3, 1953, has announced its intention of completing the process of transferring to the Governments of the three Associated States all remaining powers to perfect their independence to their own satisfaction."[21]

212

"This unequivocal statement," writes Eisenhower, "would, I hoped, demonstrate once and for all that the fighting in the unhappy region was not for reimposing French domination." [22]

These and other similar diplomatic acts were approved each time by the American Administration as sufficient and convincing. But again and again, Eisenhower's moral conscience needed another tranquilizer, another reassurance on this score. After all, he writes,

"it was almost impossible to make the average Vietnamese peasant realize that the French, under whose rule they had lived for some eighty years, were really fighting in the cause of freedom"

and still less was it possible to persuade the Communists to concede this.[23] So again, on April 12, 1954, Eisenhower had need of reassurance.

"The French must accelerate their independence programs so there could be no interpretation that United States assistance meant support of French colonialism."[24]

But only two days later, on April 14, Dulles reported from Paris that the Vietnamese were satisfied with France's further measures for granting complete independence. And on June 4 a treaty, signed by Bidault in the presence of the American Under-Secretary of State as sponsor, finally seems to have given full satisfaction to the President. Its language could not have been stronger.

"La France reconnait le Viêt-nam comme un État pleinement indépendant et souverain investi de toutes les compétences reconnues par le droit international."† [25]

During all this time, the peculiarity of the situation was that the colonialist French had been inclined to abandon Indochina, whereas America, the anti-colonialist power, had done everything possible to keep them there.

This public confession of the President does not absolve

---

† "France recognizes Vietnam as a fully independent and Sovereign State in possession of all qualifications and powers known in international law."

the historian from training his attention on all facts of the situation and diagnosing the true reasons which might have brought about or influenced the policy pursued by the actors in the events. Memoirs of statesmen are always revealing but do not necessarily reveal all elements of their policy-making decisions. This is especially true when statesmen pretend to be guided by moral principles divorced from national interest. They conceive actions in moralistic terms, though they act mostly in the interest of political power. Anticolonialist emotions, fear of resemblance to imperialists, and eagerness to satisfy their belief in their own morality, did play, no doubt, a role in Eisenhower's and Dulles' decision-making process. Yet, accepting them as motives does not necessarily give us the whole truth. Eisenhower's explanation may be merely an ideological justification and rationalization. In the Indochina crisis the main spring seems to have been domestic politics.

It is not impossible that President Eisenhower did not connect consciously in his own mind his approach to the diplomacy of Indochina with his desire to serve the interests of the Republican Party. Influence of domestic politics might have been hidden from his thinking when he acted under their impact. Yet, there were direct connecting links of which he must have been conscious.

Domestic politics are recognizable in his concern to distinguish between intervention with Air Force, Navy or even Marines on the one hand, and employment of ground troops on the other. A special feature of the American military scene connects this distinction with domestic politics. The commitment of the Army—of ground forces—to foreign operations is, as a domestic political consideration, far more sensitive than the use in foreign operations of the Navy, Air Force and the Marines. The public image of the three special services is that of athletes who have fancy uniforms, and who are, for the most part, volunteers whose business it is to undertake risks. They are in popular imagination like duelists, prize-fighters, explorers, Himalayan climbers. They are contenders for glory and medals of honor. Nobody wants to expose them to danger but their business habitually puts them in hot spots which is only to be expected. The ground forces, on the other hand, recruited as draftees, are seen in an entirely different light. They are fathers, businessmen, husbands, and sons whom bad luck and tricky foreign entanglements take away from their children, businesses, wives and mothers.

With this difference in mind, it is understandable, even though illogical, that the engagement of the Navy, Air Force, or the Marines in some kind of warlike venture does not make the Government unpopular. It results in no detriment at the polls. On the other hand, for a Congressman, Senator or other elected official to take the responsibility for sending ground forces, draftees, army men to foreign lands, requires a lot of political courage. Dulles and Admiral Radford who were perhaps not overly sensitive to domestic politics, did not shrink from the possibility that American ground forces might be committed to save Indochina from Communist conquest.[26] But, for Eisenhower, the head of the Republican Party, the predicament was serious. Again and again his memoires show his concern.

> "The ever present, persistent and gnawing possibility was that of employing our *ground forces** in Indochina. I would never agree to send our ground troops . . . without congressional action."[27]

And,

> "another consideration in any conceivable intervention was the type of forces which might be employed. . . . I could not at that moment [1954] see the value of putting United States *ground forces** in Southeast Asia."[28]

And again in his April 4, 1954 letter to Churchill:

> "I do not envisage the need of any appreciable *ground forces** on your or our part."[29]

Sherman Adams also stated that Eisenhower had "no intention of sending ground forces independently" into Indochina. He quotes Eisenhower as saying:

"The Free World must understand that our most effective role did not lie in furnishing *ground troops*."[*30]

In February 1954 when Under Secretary of State, Bedell Smith was reappraising the situation with a small group invited by President Eisenhower to consider the Indochina problem, he told the British Ambassador "that there was no intention of sending American troops into Indochina; the President would not do it even if he had the power." According to the *New Republic*[30a] the feverish insistence on united action aimed at some kind of international arrangement that one way or other would make it possible for the United States to avoid the use of ground forces. Dulles, in an address to the nation given March 8, 1955, and called "Report from Asia," pointed out that in the event of war in Southeast Asia "the United States' contribution will be primarily in terms of sea and air power."[30b] Little did he foresee the military necessities of the second, the American war in Vietnam.

Nor was the President alone in his concern. When the Congressional leaders met Dulles and Admiral Radford on April 3 their principal interest was not the employment of Air Force and Navy but the use of ground forces.[31] Thus, it is not surprising that six authors looking for an explanation of the President's decision not to intervene in Indochina, are in agreement "that the most important consideration" was the unwillingness of Eisenhower and Congress to use American ground forces and draftees."[32]

As long as he was under the influence of Admiral Radford, and only bombardment from the air by Navy bombers was contemplated, President Eisenhower was ready to consent to the intervention because it would not have produced greatly disturbing reactions among the electorate and would not have been evaluated as a disadvantage by the party stalwarts even if in the process a few planes were lost.

The second concealed connection between Eisenhower's Indochina policy in 1954 and domestic party politics made its way to his mind through his "fundamental concept" about

216

the Presidency which would not permit him military action without clear Congressional consultation and approval.[33] There cannot be any doubt that at the threshold of the 1954 elections a new Korea-type war in a far away land, where only remote and largely indirect American interests were involved, would hurt the chances of Republican candidates. Sherman Adams, the principal presidential aide, reports that "during the six-month period before the SEATO Conference in 1945," (that is, from March through September 1953, encompassing the entire period of the 1954 Indochina crisis) "Dulles held more than ninety meetings with Congressional leaders of both parties."[34] It is probable that such frequent consultations by someone as self-assured and independent as Dulles were not arranged on his own initiative, but under prompting by Eisenhower. The determined resistance of the legislators on April 3 against the Radford-Ely intervention plan was certainly influenced by domestic politics.

But over and above the indirect influence of domestic political considerations, principally the use of ground forces and constitutional inhibitions, this study has amply demonstrated Eisenhower's and Dulles' concern about the reaction among the Republican legislators to the United States' diplomacy at Geneva. The studied absence of Dulles from Geneva, his snubbing of the Chinese Delegations, Eisenhower's and Dulles' pretense that China was present at Geneva not as a negotiating power but as an indicted aggressor at the bar of world opinion, the refusal to sign the Geneva document but sanctioning it by indirect declarations—all this was done because of partisan party reflexes. It is a safe assumption that the same impulse gave impetus to other secondary moves which were also part of the Dulles diplomacy in 1954.

Foreign policy susceptibility to domestic political influences is in a democratic system of government neither avoidable nor is it, generally speaking, considered reprehensible. The limit is set by the duty of the governments to "resist the temptation to sacrifice what it considers good

217

policy upon the altar of public opinion, abdicating leadership and exchanging short-lived political advantage for the permanent interests of the country . . . A good government must recognize that the conflict between the requirements of good foreign policy and the preferences of public opinion is in the nature of things and, hence, unavoidable."[34a] Yet, as was pointed out in this study, domestic and foreign observers of our Indochina policy found it blameworthy that Eisenhower and Dulles yielded to the partisan pressure of a group of Republican legislators.

In all other democratic countries there is acceptance with good grace of such phenomena. But the United States is the leader of the Free World, and leaders have special responsibilities and are expected to observe special rules of conduct. The government which claims the leadership of a group of countries violates its moral obligations if, instead of representing the overall interests of the group, determined in good faith as such, it submits to such partisan pressure of a sectarian fraction of its own citizenry which avowedly and manifestly disregards the good of the group as a whole.

This special restraint of the coalition's leader has its corresponding parallelism in domestic politics. Individuals, associations and groups with members tied to each other by profession, class, religion or any other bonds are not thought to act reprehensibly if they use their numerical, economic, or intellectual power to advance their individual or group interests. But the head of a state is not supposed to do it and if he does, when even if by the strictest standards of the community to which he belongs his action would otherwise be legal, ethical, and respectable, his special position of leadership makes it improper and unseemly.

Not long ago this special rule was not recognized in regard to anyone but heads of state and their immediate families. Cabinet members, legislators, decision-makers even in the highest echelons were not subject to special restricting rules as long as conflict of interest did not enter the picture, making one or other of their activities a misuse of the trust which was placed in them. Recently, the prohibition has been extended beyond the conflict of interest to the area of *possible* conflict. This is being done though this wide rule eliminates from public service those whose probity is above doubt, but whose own situation, or whose family's situation could create, theoretically, an incompatibility between their personal commitments and their public office.

But the office of a head of state extends to the entire field of human activity. There is no area where possibility of conflict would not be imaginable. In view of this, he can be impartial and *un*influenced by particular personal ambitions only if his office elevates him for his whole life above such considerations. This is the reason that some political scientists find special merit in the institution of constitutional monarchy:[35] the king cannot rise higher, he need not pursue particular personal interests. His personal advancement cannot come but from the ascent of his country. He may make wrong decisions, but as far as human ability permits he will have one aim in life only, the good of his country.

It is an extension of the same theory to the international field to require a somewhat similar disinterestedness from the government of a country which has assumed the leadership position of an alliance. It cannot go as far as the rule it applies to the individual head of a state. It is impossible to demand that the leader-government should neglect the interests of its own country. But it is fair to demand that the leader-government should ignore its own domestic political sectarian considerations, when it acts on behalf of a coalition group.

The Indochina policy of the Eisenhower administration insofar as it was subservient to domestic political partisanship was in conflict with the leadership position of the United States. This justified the refusal of Britain and France to follow in Geneva Dulles' policy and vindicates its censure on this account.

The Third Question. What Eisenhower termed "American moral position" predetermined another tenet of United

States policy in Southeast Asia: the insistence on the formation of a coalition supporting United States intervention. "A coalition," wrote Eisenhower, "would give moral meaning to intervention.[36]" Why, then, did the Eisenhower-Dulles administration abandon, after the Geneva Conference, the goal of "united action" so strongly sought before?

So long as there was hope that SEATO might become a coalition, with teeth in it, to provide united action against Communist China, no other supporting united action would have been necessary. On account of the Manila Treaty, Eisenhower believed

> "the dilemma of finding a moral, legal and practical basis for helping our friends of the region need not face us again."

Should the communists commit agression in Southeast Asia, America now had the "legal, moral and practical" basis to intervene, without—so the President thought—begging Britain for "token support," or at least for "acquiescence."[37] Dulles, too, emphasized this specific purpose of the Manila Treaty. In a statement, quoted by C. L. Sulzberger, the Secretary said:

> "SEATO's *principal** purpose was to provide our President *legal** authority to intervene in Indochina."[38]

Eisenhower's and Dulles' aversion to special association with "colonialists" is the only possible explanation of these two self-serving policy statements. They thought that if America walked arm in arm with a mixed Asiatic-European group, even though they were only our honorary associates, the group would be trusted by the Asian and African States. In addition, American intervention would be immune from accusations of being imperialist, colonialist or paternalistic. They believed that any antagonism to American influence and power was the product of guilt imputed because of British-French association. Their mistaken self-persuasion made out of the anti-colonialist cant the dominating policy-line of the United States, leading it into the maze out of which France, by the Geneva settlement, had just succeeded in extricating itself.

The false pretensions of this anti-colonialist policy—with its paralyzing effect—was the dominant factor which resulted in the isolation of the American commitment in Vietnam. President Eisenhower and Secretary Dulles knew that the single-handed sponsorship of the independence and survival of South Vietnam would take the United States to the point of no return. Indeed, Dulles said that

> "if the United States sent its flag and its own military establishment,—land, sea or air, into the Indochina war, then the prestige of the United States would be engaged. . . . We could not afford thus to engage the prestige of the United States and suffer a defeat which would have worldwide repercussions."[39]

Yet, they hoisted the flag. And having done this, they engaged the United States and its political prestige in the Second Indochina War. Today, in 1965, we are still in it.

17

W~E~ MOVED INTO THE I~NDOCHINA~ CRISIS AS THE NATURAL corollary of the pronouncements made by Dulles before and during the election campaign; the *bold* policy set forth by him was both his personal creed and the Republican Party election platform.† The campaign for victory policy reached its climax in his speech on January 12, 1954 announcing the threat of instant retaliation. In essence, Dulles vehemently disavowed a policy limited to mere containment of international Communism generally; and he opposed it in Asia specifically. He held out the possibility of a defeat of the Chinese Communists on the mainland of China as the truly desirable goal; he promised, as a minimum, to resist the Communist attempt to invade the sensitive area of Indochina.

In 1954 Dulles' policy did not aim at containment. Its avowed purpose was to defeat Ho Chi Minh by military victory and to roll back the Communist camp to the northern border of Indochina. The military campaign would be fought by the French and Vietnamese ground forces, with the support, if necessary, of United States aerial units and token auxiliaries from Asiatic allies and Britain.

---

† Supra, p. III.

President Eisenhower, in his budget message to Congress on January 21, 1954, stated that

> "in Indochina where the French Union and Associated States forces are holding Communist efforts to expand into the free areas of Asia, the United States is making a major contribution by providing military equipment and other military support . . . This assistance is required to enable these gallant forces to sustain an offensive that will provide the opportunity for *victory*."[1]

It was this most ambitious plan that was resisted by Britain and France and was defeated by the diplomacy which brought about success in Geneva.

But as soon as the settlement produced by the Geneva Conference was an accomplished fact, United States policy, in a sharp change, turned into a clear cut containment posture. We gave up the victory plan. No attempt was made to encourage South Vietnam to attack Ho Chi Minh's North Vietnam and to unite Vietnam by rolling back the Communists to the southern border of Red China. On the contrary, American encouragement given to the migration of close to one million Vietnamese Catholics to the south demonstrated American acquiescence in the loss of North Vietnam to the Communists. The promise by the American delegation in the Special Declaration of Geneva not to disturb by force the settlement achieved by the Conference proves this point without the slightest shadow of doubt.†

What is important to understand, further, is that at no time after Geneva, between 1954 and 1959-60, was the slightest endeavour made to use diplomacy in order to turn the confrontation of the Free World with the Communist Powers in Indochina into a state of tolerable coexistence. The processes of diplomacy were not only ignored but explicitly rejected. Vice President Nixon summed up the American position for the future of Indochina. "It is impossible to lay down arms *until victory is completely won*."[2a] A

---

† Supra p. 154.

few weeks later, on December 23, 1953, in a nationwide radio and television address he gave firm expression to this thesis:[2b]

> "The time has passed when we would try to reach agreement with the Communists at the Conference table by surrendering to them. We are paying in Asia for that kind of diplomacy right now . . ."

Dulles' speech on March 29, 1954, the curtain raiser of his new Indochina policy, reviewed the previous twenty years of the political relationship with Soviet Russia. He recalled the recognition of Soviet Russia in 1933, on the basis of an agreement with Soviet Foreign Minister Maxim Maximovich Litvinow. He recalled the experience with the Yalta Agreement in regard to Central Europe and Russian relationship to China. He recalled the violation of the armistice agreement in Korea by China.

> "It would be reckless for us", he said, "to ignore the events of recent years which filled our archives with vain promises. And I say, *we are not in the market for any more.** It is now, in 1954, the policy of the United States not to exchange United States performance for Communist promises."[3]

President Eisenhower seemed to be in complete agreement:

> "I had long ago learned, he wrote,[4] that no agreement with Communists is worth the paper it is written on unless it contains its own self-enforcing (sic) procedures".

To *his* knowledge—so he wrote—"Communists do not keep their promises."[5] 6

The United States Special Declaration at Geneva specifically disowned the thirteenth paragraph of the General Declaration of the Conference, in which the members of the Conference agreed to consult one another on measures to insure that the agreement on the cessation of hostilities be respected.† This studied disavowal of the possibilities of diplomatic contact was but one item in our general resistance to diplomacy.

---

† Supra p. 147-8.

225

A second important step was the lockout of the French presence in Indochina. Almost a century-long connection between Indochina and France had created many personal and institutional links between the two countries. These links could have been used to serve the maintenance or strengthening of the influence of the south in North Vietnam and could have fostered friendly relations between the two halves of the truncated country, promoting an atmosphere which is not an unimportant corollary to diplomatic activity.

Our third contribution to the obstruction of diplomacy was the delivery of South Vietnam to the dictatorial reign of Diem, whose domestic policy alienated all Vietnamese groups which did not submit to his rigid dictatorship. In theory, measures of persecution and repression were aimed at the Communists only, but, in fact, they affected Buddhists, followers of other sects, democrats, socialists, liberals and even such Vietnamese who had family and friendly contacts on the other side of the Seventeenth Parallel.

All this might have been good policy if it could reasonably have been hoped that South Vietnam's security and peaceful existence had a good chance to survive the initial crisis, and that its anti-communist strength would be well supported after a few years by social unity, a healthy economic situation and reliable army strength. But tribal feuds, internal dissensions, persecution of religious and other minorities, weaknesses of the army and failure of military conscription were no secret to the Department of State and the American training mission.[†] Press reports and a number of literary presentations of life in Vietnam should have been recognized as danger signals.

In spite of the dangerous geographic proximity of China and the earlier dependence of Ho Chi Minh on Chinese military support, there was, in 1954, some possibility that Ho Chi Minh's government might have been amenable to diplomatic contacts looking to real stabilization. He had in his government several non-Marxists who might have helped

† Supra, Chapter 12.

such an undertaking. Vietnam's millennial history is filled with intermittently successful attempts to free the country from Chinese domination. "The most important question facing *both** North and South Vietnam", wrote an anti-Diem and anti-Communist Vietnamese of high repute, "is how to safeguard the future of the *whole** Vietnamese nation now threatened by such number and such great dynanism (of the Chinese)."[6]

North Vietnam's double-satellite relationship (to Moscow and Peking) potentially creates a limited measure of independence from both. The Vietnamese Communists turned to Russia and her European satellites for the help they needed after Geneva in order to recover from the devastations of a seven-year civil war.[7] With this help North Vietnam may now be increasingly independent of China. Even if the rank and file of the leadership were impervious to the pride of independence, it is a safe assumption that Ho Chi Minh himself, now an "elder statesman" of the Communist world, is not unlike other national leaders: he most certainly does not enjoy being a mere puppet. He seems to have the talent and subtlety to maneuver between the Scylla and Charybdis of commitment to China and Russia.[8] Thus, diplomacy directed at real neutralization of Vietnam, even if not fully approved by Peking, might have achieved some success in the years 1955 to 1960. Of course, to the irreconcilable fanatic, Diem, any contact with Ho Chi Minh would have been anathema. But American policy was not necessarily condemned to serve Mr. Diem's nervous system, especially since there was plenty of opposition to him among his own countrymen.

This presentation of the possibilities inherent in the Vietnam political situation serves the purpose of indicating the advantages which might have been realized by diplomacy. But the roadblocks were effective; and we adhered to a rigid and frozen version of containment. We forgot Churchill's famous motto: "We arm to parley."

There is today no way to terminate this war but by political settlement using diplomacy. John Foster Dulles refused this road to success and twice suffered defeat in Indochina. He lived to endure the first defeat, that is, the success of the Geneva settlement in 1954. He is saved from suffering the second personally. As in true tragedies, both debacles were caused not by his weakness but by his innate moral and spiritual strength, which made his anti-Communist fervor a blinding dogma and deprived him of flexibility when wisdom demanded it.

The idea of political solution is but a principle. The time for diplomacy, for a new policy, will be reached when, in regard to Southeast Asia, Russia, Ho Chi Minh and the Atlantic Community have recognized an identity of interests.

The thesis that diplomacy for adjustments and settlements of local problems is the only way to save the world from catastrophy was put in eloquent words by Sir Winston Churchill in a speech on January 28, 1948 in the House of Commons:

> "It is idle to reason or argue with the Communists. It is, however, possible to deal with them on a fair, realistic basis, and, in my experience, they will keep their bargains as long as it is in their interest to do so, which might, in this grave matter, be a long time once things are settled . . .
> There are very grave dangers . . . in letting everything run on and pile up until something happens, and it passes, all of a sudden, out of your control.
> With all consideration of the facts, I believe it is right to say today that the best chance of avoiding war is, in accord with the other Western democracies, to bring matters to a head with the Soviet Government, and, by formal diplomatic processes, with all their privacy and gravity, to arrive at a lasting settlement. There is certainly enough for the interests of all if such a settlement could be reached. Even this method, I must say, however, would not guarantee that war would not come. But I believe it would give the best chance of preventing it, and that, if it came, we should have the best chance of coming out of it alive."[9]

This was great wisdom in 1948; it is perhaps even wiser counsel in 1965.

Appendices

Appendices

Letter of President Dwight D. Eisenhower to Sir Winston Churchill, dated April 4, 1954.

I am sure . . . you are following with the deepest interest and anxiety the daily reports of the gallant fight being put up by the French at Dien Bien Phu. Today, the situation there does not seem hopeless.

But regardless of the outcome of this particular battle, I fear that the French cannot alone see the thing through, this despite the very substantial assistance in money and materiel that we are giving them. It is no solution simply to urge the French to intensify their efforts. And if they do not see it through and Indochina passes into the hands of the Communists the ultimate effect on our and your global strategic position with the consequent shift in the power ratios throughout Asia and the Pacific could be disastrous and, I know, unacceptable to you and me. . . . This has led us urgently to take serious and far-reaching decisions.

Geneva is less than four weeks away. There the possibility of the Communists driving a wedge between us will, given the state of mind in France, be infinitely greater than at Berlin. I can understand the very natural desire of the French to seek an end to this war which has been bleeding them for eight years. But our painstaking search for a way out of the impasse has reluctantly forced us to the conclusion that there is no negotiated solution of the Indochina problem which in its essence would not be either a face-saving device to cover a French surrender or a face-saving device to cover a Communist retirement. The first alternative is too serious in its broad strategic implications for us and for you to be acceptable. . . .

Somehow we must contrive to bring about the second alternative. The preliminary lines of our thinking were sketched out by Foster in his speech last Monday night when he said that under the conditions of today the imposition on Southeast Asia of the political system of Communist Russia and its Chinese Communist ally, by whatever means, would be a grave threat to the whole free community, and that in our view this possibility should now be met by united action and not passively accepted. . . .

I believe that the best way to put teeth in this concept and to bring greater moral and material resources to the support of the French effort is through the establishment of a new, ad hoc grouping or coalition composed of nations which have a vital concern in the checking of Communist expansion in the area. I have in mind in addition to our two countires, France, the Associated States, Australia, New Zealand, Thailand and the Philippines. The United States government would expect to play its full part in such a coalition. . . .

The important thing is that the coalition must be strong and it must be willing to join the fight if necessary. I do not envisage the need of any appreciable ground forces on your or our part. . . .

If I may refer again to history; we failed to halt Hirohito, Mussolini and Hitler by not acting in unity and in time. That marked the beginning of many years of stark tragedy and desperate peril. May it not be that our nations have learned something from that lesson? . . .

With warm regard,

IKE

II

Final Declaration of the Geneva Conference, July 21, 1954.

Final declaration, dated July 21, 1954, of the Geneva Conference on the problem of restoring peace in Indochina, in which the representatives of Cambodia, the Democratic Republic of Viet-Nam, France, Laos, the People's Republic of China, the State of Viet-Nam, the Union of Soviet Socialist Republics, the United Kingdom and the United States of America took part.

1. The Conference takes note of the agreements ending hostilities in Cambodia, Laos, and Viet-Nam and organizing international control and the supervision of the execution of the provisions of these agreementts.

2. The Conference expresses satisfaction at the ending of hostilities in Cambodia, Laos, and Viet-Nam. The Conference expresses its conviction that the execution of the provisions set out in the present declaration and in the agreements on the cessation of hostilities will permit Cambodia, Laos, and Viet-Nam henceforth to play their part, in full independence and sovereignty, in the peaceful community of nations.

3. The Conference takes note of the declarations made by the Governments of Cambodia and of Laos of their intention to adopt measures permitting all citizens to take their place in the national community, in particular by participating in the next general elections, which, in conformity with the constitution of each of these countries, shall take place in the course of the year 1955, by secret ballot and in conditions of respect for fundamental freedoms.

4. The Conference takes note of the clauses in the agreement on the cessation of hostilities in Viet-Nam prohibiting the introduction into Viet-Nam of foreign troops and military personnel as well as of all kinds of arms and munitions. The Conference also takes note of the declarations

made by the Governments of Cambodia and Laos of their resolution not to request foreign aid, whether in war material, in personnel, or in instructors except for the purpose of effective defense of their territory and, in the case of Laos, to the extent defined by the agreements on the cessation of hostilities in Laos.

5. The Conference takes note of the clauses in the agreement on the cessation of hostilities in Viet-Nam to the effect that no military base at the disposition of a foreign state may be established in the regrouping zones of the two parties, the latter having the obligation to see that the zones allotted to them shall not constitute par of any miliary alliance and shall not be utilized for the resumption of hostilities or in the service of an aggressive policy. The Conference also takes note of the declarations of the Governments of Cambodia and Laos to the effect that they will not join in any agreement with other states if this agreement includes the obligation to participate in a military alliance not in conformity with the principles of the Charter of the United Nations or, in the case of Laos, with the principles of the agreement on the cessation of hostilities in Laos or, so long as their security is not threatened, the obligation to establish bases on Cambodian or Laotian territory for the military forces of foreign powers.

6. The Conference recognizes that the essential purpose of the agreement relating to Viet-Nam is to settle military questions with a view to ending hostilities and that the military demarcation line should not in any way be interpreted as constituting a political or territorial boundary. The Conference expresses its conviction that the execution of the provisions set out in the present declaration and in the agreement on the cessation of hostilities creates the necessary basis for the achievement in the near future of a political settlement in Viet-Nam.

7. The Conference declares that, so far as Viet-Nam is concerned, the settlement of political problems, effected on the basis of respect for the principles of independence, unity, and territorial integrity, shall permit the Vietnamese people to enjoy the fundamental freedoms, guaranteed by democratic institutions established as a result of free general elections by secret ballot.

In order to insure that sufficient progress in the restoration of peace has been made, and that all the necessary conditions obtain for free expression of the national will, general elections shall be held in July 1956, under the supervision of an international commission composed of representatives of the member states of the International Supervisory Commission referred to in the agreement on the cessation of hostilities. Consultations will be held on this subject between the competent representative authorities of the two zones from April 20, 1955, onwards.

8. The provisions of the agreements on the cessation of hostilities intended to insure the protection of individuals and of property must be most strictly applied and must, in particular, allow every one in Viet-Nam to decide freely in which zone he wishes to live.

9. The competent representative authorities of the northern and southern zones of Viet-Nam, as well as the authorities of Laos and Cambodia, must not permit any individual or collective reprisals against persons who have collaborated in any way with one of the parties during the war, or against members of such persons' families.

10. The Conference takes note of the declaration of the French Govern-

ment to the effect that it is ready to withdraw its troops from the territory of Cambodia, Laos, and Viet-Nam, at the request of the governments concerned and within a period which shall be fixed by agreement between the parties except in the cases where, by agreement between the two parties, a certain number of French troops shall remain at specified points and for a specified time.

11. The Conference takes note of the declaration of the French Government to the effect that for the settlement of all the problems connected with the reestablishment and consolidation of peace in Cambodia, Laos, and Viet-Nam, the French Government will proceed from the principle of respect for the independence and sovereignty, unity, and territorial integrity of Cambodia, Laos, and Viet-Nam.

12. In their relations with Cambodia, Laos, and Viet-Nam, each member of the Geneva Conference undertakes to respect the sovereignty, the independence, the unity, and the territorial integrity of the above-mentioned states, and to refrain from any interference in their internal affairs.

13. The members of the Conference agree to consult one another on any question which may be referred to them by the International Supervisory Commission, in order to study such measures as may prove necessary to insure that the agreements on the cessation of hostilities in Cambodia, Laos, and Viet-Nam are respected.

III

Statement of President Dwight D. Eisenhower in regard to the result of the Geneva Conference

I am glad, of course, that agreement has been reached at Geneva to stop the bloodshed in Indo-china.

The United States has not been a billigerent in the war. The primary responsibility for the settlement in Indochina rested with those nations which participated in the fighting. Our role at Geneva has been at all times to try to be helpful where desired and to aid France and Cambodia, Laos, and Viet-Nam to obtain a just and honorable settlement which will take into account the needs of the interested people. Accordingly, the United States has not itself been party to or bound by the decisions taken by the Conference, but it is our hope that it will lead to the establishment of peace consistent with the rights and the needs of the countries concerned. The agreement contains features which we do not like, but a great deal depends on how they work in practice.

The United States is issuing at Geneva a statement to the effect that it is not prepared to join in the Conference declaration, but, as loyal members of the United Nations, we also say that, in compliance with the obligations and principles contained in article 2 of the United Nations Charter, the United States will not use force to disturb the settlement. We also say that any renewal of Communist aggression would be viewed by us as a matter of grave concern.

As evidence of our resolve to assist Cambodia and Laos to play their part, in full independence and sovereignty, in the peaceful community of free nations, we are requesting the agreement of the Governments of Cambodia and Laos to our appointment of an Ambassador or Minister to be resident at their respective capitals (Phnom Penh and Vientiane). We already have a Chief of Mission at Saigon, the capital of Viet-Nam, and this Embassy will, of course, be maintained.

The United States is actively pursuing discussions with other free nations with a view to the rapid organization of a collective defense in Southeast Asia in order to prevent further direct or indirect Communist aggression in that general area.

Notes

INTRODUCTION

[1] John Foster Dulles, "A Policy of Boldness," *Life Magazine*, May 19. 1952.

[2] William Clark, *Less Than Kin—A Study of Anglo-American Relations*, (Hamish-Hamilton, London, 1957).

[3] Hans J. Morgenthau, *Politics Among Nations* (third edition, 1960), p. 184.

Chapter 1

[1] Herbert Nicholas, *Britain and the U.S.A.* p. 58.

[2] Anthony Eden, *Full Circle*, p. 23.

[3] Ibid, p. 23.

[4] *Vital Speeches*, January 1, 1954, pp. 165-166.

[4a] *State Department Bulletin*, 1953, I. pp. 213-215. Eisenhower, *The White House Years: Mandate for Change*, 1953-1956, p. 141.

[5] Richard Goold Adams, *The Time of Power—A reappraisal of John Foster Dulles*, p. 58; Dulles' nationwide speech over radio and television, May 7, 1954, *Department of State Bulletin*, 1954, I. p. 740.

[6] Eden, op. cit. p. 61.

[7] Eden, op. cit. p. 64.

[8] Sherman Adams, *First Hand Report*, p. 132.

[9] Eisenhower, op. cit. p. 250.

[10] Walter Lippman, *Isolation and Alliance*, pp. 22-23; 34-35; 39.

[11] Eisenhower, op. cit. p. 349.

[12] Bernard Shaw, *John Bull's Other Island*, Selected Plays (Dodd, Mead), p. 471.

Chapter 2

[1] Eisenhower, op. cit. pp. 338, 372.
[2] *Department of State Bulletin,* June 30, 1952, p. 1010.
[3] Eisenhower, op. cit. p. 167.
[4] *London Times,* April 8, 1954.
[5] Eden, op. cit. p. 97.
[6] *Department of State Bulletin,* 1959, I, p. 12.
[7] Eisenhower, op. cit. p. 333.
[8] *Department of State Bulletin,* 1954, I, p. 589.
[9] Eisenhower, op. cit. p. 343.
[10] Ibid, p. 371.
[11] Eden, op. cit. p. 97.
[12] R. Rovere, *The Eisenhower Years,* p. 175.
[13] Eisenhower, op. cit. p. 343.
[14] *Débats Parlementaires,* 1954, pp. 4603-4606.
[15] Lacouture-Devillers, op. cit. p. 43.
[16] Eisenhower, op. cit. p. 343.
[17] W. H. Chamberlain, *New Leader,* April 19, 1954.
[18] *State Department Bulletin,* March 8, 1954, p. 346.
[19] Speech on March 3, 1954 to the Women National Republican Club, *Department of State Bulletin,* March 15, 1954.
[20] Lacouture-Devillers, op. cit. p. 113.
[21] R. H. Fifield, *The Diplomacy of Southeast Asia,* p. 291.
[22] Eden, op. cit. p. 100.
[23] Eisenhower, op. cit. p. 344.
[24] Eden, op. cit. p. 100.
[25] Henri Navarre, *Agonie de l'Indochine,* p. 255.

Chapter 3

[1] Lacouture-Devillers, op. cit. pp. 30-31.
[2] Eisenhower, op. cit. pp. 338, 372
[3] Testimony Dulles, Committee on Foreign Affairs, House of Representatives, April 5, 1964, p. 7.
[4] Lacouture-Devillers, op. cit. p. 38; B. B. Fall op. cit. p. 221.
[5] Débats Parlementaires, Conseil de la République 1953, p. 1748.
[6] The reader can find full presentation of both sides of the argument in the Memoirs of Joseph Laniel, *Le Drame Indochinois,* 1957 and General Henri Navarre, *L'Agonie En Indochine,* 1956.
[7] Eisenhower, op. cit. p. 339.
[8] *New York Times,* February 10 and March 24, 1954.
[9] *New York Times,* February 11, 1954; Eisenhower, op. cit. p. 343.
[9a] Lacouture-Devillers, op. cit. p. 68.
[10] Ely, op. cit. p. 64.
[11] Ibid, op. cit. p. 76; Lacouture-Devillers, op. cit. p. 73.
[12] Ely, op. cit. pp. 65 and 72.
[13] Lacouture-Devillers, op. cit. p. 72.

[14] Ibid, p. 71.
[15] Testimony Dulles, Committee on Foreign Affairs, House of Representatives, April 5, 1954.
[16] Lacouture-Devillers, op. cit. p. 95.
[17] Ely, op. cit. p. 86; Lacouture-Devillers, op. cit. p. 75.
[18] Ibid, p. 86-87.
[18b] Lacouture-Devillers, op. cit. p. 75.
[19] Lacouture-Devillers, op. cit. pp. 71-72.
[20] Vital Speeches, April 15, 1954 (XX-13) p. 387.
[21] *New York Times*, March 31, 1954.
[22] Sherman Adams, op. cit. p. 120.
[23] *Washington Post* and *Times Herald*, June 7, 1954.
[24] Eisenhower, op. cit. p. 353.
[24] Ibid, p. 353.
[24a] *New York Times*, April 18, 1954.
[25] Ibid, April 18, 1954.
[26] Ibid, April 20, 1954.
[27] Ibid, April 21, 1954.
[28] Sherman Adams, op. cit. p. 122.
[29] Eisenhower, op. cit. p. 343.
[30] Ely, op. cit. pp. 66, 72.
[31] Ibid, p. 67.
[32] B. B. Fall, op. cit. p. 226-227; Lacouture-Devillers, op. cit. p. 197.
[33] *New York Times*, April 4, 1954.
[34] *New York Herald Tribune*, April 4, 1954.
[35] Walter Lippmann, *Isolation and Alliances*, p. 34-35.
[36a] *Le Monde*, April 1, 1954.
[36b] Eden, op. cit. pp. 102-103.
[37] Sherman Adams, op. cit. p. 130.

Chapter 4

[1] Eisenhower, op. cit. pp. 346-347.
[2] Eden, op. cit., p. 103.
[3] Mutual Security Act of 1954, Hearings, Committee on Foreign Affairs, pp. 1-25.
[4] *Department of State Bulletin*, Press Release 182, April 7, 1954.
[5] *London Times*, April 8, 1954.
[6] *New York Times*, April 8, 1964.
[7] *London Times*, April 9, 1954.
[8] *London Times*, April 9, 1954.
[9] Eisenhower, op. cit., p. 349.
[10] Speech by Dulles at Syracuse, N.Y., April 15, 1954 (*Department of State Bulletin*, April 26, 1954).
[11] *Le Monde*, April 10, 1954.
[12] Eisenhower, op. cit. p. 346.
[13] Ibid, op. cit. p. 348.
[14] *Keesing's Contemporary Archives*, Vol. 9, p. 13546.

[15] *London Times,* April 15, 1954.
[16] C. S. Roberts, *The Reporter,* September 14, 1954.
[17] Eden, op. cit. p. 110.
[18] *New York Times,* April 2, 1954.
[19] E. Lefever, *Ethics and U. S. Foreign Policy,* (Meridian Books, New York, 1957) p. 46.
[20] Eisenhower, op. cit. p. 349.
[21] *LIFE Magazine,* James Shepley, "Strained Seams in the Great Alliance," May 31, 1954, p. 21.
[22] *LOOK Magazine,* Fletcher Knebel, "We Nearly Went to War Three Times," February 8, 1955.
[23] *New York Times,* May 4, 1954.
[24] Eisenhower, op. cit. p. 142.
[25] Eden, op. cit. p. 116.
[26] Eisenhower, op. cit. p. 355.
[27] Eden, op. cit. pp. 124-126.

Chapter 5

[1] Eden, op. cit. pp. 113-115.
[2] Ibid, p. 117.
[3] Ibid, p. 119.
[4] Eisenhower, op. cit. p. 351.
[5] Laniel, op. cit., pp. 87-88.
[6a] Eden, op. cit., p. 119.
[6b] *Life,* Jan. 16, 1956.
[7] Laniel, op. cit., p. 88. Eden, op. cit. p. 119.
[8] *Keesing's Contemporary Archives,* Vol 9, p. 13547.
[9] *London Times,* April 27, 1954.
[10] Ibid, April 28 and April 29, 1954.
[11] Ibid, April 26, 1954.
[12] *New York Terald Tribune,* May 2, 1954.
[13] Eden, op. cit., pp. 121-122.

Chapter 6

[1] Eden, op. cit., p. 123.
[2] *London Times,* May 5, 1954.
[3] *New York Herald Tribune,* May 6, 1954.
[4] *London Times,* June 24, 1954.
[5] Eisenhower, Press Conference, May 5, 1954; *Dept. of State Bulletin,* May 17, 1954, p. 740.

[6] Eisenhower, op. cit., p. 364.
[7] *New York Herald Tribune*, May 6, 1954.
[8] *London Times*, May 6, 1954.
[9] Ibid, May 11, 1954.   .
[10] Ibid, May 11, 1954.
[11] *New York Herald Tribune*, May 12, 1954.
[12] *London Times*, May 14, 1954.
[13] *London Times*, May 18, 1954.
[14] *London Times*, May 26, 1954.
[15] *New York Herald Tribune*, May 26, 1954.
[16] Lacouture-Devillers, op. cit., pp. 199-200.
[17] *New York Times*, June 1, 1954.

Chapter 7

[1] *New York Herald Tribune*, May 3; *London Times*, May 6, 1954.
[2] *New York Times*, May 20, 1954.
[3] *New York Herald Tribune*, May 20, 1954.
[4] Eisenhower, op. cit., p. 352.
[5] Ibid, p. 352.
[6] Ibid, p. 359.
[7] *New York Herald Tribune*, May 20, 1954.
[8] *London Times*, April 29, 1954, p. 5.
[9] Eisenhower, op. cit., p. 354.
[10] *New York Times*, May 25, 1954.
[11] *London Times*, May 18, 1954.
[12] Ibid, May 18, 1954.
[13] *London Times*, May 22, 1954.
[14] *London Times*, August 11, 1954.
[15] *London Times*, August 11, 1954.
[16] Lacouture-Devillers, op. cit., p. 170. (Translation by author.)
[17] *London Times*, May 17, 1954.
[18] *New York Herald Tribune*, May 18, 1954.
[19] *London Times*, May 17, 1954.
[20] Eisenhower, op. cit., pp. 358-9.
[21] Ibid, p. 359.
[22] Ibid, p. 359.
[23] Ibid, p. 359.
[24] *New York Herald Tribune*, May 16, 1954.
[25] Eden, op. cit., p. 134.
[26] Ibid, p. 134.
[27] *London Times*, May 17, 1954.
[28] *New York Herald Tribune*, May 19, 1954.
[29] *London Times*, May 21, 1954.
[30] *London Times*, April 10, 1954.
[31] Eisenhower, op. cit., p. 345.
[32] *Le Monde*, April 7, 1954.

[33] Eisenhower, op. cit., pp. 360-361.
[34] *New York Herald Tribune,* June 3, 1954.
[35] *London Times,* May 21, 1954.
[36] *New York Herald Tribune,* May 23, 1954.
[37] Eden, op. cit., p. 143.
[38] *London Times,* June 19, 1954; State Department Bulletin, June 28, 1954, p. 990.
[39] Speech of Mendès-France, Assemblée Générale, July 25, 1954.
[40] Hearings before the Foreign Relations Committee of the Senate, June 4, 1954, p. 11.
[41] *New York Herald Tribune,* June 9, 1954.
[42] *New York Herald Tribune,* June 6, 1954.
[43] *New York Herald Tribune,* June 13, 1954.
[44] Marquis Childs, *The Ragged Edge,* Doubleday, Garden City, N. Y., 1955., p. 137.
[45] Eden, op. cit., p. 135.
[46] Ibid, p. 142.
[47] Ibid, pp. 142-3.
[48] *London Times,* May 14, 1954.
[49] *London Times,* June 1, 1954.
[50] Eden, op. cit., p. 145.
[51] Ibid., p. 144.
[52] Dulles, News conference, *Department of State Bulletin,* June 28, p. 990.
[53] Eden, op. cit., p. 146.
[54] Ibid, p. 160.

Chapter 8

[1] *London Times,* April 29, 1954.
[2] *London Times,* May 7, 1954.
[3] *London Times,* May 4, 1954.
[4] *New York Herald Tribune,* May 5, 1954.
[5] *New York Herald Tribune,* May 6, 1954.
[6] Ibid, May 6, 1954.
[7] Eden, op. cit., p. 150.
[8] Marquis Childs, op. cit., p. 164.
[9] R. Murphy, *Diplomat Among Warriors,* Doubleday, Garden City, N. Y., 1964, pp. 383-384.
[10] *New York Times,* May 7, 1954.
[11] *New York Herald Tribune,* May 19, 1954.
[12] Eden, op. cit., pp. 125-127.
[13] *London Times,* April 28, 1954.
[14] *London Times,* May 18, 1954.
[15] House of Commons, May 17, 1954.
[16] *New York Herald Tribune,* May 19, 1954.
[17] *London Times,* May 21, 1954; *New York Times,* May 20, 1954.
[18] *New York Herald Tribune,* June 20, 1954.

[19] *Department of State Bulletin*, June 28, 1954.

[20] Press Conference, April 7, *New York Times*, April 8, 1954.

[21] House of Commons, June 23, 1954; *Keesing's Contemporary Archives*, Vol., 9, p. 13662.

[22] Eisenhower, op. cit., p. 355.

[23] *New York Times*, January 14, 1960.

[24] Eden, op. cit. p. 116; Ch. M. Roberts, *Washington Post*, June 7, 1954.

[25] Sh. Adams, op. cit., p. 122.

[26] *Department of State Bulletin*, August 23, 1954, p. 261.

[26a] H. Nicolson *The Congress of Vienna*, Constable London, 1947, p. 153.

[27] House of Commons Debate, June 23, 1954; *Keesing's Contemporary Archives*, Vol. 9, p. 13662.

[28] *New York Times*, June 25, 1954.

[29] Marquis Childs, op. cit. p. 137.

[30] *Department of State Bulletin*, June 28, 1954, p. 972.

[31] *New York Herald Tribune*, June 16, 1954.

[32] Sh. Adams, op. cit., p. 123.

[33] House of Commons Debate, June 23; *Keesings' Contemporary Archives*, Vol. 9, p. 13662.

[34] *London Times*, June 8, 1954; Congressional Hearings, Senate Foreign Relations Committee, June 4, 1954, p. 24.

[35] *LIFE Magazine*, James Shepley, p. 21, May 31, 1954.

[36] *London Times*, June 8, 1954.

[37] *Keesing's Contemporary Archives*, Vol. 9, p. 13662.

[38] *Congressional Record*, June 29, 1954, p. 9182.

[39] Press Conference, June 15, 1954, *Department of State Bulletin*, June 28, 1954, p. 990.

Chapter 9

[1] Eisenhower, op. cit. p. 332.

[2] *Department of State Bulletin*, Press Release 321, June 15, 1954.

[3] Eisenhower, op. cit. p. 367.

[4] Ibid, op. cit. p. 368.

[5] *Department of State Bulletin*, June 26, 1954, p. 990.

[6] *TIME Magazine*, July 5, 1954.

[7] *London Times*, June 26, 1954.

[8] *Congressional Record*, June 29, 1954, p. 9206.

[9] *London Times*, June 26, 1954.

[10] Dulles, Senate Foreign Relations Committee, June 5, 1954, p. 11.

[11] Eisenhower, op. cit., p. 342.

[12] *London Times*, June 26, 1954.

[13] *Congressional Record*, June 29, 1954, p. 9205.

[14] *New York Times*, July 1, 1959.

[15] Dulles, Broadcast to the Nation, Sept. 15, 1954.

[16] Eisenhower, op. cit. p. 368.

[17] *London Times*, July 13, 1954.

[18] Eden, op. cit., p. 148.

[19] Eisenhower, op. cit., p. 368.
[20] Eden, op. cit., p. 150.
[21] *Congressional Record,* June 29, 1954 pp. 9204-9205.
[22] *London Times,* June 24, 1954 (cable Washington June 24).
[23] Sh. Adams, op. cit., p. 127.
[24] *London Times,* June 29, 1954.
[25] Ibid, July 15, 1954.
[26] Ibid, June 28, 1954.
[27] Ibid, July 2, 1954.
[28] Ibid, July 13, 1954.
[29] *New York Herald Tribune,* July 9, 10, 11, 1954.
[30] *London Times,* July 12, 1954.
[31] Eisenhower, op. cit., p. 369.
[32] Eden, op. cit., p. 160.

Chapter 10

[1] Eisenhower, op. cit., p. 573.
[2] *LIFE Magazine,* January 16, 1956, "How Dulles Averted War Three Times; New Disclosures Show He Brought U. S. Back From The Brink."
[3] R. Goold Adams, *The Time of Power,* Weidenfeld & Nicholson, 1962, p. 74; Drummond-Coblentz, *Duel at the Brink,* p. 113.
[4] *New York Times,* April 28, 1954.
[5] *Christian Science Monitor,* April 27, 1954.
[6] Sherman Adams, op. cit., p. 117.
[7] Eisenhower, op. cit., p. 342.
[8] Sherman Adams, op. cit., p. 118.
[9] *Department of State Bulletin,* July 30, 1954, p. 259.
[10] *Le Monde,* December 21, 1954.
[11] Lacouture-Devillers, op. cit., p. 367.
[12] *New York Herald Tribune,* April 9, 1964.
[13] Herbert Nicholas, *Britain and the U.S.A.,* John Hopkins Press, Baltimore, 1963, p. 99.

Chapter 11

[1] *Keesing's Contemporary Archives,* Vol. 9, p. 13662.
[2] Lacouture-Devillers, op. cit., p. 123; Speech of Mendès-France, l'Assemblée Nationale, December 21, 1954; Le Monde, December 22, 1954.
[3] *Documents on American Foreign Relations,* 1954, p. 313.
[4] *New York Times,* July 17, 1955; ibid, August 11, 1955.
[5] *Documents on American Foreign Relations,* 1954, p. 317.

6 Ibid, p. 313.
7 News Conference, August 30, 1955; *New York Times*, September 1, 1955.
8 C. L. Sulzberger, *New York Times*, July 17, 1955.
9 *Department of State Bulletin*, June 11, 1956, p. 974.
10 *New York Times*, March 9, 1956.
11 *London Times*, April 10, 1956; *New York Times*, April 11, 1956.
12 Lacouture-Devillers, op. cit., p. 320.
13 Eden, op. cit., pp. 159-160.
14 *Documents on American Foreign Relations*, 1954, pp. 283-318; Lacouture-Devillers op. cit. p. 276.
15 Ibid, p. 315.
16 Drummond-Coblenz, op. cit., p. 120.
17 *Documents on American Foreign Relations*, 1954, pp. 282-283.
18 Ibid, pp. 64-65.
19 Eisenhower, op. cit., pp. 338 and 372.
20 *Documents on American Foreign Relations*, 1954, p. 317.

Chapter 12

1 Report of Senator Theodore Francis Green to 84th Congress, 2nd Session, on a Study Mission, January 13, 1956, p. 14.
2 John D. Montgomery, *The Politics of Foreign Aid*, Praeger, New York, 1962, p. 44.
3 *Indochina Report of Senator Mike Mansfield on a Study Mission to the Associated States of Indochina, Vietnam, Cambodia and Laos*, October 27, 1953, 83rd Congress 1st Session, Senate Foreign Relations Committee; *Report on Indochina*, Senate Foreign Relations Committee, 1954.
4 Rapport, Commission de Finance, l'Assemblée Nationale, *Le Monde* December 19, 1954.
5 *Vietnam, Cambodia and Laos*, Report by Senator Mike Mansfield to Senate Foreign Relations Committee, 84th Congress, 1st Session, October 6, 1955.
6 *London Times*, April 28, 1954.
7 Ibid, April 30, 1954.
8 Eden, op. cit., p. 121.
9 *London Times*, May 18, 1954.
10 Ibid, July 17, 1954.
11 *Documents on American Foreign Relations*, 1954, p. 314.
12 Ibid, p. 316.
13 Lacouture-Devillers, op. cit., p. 294.

Chapter 13

1 Eden, op. cit., p. 103.
2 Ibid, p. 104.

[3] Norman D. Palmer, "Indian Attitudes Toward Colonialism" (in Strausz-Hupé and Hazard, *The Idea of Colonialism*, Praeger, New York, 1958, p. 295).

[4] Eden, op. cit., p. 107.

[5] *London Times*, June 24, 1954.

[6] Eden, op. cit., p. 128.

[7] *New York Times*, August 6, 1954.

[8] *London Times*, June 24, 1954.

[9] Eden, op. cit., p. 148.

[10] *London Times*, July 13, 1954.

[11] Eisenhower, op. cit., p. 368.

[12] *New York Herald Tribune*, July 1, 1954.

[13] *Documents on American Foreign Relations* 1954, pp. 319-323.

[14] *State Department Bulletin*, 1954, p. 432.

[15] *London Times*, November 9, 1954.

[16] Lacouture-Devillers, op. cit., p. 294.

[17] *London Times*, July 9, 1955.

[18] *London Times*, November 9, 1954.

[19] Quoted by Kenneth Younger, House of Commons, *London Times*, November 9, 1954.

[20] Sh. Adams, op. cit., p. 126; Speech of Dulles, *State Department Bulletin*, July 26, 1954, p. 121.

[20a] The Brookings Institution, *United States Foreign Policy, 1945-1955*, p. 313.

[21] *New York Times*, January 1, 1955; *London Times*, January 1, 1955.

[22] *London Times*, January 1, 1955.

[23] *New York Times*, April 24; August 14, 1964.

[24] Ibid., May 30, 1962.

[25] *Foreign Affairs*, January 1960, pp. 244-253.

[26] Sulzberger, *New York Times*, May 30, 1962.

Chapter 14

[1] *Documents on American Foreign Relations*, 1954, p. 312.

[2] Paul Ely, *l'Indochine dans la Tourmente*, Plon, Paris 1964.

[3] *Report to Senate Committee on Foreign Relations*, October 6, 1955, p. 1.

[4] Ibid, pp. 1-2.

[5] *Foreign Affairs*, January 1957, p. 285.

[6] Ely, op. cit., pp. 305-306.

[7] *Foreign Affairs*, January 1957, pp. 287-289.

[8] *France Presse*, August 31, 1954; Ely op. cit., pp. 238-243.

[9] Ely, op. cit., p. 260.

[10] *Department of State Bulletin*, October 4, 1954, p. 491 and October 11, p. 534.

[11] Ely, op. cit., p. 298.

[12] Ibid, pp. 303; 307-317; D. Wise and Th. B. Ross, *The Invisible Government*, Random House, New York, 1964, p. 157.

13 *New York Times*, May 8, 1955, p. 4.
14 *Department of State Bulletin*, March 14, 1955.
15 *New York Times*, May 8, 1955, p. 4.
16 *Report by Senator Mike Mansfield to Senate Committee on Foreign* Relations, October 1954, repeated and quoted in Report, October 6, 1955.
17 *New York Times*, May 8, 1955; ibid June 8, 1955 (Sulzberger); address of Walter S. Robertson, Assistant Secretary for Far-Eastern Affairs, *Department of State Bulletin*, July 11, 1955, p. 1002; D. Wise—Th. B. Ross, op. cit., pp. 157-158.
18 Ely, op. cit., p. 309.
19 *New York Times*, May 8, 1955.
20 Eisenhower, op. cit., p. 371.
21 *New York Times*, September 27, 1954.
22 Ibid, October 25, 1954.
23 Ibid, October 27, 1954.
24 *London Times*, December 14, 1954.
25 *New York Times*, December 21, 1954; *Le Monde*, December 19-20, 1954.
26 *Department of State Bulletin*, January 10, 1955, p. 51.
27 Bernard B. Fall, op. cit. p. 318-9.
28 Direct quotation by C. L. Sulzberger, *New York Times*, June 3, 1964.
29 Ely, op. cit. pp. 315-6.
30 *Department of State Bulletin*, June 11, 1956, pp. 972-74.
31 *Le Monde*, December 21, 1954.
32 *London Times*, March 3, 1955.
33 Ibid, April 30, 1955.
34 Ibid, May 13, 1955
35 *New York Times*, May 14, 1955.
36 Ibid, May 18, 1955.
37 Ibid, April 24, 1964.

Chapter 15

1 Eisenhower, op. cit., 352.
2 John Foster Dulles, *Department of State Bulletin*, June 21, 1954, p. 936.
3 *Department of State Bulletin*, November 3, 1953, p. 743, Speech of Dulles in Cleveland at Convention of C.I.O., November 18, 1953.
4 Eisenhower, op. cit., p. 373.
5 Ibid, p. 374.
6 Hans Kohn," Reflections on Colonialism," in Strausz-Hupé and Hazard, *The Idea of Colonialism*, op. cit., p. 3.
7 Julius W. Pratt, "Anticolonialism in United States Policy", Strausz-Hupé and Hazard, *The Idea of Colonialism*, World Publishing Co., New York, 1951. p. 130.
8 *United Nations Charter*, Chapter I, paragraph 2.
8a Julius W. Pratt, op. cit. pp. 114-151.
9 Ibid.

[9a] Hans J. Morgenthau, Politics Among Nations, p. 65.
[9b] Ibid., p. 65.
[10] Joseph Schumpeter, *Imperialism,* World Publishing Company, New York, 1951, pp. 6-7.
[11a] Eisenhower, op. cit., p. 374.
[11b] R. W. Van Alstyne, *The Rising American Empire,* Blackwell, Oxford, 1960, p. 9.
[12] Eisenhower op. cit., p. 364.
[13] Ibid, p. 352.
[14] Ibid, p. 374.
[15] Walter Lippmann, *New York Herald Tribune,* June 14, 1954.

Chapter 16

[1] Elliott Roosevelt, *As He Saw It,* Duell, Sloan & Pearce, New York, 1946, p. 115.
[2] Bernard B. Fall, op. cit. pp. 49-54.
[3] General Joseph W. Stilwell *Stilwell Papers,* (New York, Sloane, 1948) p. 246.
[4] B. Fall, op. cit. p. 458.
[5] *The Fortnightly,* April 1954, p. 77.
[6] Lacouture-Devillers, op. cit. p. 31.
[7] Eisenhower, op. cit. pp. 166-167.
[8] Senator Mike Mansfield, *Report on Vietnam and Southeast Asia,* 1963, p. 2.
[9] Eisenhower, op. cit., p. 169.
[10] Ibid, p. 336.
[11] Ibid, p. 336.
[12] Ibid, p. 336.
[13] Ibid, pp. 340, 341, 351, 352, 353 and 363.
[14] *Department of State Bulletin,* June 28, 1954, p. 972.
[15] Eisenhower, op. cit. p. 362.
[16] Eisenhower, op. cit. p. 374.
[17] *London Times,* June 4, 1954.
[18] Sherman Adams, op. cit., p. 247.
[19] Eisenhower, op. cit., p. 336.
[20] Ibid, p. 170.
[21] Text quoted: Laniel, op. cit. pp. 11-12.
[22] Eisenhower, op. cit., p. 169.
[23] Ibid. p. 337.
[24] Ibid. p. 347.
[25] *Le Monde,* April 29 and June 5, 1954.
[26] R. Rovere, op. cit. pp. 192-193.
[27] Eisenhower, op. cit., p. 345.
[28] Ibid, p. 341.
[29] Ibid, p. 346.

30 Sherman Adams, op. cit. p. 123.
30a *New Republic*, April 12, 1954.
30b *New York Times*, March 9, 1955.
31 Ch. Roberts, *Washington Post*, June 7, 1954 and Eisenhower, op cit. p. 343.
32 Robert E. Osgood, *Limited War*, University of Chicago Press, 1957, p. 220; Shepley, op. cit., p. 70ff; R. Donovan, *Eisenhower, The Inside Story*, Harper, New York, 1956, p. 266; Chalmer Roberts, *Washington Post*, June 7, 1954; also *Reporter*, September 15, 1954, pp. 31-35; Marquis Childs, *The Ragged Edge*, Doubleday, 1955, p. 134; M. B. Ridgeway, *Memoirs*, Harper, New York, 1956, pp. 376-7.
33 Eisenhower, op. cit. p. 345.
34 Sherman Adams, op. cit., p. 123.
34a Hans J. Morgenthau, op. cit., p. 146.
35 Hans Nawiasky, *Staatslehre 1955*, Teil II, Band 2 Bonziger, Zurich, 1955, pp. 133-134; Carl J. Friedrich, *Constitutional Government and Democracy*, Little, Brown, Boston, 1941, pp. 397-399.
36 Eisenhower, op. cit. p. 341.
37 Ibid, p. 374.
38 *New York Times*, June 3, 1964; R. E. Osgood, op. cit. p. 228.
39 Dulles, quoted by Eisenhower, op. cit. p. 245.

Chapter 17

1 *Department of State Bulletin*, January 1954, I. p. 144.
2a *New York Times* Nov. 8, 1953.
2b Ibid, p. 12.
3 *Vital Speeches*, April 15, 1954, p. 388.
4 Eisenhower, op. cit. p. 357.
5 Ibid, p. 349.
6 Nguyen N. Bich, "Vietnam," *The China Quarterly*, Jan.-Mar. 1952, p. 105.
7 Ibid, p. 25.
8 Editorial, ibid, p. 1.
9 Hansard, Vol. 446, p. 562-563. Morgenthau op. cit. p. 570.

Bibliography

Books, Periodicals, Newspapers, Publications of Governments Used As Direct Sources of Information

ADAMS, Sherman, *First Hand Report*, Harper, New York, 1961.

BICH, Nguyen N., *Vietnam*, The China Quarterly, Jan.-March., 1952.

CHILDS, Marquis, *The Ragged Edge*, Doubleday, New York, 1955.

CLARK, William, *Less Than Kin*, Hamish-Hamilton, London, 1957.

Documents on American Foreign Relations, 1954, Harper, New York, 1955.

DONOVAN, Robert, *Eisenhower, The Inside Story*, Harper, New York, 1956.

DRUMMOND-COBLENTZ, (Roscoe Drummond and Gaston Coblentz), *Duel At The Brink*, Doubleday, New York, 1960.

EDEN, Anthony, *Full Circle*, Houghton Mifflin, Boston, 1960.

EISENHOWER, Dwight D., *The White House Years: Mandate For Change, 1953-1956*, Doubleday, New York, 1963.

ELY, Paul Général, *L'Indochine Dans La Tourmente*, Plon, Paris, 1964.

EPSTEIN, Leon D., *British Politics In The Suez Crisis*, University of Illinois.

FALL, Bernard B., *The Two Vietnams*, Praeger, New York, 1963.

FIFIELD, Russell H., *Southeast Asia In United States Policy*, Praeger, New York, 1963

FRIEDRICH, Carl J., *Constitutional Government and Democracy*, Little Brown, Boston, 1941.

GOOLD-ADAMS, Richard, *The Time of Power*, Weidenfeld-Nicolson, London, 1962.

KOHN, Hans, *Reflection On Colonialism*, Strauss-Hupé and Hazard, *The Idea of Colonialism*, Praeger, New York, 1958.

KNORR, Klaus, "Theories On Imperialism," *World Politics*, Vol. 4, 1952.

LACOUTURE-DEVILLERS, (Jean Lacouture, Philippe Devillers), *La Fin D'une Guerre—Indochine, 1954*, Seuil, Paris, 1960.

LANIEL, Joseph, *Le Drame Indochinois*, Plon, Paris, 1957.

LEFEVER, Ernest, *Ethics and United States Foreign Policy*, Meridian Books, New York, 1957.

LIPPMANN, Walter, *Isolation and Alliances*, Little-Brown, Boston, 1952.

MORGENTHAU, Hans J., *Politics Among Nations*, Knopf, New York, 1962.

MONTGOMERY, John D., *The Politics of Foreign Aid*, Praeger, New York, 1962.

MURPHY, Robert, *Diplomat Among Warriors*, Doubleday, New York, 1964.

NAVARRE, Henri, *Agonie De L'Indochine*, Plon, Paris, 1956.

NAWIASKY, Hans, *Staatslehre, Bonzieger*, Zurich, 1955.

NICHOLAS, Herbert, *Britain and the U.S.A.*, Johns Hopkins Press, 1963.

NICOLSON, Harold, *The Congress of Vienna*, Constable, London, 1946.

OSGOOD, Robert E., *Limited War*, Univ. of Chicago Press, 1957.

ROVERE, Richard H., *The Eisenhower Years*, Farrar, Straus & Cudahy, New York, 1956.

SCHUMPETER, Joseph, *Imperialism*, World Publishing Co., New York, 1951.

STRAUSS-HUPE and HAZARD, *The Idea of Colonialism*, Praeger, New York, 1958.

PALMER, Norman D., *Indian Attitudes Toward Colonialism* (*Strauss-Hupé and Hazard, The Idea of Colonialism*), Prager, New York, 1958.

PRATT, Julius W., *Anticolonialism In United States Policy* (*Strauss-Hupé and Hazard, The Idea of Colonialism*), Prager, New York, 1958.

RIDGEWAY, General M. B., *Memoirs*, Harper, New York, 1958.

REITEL, KAPLAN, COBLENTZ, *United States Foreign Policy 1945-1955*, The Brookings Institution.

ROOSEVELT, Elliot, *As He Saw It*, Duell, Sloan & Pearce, New York, 1946.

SCIGLIANO, Robert, *South Vietnam*, Houghton Mifflin, Boston, 1963.

SHAW, Bernard, *John Bull's Other Island, Selected Plays*, Dodd, Mead, New York.

STILLWELL, General Joseph W., *Stillwell Papers*, Sloane, New York, 1948.

VAN ALSTYNE, R. W., *The Rising American Empire*, Blackwell, Oxford, England, 1960.

WISE AND ROSS, *The Invisible Government*, Random House, New York, 1964.

Christian Science Monitor

Congressional Records

Débats Parlementaires de l'Assemblée Nationale (Paris, France)

Department of State Bulletin

Foreign Affairs

Keesing's Contemporary Archives

Le Monde

LIFE Magazine

London Times

New York Herald Tribune

New Leader

Time Magazine

The China Quarterly

Vital Speeches

Washington Post

Index of Names

Acheson, Dean, 3
Adams, Sherman. See *Subject Index*
Alsop, Stewart and Joseph, 72
Armstrong, Hamilton Fish, 168

Bao Dai. See *Subject Index*
Bich, Nguyen N., 227
Bidault, George. See *Subject Index*
Binh Xuyen, 151, 174-175

Casey, Richard G., 81, 83-84
Castries, *Colonel de,* 28
Chauvel, 163
Chen Yun, 129
Chiang Kai-shek, 60
Chou En-lai, 19
Churchill, Sir Winston. See *Subject Index*
Collins, I. L. See *Subject Index*
Coty, 90

Diem Ngo Dinh. See *Subject Index*
Dulles, Allen, 31
Dulles, John Foster. See *Subject Index*

Eden, Anthony. See *Subject Index*
Eisenhower, Dwight David. See *Subject Index*
Ely, Paul. See *Subejct Index*

Fall, Bernard B., *foreword*
Faure, Edgar, 180

Gazounod, *General,* 174, 185
George, Walter F., 181
Graves, Hubert, 184
Green, Theodore, 100
Gromyko, 138
Gruenther, Alfred M., 67

Heath, Donald, 179
Henderson, William, 174-175, 180
Higgins, Marguerite, 98
Ho Chi Minh. See *Subject Index*
Hoover (under-secretary of state), 99
Hull, Cordell, 7

Knowland, William, 98

Lacouture, Jean, *foreword*
Landsdale, E., 181
Laniel, Joseph. See *Subject Index*
Lawrence, David, 98
Lippmann, Walter, 7, 98, 130
Lloyd, Selwyn, 78

MacArthur, Douglas, II, 37
McConaughy, Walter S., 18
McCormack, *Representative,* 114-115
Mansfield, Mike. See *Subject Index*
Mao Tse Tung. See *Subject Index*
Mendès-France, Pierre. See *Subject Index*
Menzies, Robert G., 83, 127
Morgenthau, Hans J., *foreword*
Morrison, Herbert, 65

Navarre, Henri. See *Subject Index*
Nehru, 165-166
Nicholson, Harold, 105
Nixon, Richard. See *Subject Index*

O'Daniel, John W., 174, 185-186

Pinneau, 140
Pleven. See *Subject Index*

Radford, *Admiral.* See *Subject Index*
Rayburn, Sam, 100

Reston, James, 37-38
Reynaud, Paul, 18
Rhee, Syngman, 124
Richard, James P., 184
Ridgway, Mathew, 31
Roberts, Chalmers M., 40
Robertson, Walter. See *Subject Index*
Roosevelt, Franklin D. See *Subject Index*

Sainteny, Jean, 176-177
Salan, *General*, 179
Schuman, Maurice, 90
Servan-Schreiber, J. J., 89
Shaw, Bernard, 8
Smith, Bedell. See *Subject Index*
Sulzberger, Cyrus, 168, 220

Talleyrand, 130
Tran Van Do, 143
Truman, Harry S. See *Subject Index*
Turton, 162-163

Ucalegon, 36

Vu Nguyen Giap. See *Subject Index*

Webb, Clifton, 81, 83
Wilson, Charles, 29, 210
Wilson, Woodrow, 6

Younger, Kenneth, 164-165

Index of Subjects

(For names of persons mentioned only once or twice see
INDEX OF NAMES)

Adams, Sherman
  Doubts of military action, 128
  On Dulles' consultations with Congressional leaders, 217
  On Dulles' contention concerning Korean armistice, 127
  On Dulles-Nixon disagreement, 42
  On U. S. opposition to "colonialism", 210
  On U. S. use of ground forces, 214-215
American-British relations. See U. S. Foreign relations
Anti-Colonialism. See Colonialism
Armed Forces. See U. S. Armed Forces
Associated States
  Admission to SEATO as "protected" not "participating" areas, 163
  British-French objection to inclusion in SEATO, 163
  Chinese objection to inclusion in SEATO, 163
  Declaration of independence by France, 26
Atlantic Community. See North Atlantic Treaty Organization
Australia
  Attitude toward emerging democracies in Asia, 159
  Failure of attempt by Dulles to achieve coalition, without Britain, 83-84
  Position on French resistance in Indochina, 13
  Refusal to join U. S. military action, 127
Australia-New Zealand-United States Mutual Security Treaty, (ANZUS), 4, 81-84

Plan for immediate collective defense of Southeast Asia, 161
Austria
  Treaty of peace, Berlin Conference on, 15

Balance of Power
  Hull's views, 7
Bao Dai
  As impartial head of state, 179
  Ho Chi Minh, relations with, 137
  Partition, position on, 136, 145
Berlin Conference, 15-17
  Dulles' consent to allow Indochina on agenda of Geneva Conference, 18
Bermuda Conference, 6
Bidault, George
  Ambiguous position on Indochina crisis, 91-92
  As foreign minister during Indochina crisis, 24, 213
  French recognition of Vietnam's independence, 213
  Indochina on agenda of Geneva Conference, 127
  On "final political status," 137
  On French settlement of Indochina crisis, 17
  Promise of French victory at Dien Bien Phu, 36
Brinkmanship, 58
  Churchill's views, 128
  Dulles' theory of efficacy, denied, 125-129
British American Relations. See U.S. Foreign Relations

Cambodia. See also Associates States
  Independence secured at Geneva Conference, 123

Independent country with anti-Communist government, 171
Withdrawal of Communists, 95

China (Communist) See also Geneva Conference; Indochina; Vietnam
Dulles' statement on admission to Geneva Conference, 19
Molotov's proposal for five-power conference to include, 16
Recognition by Ho Chi Minh, 10

China (Nationalist)
Possible use of forces in Indochina, 60

Christian Science Monitor
On British policy in Indochina, 72
On Dulles' contention regarding Korean armistice, 127

Churchill, Sir Winston
And the Suez crisis, 113
"Brink" myth, 128
Concessions to Dulles on SEATO, 161
Determination to step into Dulles-Eden dispute, 111
In prasie of Eden, 120
Influence in averting U.S.-British conflict over Vietnam, 2
On international guarantees, 153
On participation in SEATO of India, Ceylon, Pakistan and Burma, 120, 127
On publicizing SEATO before Geneva Conference, 116
On "united action" in Southeast Asia, 116
Opposition to Eden on SEATO, 114
Report to House of Commons on reconciliation visit, 118-119
Support of Eden's policies, 120

Churchill-Eden Reconciliation Visit to Washington, 113-119
Achievement of purpose, 119
Agreement on acceleration of SEATO, 117
Agreement on immediate "study" of Southeast Asia Defense Pact, 160-161
Agreement to partition of Vietnam, 117
Eisenhower's hopes, 113
Joint U.S.-British declaration on independence of Asian nations, 144
Purpose of visit, 119
U.S. press reactions to motivation, 115-116

Coalition. See also United Action
As endowing U.S. policy with moral force, 203
As necessary to prove non-imperialistic aims, 201-202
Attempt by Dulles to achieve substitute plan by participation of Australia and New Zealand, 81-84
Debacle at Dien Bien Phu gives new opportunity to Dulles, 67
Declaration for united action against China in self-defense, proposed by Dulles, 53
Dulles' attempt to obtain British consent through France, 70 ff
Dulles' objection to India, 60
Dulles' plan, preceding Geneva Conference, 157
Dulles' policy of Southeast Asia coalition to defeat Communism, 44 ff
Eisenhower's plea to Churchill, 51-52
Eisenhower's proposal for member countries, 52
Failure of U.S. to follow up "united action" policy after Geneva, 192
Formal proposal to Britain and France by State Dept., 52
"Moral meaning" attaching to intervention by means of, 220
Staff talks in Britain used by U.S. to organize action towards, 77
Substitute plan excluding Britain, and failure, 81-84

Coexistence
U.S. resistance to, 224

Cold War
Stalinist imperialism as origin of, 2

Collins, I. L.
Confidence in General Ely, 175, 179, 180
On Dulles' unconditional support of Diem, 181-182

Colonialism
American Revolution as "separation" not "revolution", 194
Anti-colonialism as a policy, 195-196
"Anti-colonialism" as false pretense, 220-221
Anti-colonialism, origin of principle in U.S. policies, 197
Attitude towards as endowing U.S. with "moral position", 193, 198, 201, 210-211
British settlers in new world not "colonies", 193
Defined, 195 ff
Denmark-Norway relationship as comparable to U.S.-British "colonial" ties, 195
Difference between British settlers in U.S. and native inhabitants of colonial countries, 193
Erroneous use of "colonies" in connection with British settlers in new world, 193
Excessive emphasis by Eisenhower on U.S. "anti-colonialism", 210-212
Fear of identification with motive for non-intervention in Indochina, 212
Fear of U.S. identification with as prompting policy in South Vietnam, 201
Myth of American anti-colonialism, 211
U.S. declared attitude towards, 197-198
U.S. fear of accusation as motive for non-intervention in Indochina, 212
U.S. mistaken opinion of French colonial policies in Indochina, 205
U.S. policy as not anti-colonial, 196-197
U.S. tradition concerning, 192-193, 198

Colonies. See Colonialism

Communism
Eisenhower-Dulles change in U.S. attitude toward, *foreword*
Eisenhower-Dulles on, 7

Concert of Powers. See also Coalition; United Action
As an indication of non-imperialistic aims, 201-202
Conference of Ambassadors, Washington, 62-63
Eden's statement on, 108
Conflict of Interest
Leadership responsibility of public officials, 218-219
Possibility of conflict concept, 219
Containment
U.S. policy prior to and after Geneva, 223-228

Declaration by United Nations on National Self-Government, 197
Denmark
Relationship to Norway and Sweden, 195
Diem, Ngo Dinh
Actual power in relation to the French, 174-176
As leader, 180
As potential war time leader, 180
As President, contempt of by Army and Sect leaders, 174
Danger from the North, 150
Elections, position on, 138
Evaluation of government of, 150, 152, 174, 179
Lack of popular support, 180
Opposition to Binh Xuyen, 175
Statesmanship, making Vietnam a pro-American power, 175
Successful state of affairs in South Vietnam, 141

Dien Bien Phy
Circumstances of ominous nature of situation, 27
Last-minute talks on British and American intervention, 68-69
Navarre's change of plans, 27
Navarre's opinion of Geneva Conference, 21
Radford's plan for single bombardment rejected by congressional leaders, 49
U.S. awareness of worsening situation, 28
U.S.-French negotiations following defeat of Dulles' "coalition plan" in London, 70

257

Diplomacy
  As only means for settlement of
    conflict in South Vietnam, 227-
    228
  U.S. resistance to, 225 ff
Domino theory, 55, 59, 102, 122
Dulles, John F.
  Admission of failure on "momen-
    tous decisions", 127
  Admission of failure to gain sup-
    port for coalition, 92
  Admission of strong dependence
    on France, 187
  Anti-Communist pact, 165-166
  Appointment as Secretary of State,
    foreword
  Attempt to achieve coalition
    through participation of Aus-
    tralia and New Zealand, 81-84
  Attempt to explain away defeat
    of united action plan prior to
    Geneva Conference, 62-64
  Attempt to convene nine ambas-
    sadors for collective defense of
    Southeast Asia prior to Geneva
    Conference, 62-63
  Attempt to persuade Eden on im-
    mediate British-American action
    in Indochina, at Geneva Con-
    ference, 73
  Awareness of Military situation in
    Vietnam, 149
  Bold policy, personal creed and
    Republican Party electoral plat-
    form, 223
  Brink diplomacy, 58, 125-129
  Coalition policy, 45-46
    See also Coalition; Southeast
    Asia
  Containment policy, 223-228
  Dependence on Diem, 181
  Development of theme of "colon-
    ialism" against Britain and
    France, 99
  Eden's disagreement regarding
    Southeast Asia defense or-
    ganization, 61 ff
  Effect of defeat of united action
    plan on, 64-65
  Effect on Suez crisis of antagon-
    ism to Eden, 131
  Elections, position on, 140

Faure, Conference with, 182
Freedom in Asia, position on,
  foreword
"Gates" to U.S. sole defense of
  South Vietnam, 154, 169ff, 190
Geneva Conference policy, 93,
  121, 127, 142-143, 217
"Hoisting the flag," 221
Influence in excluding Britain
  from ANZUS treaty, 4
Insistence on immediate united
  British-American action, 73
Interpretation of Churchill-Eden
  reconciliation mission to U.S. as
  action to begin Southeast Asian
  alliance, 75, 77, 110, 117
Lack of interest in French aims
  in Indochina, 34
Meeting with Eden and Mendès-
  France in Paris, 122
Mission to Europe to force de-
  cision against Indochina prior
  to Geneva Conference, 59 ff
Mutual Security Act of 1954, re-
  quest for approval, House hear-
  ing, 53 ff
Negotiations with France follow-
  ing defeat of coalition plan in
  London, 69 ff
Nehru, attitude toward, 128
Nightmarish attitude toward Com-
  munist China, 102-103
Obsessive and shortsighted view
  of Communism, 59
On "agonizing reappraisal" of U.
  S.-French relationship, 3, 5
On twenty years of relationship
  with Soviet Union, 225
On "U.S. principles", 144
On use of U.S. ground forces, 215
Opposition to British participation
  and presence in Vietnam, 190
Opposition to Communism as ob-
  literating all other considera-
  tions in Indochina, 43-45
Personal relations with Eden, 65,
  67, 107
  influence on Suez decision, 65,
  131
Preoccupation with Southeast
  Asia pact and neglect of French
  position in Indochina, 35

258

Refusal to grant French request for American aerial action in Dien Bien Phu, 37

Refusal to sign any guarantee with Chou En-lai, 110-111

Resistance to peaceful settlement of Vietnam situation, motivation, 43

Return to Paris upon insistence of Britain and France, 121

SEATO, determination and victory, 115, 117, 155-159, 161-162, 166, 220

Speech at North Atlantic Council, Dec. 1953, 3

Speech to Republican Women's Centennial Conference, 55

Speech to World Affairs Council on United defense of Southeast Asia, 66

Statement on admission of Red China to Geneva Conference, 19

Substitute plans for circumventing Britain's opposition to U. S. "united action" project, 81-86

Testimony before Foreign Relations Committee, 115-116

"United action" theme on U. S. intervention in Indochina, 38-41, 46 ff

Unwillingness to recognize political and military situation in Dien Bien Phu, 35-36

Vietnam army to be trained by U.S., 184-185

Eden, Anthony, *foreword*

American reactions to. See U. S. reactions, *below*

Attempt to re-establish partnership with U. S. in Indochina, 184

Attitude toward Molotov's proposal for 5-power conference, 16

Closing statement at Geneva Conference, 122

Conversations with Molotov and Chou En-lai, 121

Diplomacy and determination to reach solution at Geneva Conference, 105

Discussion with Dulles concerning Indochina Conference, 118

Explanation to Kenneth Younger on reciprocal guaranty, 164

Final declaration at Geneva, attempt to obtain signatures of U.S. and China, 142

Harmonious relationship with Bedell Smith, 107

House of Commons debate on SEATO, 163-164

"Municheer", designation as, 136

On absence of normal diplomatic relations between a number of countries, 136

On Acheson's attitude toward British-U.S. relationship, 3

On American repudiation, 146

On French resistance in Indochina, 14

On Locarno-type system of guarantees, 118

Opposition to "momentous decision", 127

Opposition to "united action" plan pronounced by Dulles, 48, 61-63, 69, 160

Personal relations with Dulles, 65, 67, 107, 142

Plan of settlement, interpretation in Washington, 115

Position on SEATO, 61, 69, 115, 157-160

Reaction to French-American secret talks on military intervention, 86

Success in making Indochina subject to diplomatic negotiations, 20

U.S. leaders' reaction to, 99

U.S. press reactions to, 94, 114

U.S. share in political downfall, 65

Eisenhower, Dwight D.

Agreement with Radford-Ely plan, 46

Anti-colonialism as policy line, 220-221

Anti-Communism as objective, 59, 102-103, 124, 130, 207

Assurance of Diem of unconditional support, 183

Attempt to win France to united action plan, 90
Defense of Indochina as basis of Southeast Asia policy, 208-209
Denial of proposal to intervene in Indochina with air attack, 69-70
Distrust of Communist agreements, 102
Domestic political considerations, 155, 214-219
Election, *foreword*
"Fundamental concept" about Presidency, 216-217
Inability to acquiesce to British-French policy of settlement of Indochina dispute as hampering Dulles at Geneva, 95-96
Interpretation of British staff talks as change in British policy regarding coalition, 77
Joint declaration with Churchill, 144-145
Lack of awareness of European strength, 59
Lack of awareness of post-war changes, 59
"legal, moral and practical" basis for intervention, 220
Message to Bao Dai, 181
No overall agreement with British, 116
Obsessive and shortsighted view of Communism, 59, 102-103
On Churchill-Eden reconciliation visit to Washington, 113-114
On "coalition", 51-52, 220
On coalition wtih Australia and New Zealand without Britain, 82
On Communist victory on Chinese mainland, 207
On disagreements among allies, 113
On elimination of French influence, 182
On French Expeditionary Forces in Indochina, 211
On full help to France, May, 1953, 207
On "momentous decision", 127
On occupation of Dien Bien Phu, 28

On opportunity for victory, 224
On U.S.-British alliance, 5-6, 113-114
On U.S. ground forces in Indochina, 215
On U.S. intervention in Indochina, 29
On U.S. "moral position", 209, 210, 219-220
Plea to Churchill for coalition in Indochina, 51-52
Preparation of public opinion for war in Indochina, 55
Reaction to French and British refusal to join "united action" plan, 56-57
Reaction to Geneva settlement proposals, 102
Reasons for failure to act in Indochina, 209 ff
Reassurance on Geneva Conference, 116
Resistance to Geneva, vindicated, 124
Response to Nixon's statement regarding American involvement in Indochina, 42
Settlement by bogus united military action, 128
SEATO, hopes for, 115, 166-167, 220

Ely, Paul, *foreword*
Agreement with Washington on policy, 179
As decision-maker, 175
Attempt to prevent Diem from abandoning task of political stability, 180
Author of French post-Geneva policy, 173
Casualties' report, 149
Conference with Dulles and Hubert Graves, 184
Counteracting resistance to policy implementation, 179
Effort to gain Dulles' approval for French policy line, 181
Implementation of policy of French withdrawal, 178
Interview with France-Press on French policy toward Vietnam, 177-178
Mission to Washington, 30-36

Norodom Palace, termination of occupancy, 178-179
On inclusion of local intelligentsia into power structure of South Vietnam, 179
Opposition to appointment of Sainteny, 176
Policies as offensive to vested interests, 178
Restraint of anti-Diem activities of officer-corps, 175
Resignation, 189
Support of American envoys, 179
Support secured for full aid to South Vietnam, 176-177

European Defense Community
Bermuda Conference on, 4
French opposition to, 129

Foreign Aid Bill
Amendment withholding aid to Communist-guaranteed Asia, 118-119
"Fourteen Points" of Wilson
Self-determination, not "anti-colonialism", 197

France
Agreement to Dulles' demand that U.S. take over strategic command in Indochina, 70
Attempt by U.S. to gain agreement on coalition despite Gt. Brit., 84-90
Decision to continue plans for negotiated settlement of Indochina crisis at Geneva, contrary to U.S. proposal, 56
Establishment of command with decision-making authority in Indochina, 172-173
Military and political weakness in Indochina crisis, 12
Position on internationalization of Indochina, 88
Position on single-handed responsibility in Indochina, 14-15
Post-war intention of granting independence to Associated States, 212
Reaction to Nguyen Giap's extension of guerrilla operations, 11
Reaction to U.S. promise to intervene in Indochina, 36

Reaction to U.S. refusal to implement Radford-Ely plan, 56
Strategy in Indochina crisis, 24
U.S. mistaken opinion of French colonial policies in Indochina, 205
France-Presse
Interview with Gen. Ely on French policy in Vietnam, 177-178

"Gates" to U.S. sole responsibility in South Vietnam, 154, 169, 190
Geneva Conference. See also Dulles, John F., Eden, Anthony, Eisenhower, Dwight D., France, Indochina, U.S. Foreign Policy
Absence of Dulles and Smith as strengthening China's position, 121
Agreement on withdrawal of Communists from Laos and Cambodia, 95
Agreement, summary of, 142-143
Agreement to end Indochina war, by Britain, France, Russia and China, 102
Agreements as gain of time for Free World, 125
Agreements as not causing subsequent events, 125
Agreement remaining unsigned, 133
Antecedents, 15-16
Documents not signed, 133
Dulles-Eden antagonism, 131. See also Dulles, John F.; Eden, Anthony
Dulles' mission to Europe to persuade action on Indochina prior to, 59-61
Dulles' non-recognition of Chinese prime minister, 93
Dulles' obstructionist tactics, 93-96, 114, 120-121. See also Dulles, John F.
Eden's diplomacy to achieve solution, 105-107. See also Eden, Anthony
Eden's tentative plan for cease-fire talks, American "reservation", 94
End of first phase, agreement on military staff talks, 95
"Final Declaration", 134, 142-143

261

as temporary arrangement, 134

documents, agreements, declarations, 142-143

obligations among participants omitted, 134, 141-143

pretense of non-political nature of, 134

repudiation by U.S. and South Vietnam, 134, 138-143

U.S. as "participant" not "signer," 141-142

U.S. unilateral declaration, domestic political overtones, 143-148

Guarantees by all governments except U.S., to preserve Indochina, 153-154

Independence of Laos and Cambodia, 123

Korean phase versus Indochinese phase in U.S. attitude toward, 16, 142

Listing of decisions, 123

Long-run results, generally, 123-124

Military agreements as beginning for political action, 135

Negative American policy at, 93-96. See also Dulles, John F.

Non-participation tactics of U.S., 120-121

Non-signed treaty, 146

Peaceful coexistence—tacit consent of negotiators, 146

Political arrangements disguised but unavoidable, 135

Restricted sessions to achieve progress found necessary, 93

Settlements arrived at, 123. See also Agreements, above; Final declaration, above

Successful negotiations seen as demonstrating error of U.S. policies, 121

U.S. assertion of influence in success of, 125

U.S. efforts to thwart settlement with China on Indochina, 17

U.S. "impatience" noted, 93-94

U.S. passive resistance to, 120-121 See also Dulles, John F.

U.S. refusal to sign any declaration, 95

U.S. stake in Korean setttlement at, 16

U.S. unilateral declaration as "first gate" to U.S. sole defense of South Vietnam, 154

U.S. unilateral declaration, domestic political overtones, 143-148

Germany

Unification, Berlin Conference, 15

Great Britain

Censure of U.S.-France negotiations, 101

Commitment to guarantee settlement after Geneva Conference, 69

Defense of British position on U. S. insistence on Southeast Asia Defense Past, 100-101

Determination to settle Indochina crisis, 59

Change in determination denied, 78

Eden's decision to study plan for military action in Southeast Asia, 118

Eden's recommendation not to participate in military intervention in Indochina, approval by Cabinet, 69

Modification of position on defense of Southeast Asia, 66

Mollifying proposal for secret bilateral talks in defense of Southeast Asia, used and misinterpreted by Eisenhower, 75

Reactions to American-French negotiations regarding intervention in Indochina, 101

Reaction to Dulles' attempt at coalition with Australia and New Zealand without Britain, 83

Reaction to U.S. proposal for united action in Indochina, 56

Recognition of need for support from Southeast Asia Commonwealth countries, 105

Staff talks to study military situation in Indochina as impetus to U.S. interpretation of British change of policy, 77

Ground troops. See U.S. Armed forces

Guerrilla war in Vietnam, 124, 141

Hanoi, 176

Hemispheric defense, 5

Herald-Tribune
  Account of French-American negotiations on intervention in Indochina, 87
  News report on "concessions" by British, 76
  Statement on modification of U.S. plan for immediate Southeast Asia Defense Pact, 79

Ho Chi Minh
  Achievement of leadership of North Vietnam by Geneva Conference, 123
  Acquisition of Hanoi area by Geneva agreement, 176
  Ambitions beyond Chinese wishes, 129
  Amenability to stabilization of external conditions, 226-227
  Bao Dai, relations with, 137
  Eden's recognition of strength, 105
  "Elder statesman," not necessarily puppet, 227
  Elections, position on, 138-139, 141
  Favored by U.S. policy, 206
  Hypothetical activities, 124
  Maneuvering between China and Russia, 227
  Partition, position on, 145
  Political history, 23
  Political situation in 1954, 152
  Reaction to U.S. inclusion of Associated States in SEATO, 163
  Recognition of rule of North Vietnam, 123
  Renewed fight to conquer South Vietnam despite Geneva agreement, 124
  U.S. policy favoring, 206

Hoa Hao Sect
  Control of rural areas, 150-151

Imperialism
  And "morality", 203
  Characteristics, 199
  Defensive imperialism of U.S., 200-201
  Definitions and delimitations, 198
  U.S. declared attitude toward, 192

U.S. policies as imperialistic, 200-201

India
  Attitude toward Ho Chi Minh's campaign in Indochina, 60
  Dulles' objection to inclusion in Geneva Conference, 60
  Eden's insistence on inclusion in Southeast Asia Defense Pact, 159
  Elimination from SEATO, British reaction, 164
  Influence on China, Dulles' theory, 125-127
  Uncertainty as to anti-Communist policy of, 158

Indochina
  Aims of Nguyen Giap, 10
  Australia, position on French resistance in, 13
  Break-down of French-American negotiations, 90-92
  Cease-fire, July 21, 1954, 172
  Churchill's statement on British policy in, 71-72
  Dulles' mission to Europe to force decision on, prior to Geneva Conference, 59 ff
  Dulles' position on "offensive" military power, *foreword*
  Dulles' theory on influence, of "brinkmanship" at Geneva, denied, 125-129
  Eden's proposal to include on agenda of Geneva Conference, 16
  Effect of Dulles' rejection of Radford-Ely plan on U.S. policy in, 50
  Eisenhower's hesitancy in sending ground troops to, 215
  Ely's position as military and political authority, post-Geneva, 173
  Four-power agreement to end fighting, 102
  French attitude towards single-handed responsibility in, 14-15
  French-British position on settlement of crisis in, 90
  French determination to limit action in, 30, 34
  French losses in, 14-15
  French occupation of, 9

French occupation of, after Geneva, 173-175

French public opinion on U. S. position, 14

French reaction to Nguyen Giap's offensive, 11

French realization of imminent defeat and request for massive American support, 30-31

French strategy by Laniel Government, 24 ff

Geographical designation, 9

Guarantees to assure future of, U.S. refusal to join, 153-154

Guerrilla war in, 9-10

Ho Chi Minh's ambitions more than China cared for, 129. See also Ho Chi Minh

Intervention precedents in history, 134-135

Japanese occupation, 9

Military arrangements as wedge for political action, 135

Military intervention by U.S. seen as psychological warfare, 125, 128-129

Motivations for U.S. change toward France, 208

Motivations for U.S. ousting of France, 201

Navarre's change of French strategy, 27. See also Navarre, Henri

Partition plan by Britain, rejected by U.S., 48 ff

Peace at any price as Mendès-France aim, 127

Possibility of American aerial intervention discussed by Ely, 32-34

Post-war decision to joint occupancy of, by U.S. and Britain excluding France, 206

Request for U.S. aid should China support Dien Bien Phu, 30

Settlement as reminiscent of earlier truce adjustments, 134

U.S. attitude on negotiated peace in, 16

U.S. policies on, conflicts and contradictions, 103

U.S. delay in assistance to France, 206-207

U.S. determination to keep France

fighting and eventually control military strategy through intervention, 84-90

U.S. domestic political situation, effect on intervention plans, 104

U.S. failure to follow up intervention threats and promises, reasons given, 209 ff

U.S. influence on France, termination of, 91

U.S. intervention as "crusade" against Communist take-over, 208

U.S. intervention promised should China appear over Dien Bien Phu, 30

U.S. military and financial aid, 25-26

U.S. official position on French resistance, 14

U.S. policy in, leading toward Vietnam involvement, *foreword*

U.S. proposal to France to agree to coalition in exchange for military intervention, 84 ff

U.S. proposal unacceptable to France, 88

U.S. reaction to Indochina crisis, 1952, 13

U.S. refusal to join guarantees to assure future of, 153-154

U.S. take-over of strategic command in Indochina as price for help in Dien Bien Phu, 70

Internationalization, 88, 120

Intervention. See also Dulles, John F., Eden, Anthony; Geneva Conference; Indochina; U.S. Foreign policy

Congressional approval required for military intervention, 217

Historical points of comparison with Indochina, 134-136

Military agreements as opening wedge for political action to follow, 135

Johnson, Lyndon B.
Attack on U.S. Indochina policy, 100

Kennedy-Johnson administration, position on SEATO, 167

Korea
  American intervention in as essentially "imperialistic", 201
  Violation of armistice by China, influence on U.S. foreign policy, 225

Laniel, Joseph, *foreword*
  Ascension to power by Indochina crisis, 24
  Obligation to end Indochina war, 18
  On internationalization of Indochina, 88
Laos. See also Associated States
  Coalition form of government, 171-172
  Defense by French government, 28
  Independence secured at Geneva Conference, 123-124
  Withdrawal of Communists, 95
Life Magazine, 125
Locarno-Type Agreements
  Best assurance of South Vietnam survival, 152-153
  Eden's plan for Indochina settlement, 109-110
  Rejection by U.S., 118-119
London Times
  On American alarm concerning recognition of Peking regime, 115
  On American demands upon France, 87
  On break-down of French-American negotiations, 90
  On British change of policy toward U.S. coalition proposal, 78
  On British reaction to Dulles' attempt at coalition with Australia and New Zealand, 82
  On "concession," by British, 76
  On French-American negotiations for intervention in Indochina, 87
  On State Dept's reaction to Eden's speech, 114
  On U.S. attitude toward Eden's agreement with China at Geneva, 114

Malayasia, 13, 124

Mandate for Change, *foreword*
  As influencing U.S. policies in Indochina after loss of China to Free World, 208
Mandate System
  "Anti-colonialism" no aim of, 197
Manila Conference. See South East Asia Defense Pact
Manila Pact. See South East Asia Defense Pact
Mansfield, Mike
  Determining policy on Vietnam, 184
  Diem's non-existent authority, 174
  Policy to eliminate "colonialist" France, 184
  Suspension of U.S. aid in event of Diem's fall, 181
Mao Tse Tung
  Activity influencing events in Indochina, 10
  On Nationalist Chinese troops in Indochina, 206
  Recognition of Ho Chi Minh's government, 207
Mendès-France, Pierre
  Account of military situation, 149-150
  Acquiescence to defense of Indochina resting on Manila Treaty, 185
  Attempt to revive Ely-Bedell Smith agreement, 183-184
  Commitment to resign if no settlement in Indochina, 121
  Disinterest in American proposals for intervention and united action, 91
  Favoring direct negotiation with Ho Chi Minh, 17
  Instructions to Ely to coordinate command with American policy, 187
  Peace at any price, 127
  Proposals on Indochina crisis, 11
  Reaction to cut of American aid to French Expeditionary Force, 185
  Reaction to "seven-point memorandum", 118
  Speech to National Assembly, Dec. 21, 1954, 129
  "Symmetry" policy, 176-177

265

Tribute to Eden, 122
Military Forces. See U.S. Armed
    Forces
Minh, Ho Chi. See Ho Chi Minh
Molotov
    Awareness of political pressures
        on Bidault, 127
    Proposals for China's entrance into
        great powers, 16
    Reaction to "seven-point memor-
        andum", 122
    Siren song to the French, 129
Morality
    Concept of, as used in U.S. foreign
        policy decisions, 193, 198, 201,
        210-211, 220
Mutual Security Administration, 207
Mutual Security Act of 1954, 53 ff
Mutual Security Treaty of Australia,
    New Zealand and United States
    (ANZUS), 4, 81-84. See also
    Australia, New Zealand

Navarre, Henri, *foreword*
    Appointment as Chief of Staff in
        Indochina, 24
    Military plan for Indochina war,
        24
    Position on French government's
        decision to negotiate with Ho
        Chi Minh, 20
    Urgent request for immediate air
        support at Dien Bien Phu, 30-
        31, 67
    Weaknesses in position of, regard-
        ing decision to negotiate, 21
New York Times
    Myth of Dulles' contention on
        Korean armistice, 126
    On defense of Indochina without
        French troops, 182
    Report by Eden on French-British
        agreement, 90
    Report on negotiations at Geneva
        Conference, 94
New Zealand
    Failure of attempt by Dulles to
        achieve coalition without Brit-
        ain, 83-84, 127
Ngo Dinh Diem. See Diem, Ngo
    Dinh
Nguyen Ai Quoc. See Ho Chi Minh

Nixon, Richard
    On American position for the
        future of Indochina, 224-225
    On French resistance in Indo-
        china, 14
    Presence when Radford orders
        American support for Indochina
        defense, 31
    Speech on American intervention
        in Indochina, 40-41
North Atlantic Treaty Organization
    Eisenhower-Dulles wavering sup-
        port of, 4
    Establishment, 2
    Meeting between Dulles and Eden,
        April 22, 1954, 67
    Recognition of need to support
        France in Indochina, 207
    Resolution supporting French re-
        sistance in Indochina, 12
North Vietnam. See also Ho Chi
    Minh
    Double-satellite relationship, 227
Norway
    As "colony" of Denmark, 195
    Union with Sweden, 195

Plan Navarre. See Navarre, Henri
Pleven
    Informed about Radford promise
        of American air assistance, 36
    Mission to Dien Bien Phu, 27
Potsdam Conference, 206
Psychological Warfare, 55 ff, 125,
    128-129

Radford, *Admiral*
    Orders American support for In-
        dochina defense, 30-31
    Plan for single bombardment of
        Dien Bien Phu, rejected by
        Congress, 49
    Position on use of ground forces,
        214-215
    Recognition of Dulles' opposition
        and Eisenhower's sympathy, 46
Republican Party
    Chinese "terror", fear of, 103
    Eisenhower's sensitivity to, 214-
        215
    Eisenhower's Vietnam policy as
        directed toward anti-colonial
        and anti-Communist viewpoint
        of, 155

Fear of Communist take-over in
Asia after victory in China, 208
"Mandate for change", *foreword*
Reaction to Dien Bien Phu situa-
tion, 37
Revolution
American Revolution as "separa-
tion" not "revolution", 194
History of similarities to Indochina
crisis, 134-136
Robertson, Walter, 37
Attack on proposal for withdrawal
of Communists from Laos and
Cambodia, 94
Ignoring of French presence, 189
Position on elections, 140
Review of U.S. policy, 128
Statement on U.S. readiness to
intervene in Indochina, 104
Roosevelt, Franklin D.
Attitude toward Russia, 2
Indochina's future ignored in
negotiations with France, 206
Offer of Indochina as "gift" to
Chiang Kai-Shek, 206
Position on French rule in Indo-
china, 205
Relationship with Churchill, 2
Rule of Law, 7

Sects
Cao Dai Sect, control of rural
areas, 150-151
Hoa Hao Sect, control of rural
areas, 150-151
Political and military power in
South Vietnam, 173-174, 180,
182
Repression under Diem, 226
Self-Determination
Wilson's "fourteen points" as, 197
Seven-Point Memorandum
Dulles' insistence on French ac-
ceptance before Geneva settle-
ment, 118
Eden's promise to abide by, at
Geneva Conference, 122
U.S. terms for assistance to
France, 85-89
Smith, Bedell
Agreement with General Ely on
policy, 179
Denial of French-American talks

on intervention in Indochina,
86
Elections, position on, 138-139
Harmonious relationship with
Eden, 107
Non-participation position at
Geneva, 143, 144, 146
On French resistance in Indo-
china, 14
On SEATO, 156
On U.S. help to France, 207
Return to Geneva, 127
Return to Washington without
signing Geneva declaration, 102
U.S. representative at Geneva
Conference, 94
U.S. unilateral declaration, 143
South Vietnam. See also North Viet-
nam; Vietnam
As buffer state against Communist
conquest of Southeast Pacific
Islands, 124, 147
Communist infiltration, 151-152
Continuing American support as-
sured by Eisenhower, 181
Corruption in, 151-152
Diem's lack of popular support,
180. See also Diem
"Final Declaration" at Geneva as
no guarantee of protection by
any of seven signatories, 154
French attempt at continuing joint
control with U.S., 183-184
French declaration of complete
support of independence of, 177;
implementation by immediate
withdrawal, 177-178
French gestures toward semi-
diplomatic relations with North
Vietnam, 176-177
French withdrawal, 177 ff; erron-
eous American beliefs regard-
ing, 175
Introduction of exclusive Ameri-
can influence, 182-183
"Sects" in, 173-174, 180, 182
Suppression of religious and poli-
tical groups opposed to Diem,
American approval, 180-181
Unfavorable comparison with
North Vietnam, 152
U.S. action causing withdrawal of
Britain, 189

U.S. action forcing total withdrawal of French, 182-189
U.S. as sole builder of anti-Communist force in Southeast Asia, 184
U.S. as sole support, 154, 169 ff, 182-183, 189
U.S.-French disagreement on policies regarding, 180-181
U.S. ouster of France and Britain as "third gate" to sole responsibility, 190
U.S. support of French withdrawal program and policies, 179-180
U.S. unilateral declaration at Geneva as "first gate" toward sole responsibility, 154
Weakness of Diem's government, 174-175
Weaknesses from beginning, 150-152, 226
Withdrawal of American aid to France, 182, 184-185
Withdrawal of British influence under U.S. action, 190
Withdrawal of Communist forces secured at Geneva Conference, 123

Southeast Asia. See also Indochina; Southeast Asia Defense Pact, Southeast Asia Treaty Organization; U.S. Foreign Policy
Agreement between U.S. and Britain to establish study conference on defense, 117-118
Britain's modification of position, 65, 117-118
Churchill-Eden visit to U.S., effect on British attitude, 115-117
Determination of U.S. to proceed without British consent, 86
Dulles' misunderstanding with Eden on defense of, prior to Geneva Conference, 62-66
Eden-Dulles communique regarding action prior to Geneva Conference, 61
Eden's plan of reciprocal guarantees, 109-110
Proposal by Britain for secret talks called "concession" by Eisenhower, 75

Shortsightedness of U.S. policy, 59
"Staff talks" in Britain used by Eisenhower to announce plans for security pact, 77
U.S. insistance on Pact before Geneva settlement, 115
U.S. misinterpretation of Britain's proposal for bilateral secret talks, 75
U.S. press reaction to Eden's agreement at Geneva, 114
Southeast Asia Collective Defense Treaty. See Southeast Asia Defense Pact
Southeast Asia Defense Pact
Admission of Laos, Cambodia and South Vietnam as "protected" areas under, 163
Anti-Communism as exclusive feature, 165-166
Dulles' hopes for as defense of Indochina, 114, 155-156
Dulles' interest only in anti-Communist aspect of, 35, 165
Dulles' "united action" plan, 157
Eden's acquiescence to "study" Dulles' plan for "immediate" action, 160-161
Eden's agreement and reservations to, 158-159
Eden's concept and aims concerning, different from Dulles', 159-160
Limitation to powers "willing to undertake military action" against Communist agression, 158, 160
Necessary protection absent specific guarantees under Geneva agreements, 162-163
Protocol and Pacific Charter approved, 162
Reactions in House of Commons, 163-164
Urgent character of, 162
Southeast Asia Treaty Organization (SEATO)
As endowing U.S. with "moral" and "legal" right to intervene in Southeast Asia, 220
As "second gate" to U.S. sole responsibility, 169

Inherent weakness and ineffectiveness, 156, 166
Non-contribution to defense of Southeast Asia, 167
South Vietnam's message on Geneva agreement, at Karachi meeting, 140
Recent moves to obtain help in Indochina, 167
Unreality as protective organization, 155, 166-169
Sphere of Influence
Hull's views, 7
Soviet Russia
Interest in successful outcome of Geneva Conference, 129
Staff Talks
British indications and American misinterpretations, 76-79
Suez Canal Crisis
American-British disagreement, *Foreword*
Dulles' attitude toward Eden as influencing decision, 65
Sweden
Union with Norway, 195

Teheran Conference, 206
Time Magazine
On Eden, 114
Truman, Harry S.
Approval of defense-support program for Indochina, 207
Attack on U.S. Indochina policy, 100
British-American relations under, 2

United Action. See also Coalition
Dulles' opposition to Radford-Ely plan to rescue French efforts in Indochina, 37-41
Dulles' plan for "total victory" against Communism, 37-41
Eden-Dulles disagreement, 61-62
Eisenhower-Dulles' attempts to win public approval of change in U.S. policy, 55 ff
Repercussions to Dulles plan, 47
U.S. Armed Forces. See also Intervention; U.S. Foreign Policy
Difference in popular attitude toward units of, 214

Reluctance to engage ground troops in Indochina, 214-216
U.S. Congress
Approval required, 49, 217
Refusal of aid to Asian governments under guarantees by Communist countries, 118-119
Rejection of mutual guarantees in Asia, 119-120
U.S. Foreign Policy. See also U.S. Foreign Relations
Aim of U.S. to save Southeast Asia from Communist domination, 129-130
"Anti-colonialism" as major influence, 220; as playing into hands of Russia and China, 196
Anti-French sympathy in Indochina before 1950, 206
"Asia last" policy, *foreword*
Australia, New Zealand, U.S. Treaty, 4, 81-84
Change in policy toward France in Indochina, after 1949, 206-207
Change toward Britain under Dulles, 3
Change under Eisenhower and Dulles, *foreword*, 1
Commitment of army as of special significance, 214-217
Commitment to help France to fullest in Indochina, 20
Conflict between Dulles and Nixon regarding American intervention in Indochina, 41
Conflict of interest, application of concept to, 218-219
Conflicting and contradictory policies regarding Indochina, 103
Congressional consent requirement, 49, 217
"Containment" policy, 223-224
Demand that France accede to U.S. command of Indochina, 70
Dictated by "America's moral position", 210-211
Distrust of Communist China, 102-103
Domestic political considerations as affecting, 148, 214-217, 223
Domestic politics, not "moral principles" as motivation for policies in Indochina, 214

Dulles' destruction of Radford-Ely plan of air action over Dien Bien Phu, 38-45

Failure to follow up "united action" policy declared earlier, 191-192

Immobility in Southeast Asia crisis, 130

Indecision and confusion in policy making, 42

Inflexibility under Dulles, 130

Influenced by experience at Yalta and Korea, 225

Intervention in Indochina—Eisenhower's response to American anxiety, 29

"Mandate for change" influence, 208

Political situation in U.S. as affecting intervention in Indochina, 104

Possibility of direct intervention by air in Dien Bien Phu, 32-34

Promise of head-on military intervention in Indochina, 25-26

Rationale for not following up intervention threats and promises, 209 ff

Rational of U.S. change-over from ally of France to dominant leader of coalition, 57-59

Reaction to Eden's plan of reciprocal guarantees in Southeast Asia, 110

Refusal to follow up Radford's promise of aerial intervention in Dien Bien Phu, 37

Rejection of mutual guarantees arrangements in Asian countries, 119

Resistance to diplomatic methods as characteristic, 225

Results of Dulles' rejection of Radford-Ely plan, 50

"United action" policy against Communist control of Southeast Asia, 38 ff

U.S. replacement of France in Indochina, statement of possibility, 41. See also South Vietnam

U.S. Foreign Relations. See also U.S. Foreign Policy

British-American relations
American reactions to strained relations, 97-98, 100
British reactions to strained relations, 97, 99-101
disagreement in Vietnam crisis, foreword, 1
disagreement over Indochina, foreword
disagreement over Suez, foreword
Eisenhower-Dulles "new look", 2
hostility toward Brtiain, 97
policy disagreements, 102

Change in U.S. position toward Allies, between 1945 and 1954, 48

Close association with Brtiain and France, 155

France, critical analysis of U.S. as ally to, 191; non-friend of France before Mao Tse Tung victory on mainland, 207-208

Misinterpretation of Britain's proposal for bilateral secret talks regarding defense of Southeast Asia, 75

Unavoidability of being an "imperialist" nation, 203

Veto, 109

Vietminh
Extension of guerrilla operations by, 10

Vietnam. See also North Vietnam; South Vietnam
Communist Party dissolution by Ho Chi Minh, 9
Desperate French military position described, 149-150
Diplomatic possibilities for peace, ignored by U.S., 226-228
Elections for unification
"free election" impossible, 139-140
Ho Chi Minh's attitude, 141
South Vietnam position on, 138, 140
U.S. stand on, 138-140
Elections provided for at Geneva Conference, never held, 137-140
Partition, by Geneva Conference, 123, 136

Partition made permanent, 138-139

Partition, U.S. rejection, 122

Political history, 226-227

Recognition of Ho Chi Minh and Republic of Vietnam by Communist China, 10

Transition from French to American responsibility, 1

Unification defeated by South Vietnam, 143

Unification as envisioned at Geneva Conference, 137

U.S. failure to undertake direct military intervention, 191

U.S. insistence on French declaration of independence of, 212-213

Vu Nguyen Giap
Extension of guerilla operations in Indochina, 10
Failure of agrarian reform in North Vietnam, 141

War
Congressional consent requirement, Eisenhower's attitude, 49

Yalta
U.S. policy in Indochina influenced by, 225

Date Due